This book is the first of two volumes comprising a collection of manuscripts by or relating to Thomas Robert Malthus (1766–1834), recently discovered in the estate of a distant nephew, consisting of correspondence, sermons, essays and lecture notes on political economy and history, some over 200 years old. The manuscripts provide insights into Malthus' personal life – especially his relationships with his parents and his tutors. They also give details of the books he studied as a student, and suggest hitherto unknown influences on his intellectual development. They suggest a solution to the question of who or what influenced him to omit the controversial theological chapters from later editions of his *Essay on Population*; and his sermons present further evidence of his religious views. Some of the manuscripts had been seen by Malthus' biographers; William Otter, William Empson, James Bonar and John Maynard Keynes quoted extracts from the family letters, and Bonar transcribed them, apparently with a view to publication. But until recently the original manuscripts of the letters had been presumed lost, and the full text of the letters and the other documents contained in this collection had remained unpublished and generally unknown.

T. R. MALTHUS:
THE UNPUBLISHED PAPERS
IN THE COLLECTION OF
KANTO GAKUEN UNIVERSITY

VOLUME I

T. R. MALTHUS:
THE UNPUBLISHED PAPERS IN THE COLLECTION OF KANTO GAKUEN UNIVERSITY

VOLUME I

edited by

JOHN PULLEN
University of New England

and

TREVOR HUGHES PARRY
Kanto Gakuen University

FOR THE ROYAL ECONOMIC SOCIETY

CAMBRIDGE
UNIVERSITY PRESS

CAMBRIDGE UNIVERSITY PRESS
Cambridge, New York, Melbourne, Madrid, Cape Town, Singapore,
São Paulo, Delhi, Dubai, Tokyo, Mexico City

Cambridge University Press
The Edinburgh Building, Cambridge CB2 8RU, UK

Published in the United States of America by Cambridge University Press, New York

www.cambridge.org
Information on this title: www.cambridge.org/9780521187473

© Cambridge University Press 1997

First published 1997
First paperback edition 2010

A catalogue record for this publication is available from the British Library

Library of Congress Cataloguing in Publication data

Malthus, T. R. (Thomas Robert), 1766-1834.
[Selections. 1997]
T R Malthus: unpublished papers in the collection of Kanto Gakuen
University, Vol. I /edited by John Pullen and Trevor Hughes Parry
140 p. cm.
Introduction in English and Japanese.
A collection of manuscripts by or relating to T R Malthus,
recently discovered in the estate of a distant nephew, and
consisting of correspondence, sermons, essays, and lecture notes on
political economy and history.
Includes bibliographical references (p. xxii).
Contents: Introduction – Correspondence relating to Malthus'
early years – Correspondence relating to Malthus' years at
Cambridge University – Later family correspondence – Themes from
the Essay on population – Miscellaneous correspondence.
ISBN 0-521-58138-9 (hbk.)
1. Malthus, T. R. (Thomas Robert), 1766-1834 – Correspondence.
2. Economists – Great Britain – Correspondence. 3. Population.
4. Economics. 5. History. 6. Religion. I. Pullen, John, 1933- .
II. Hughes Parry, Trevor, 1962- . III. Kanto Gakuen Daigaku.
IV. Title.
HB961.M352 1997
330.15'3 – dc20 97-24192 CIP

ISBN 978-0-521-58138-7 Hardback
ISBN 978-0-521-18747-3 Paperback

Contents

Contents

Preface

The papers now known as the 'Kanto Gakuen Collection of Malthus Manuscripts' were acquired by Kanto Gakuen University in March 1991. They had previously been in the possession of Mr Robert Malthus, a great-grandson of Malthus' elder brother, Sydenham. When Robert Malthus died at Ryde, on the Isle of Wight, in 1972, without direct heirs, he left his residual estate to Miss Jane Catchpole who had for many years been employed as a servant in the household of Robert Malthus and his wife. When Miss Catchpole died in 1986, also without direct heirs, these papers and other items were auctioned on the premises for charity in June 1986. Until that time the full nature and significance of the papers had not been appreciated. At the auction they were described merely as a 'Box of Old Documents'. Previously, Robert Malthus had generously made other papers available to researchers – notably, Malthus' travel diaries published by Mrs Patricia James in 1966 – but was apparently unaware of the existence or importance of these papers.

The papers were purchased at the auction by Mr Colin Frost, a bookseller of Wimbledon, London, in conjunction with Maggs Bros., booksellers of London, with a view to selling them as a joint venture. Maggs Bros. arranged for a general descriptive catalogue to be drawn up, with the assistance of Patricia James, and the collection was offered for sale in 1987. It was acquired by K. D. Duval, booksellers, of Pitlochry, Scotland who later approached Maruzen & Co., booksellers, of Japan, with a view to finding a purchaser in Japan. After some unsuccessful negotiations with a number of other Japanese universities and research institutes, Maruzen contacted Kanto Gakuen University in September 1990. The University Board realised that the acquisition of the collection would be a great honour for the University, and that by acquiring the collection as a whole, instead of allowing it to be dispersed throughout the world in small lots, the University would be protecting an international academic inheritance and contributing to the promotion of Malthus studies.

The University therefore decided to send a delegation to Scotland to inspect the papers and to negotiate their purchase. The delegation, consisting of Mr Masahisa Matsudaira (Director of the Board), Mr Trevor Hughes Parry (Lecturer in English), and myself (then Head of the Library), inspected the papers on 10–11 December 1990, and made the final arrangements with K. D. Duval for their purchase. The papers were subsequently conveyed from Scotland to the offices of Maruzen & Co., and finally to the University in March 1991, where they are now housed under specially designed conditions to ensure their safety and preservation.

As soon as practicable after the arrival of the papers at Kanto Gakuen University, a publication project was commenced. From the outset it was the University's intention not to jealously guard the papers in a secret vault, but to make them available to the world-wide community of Malthus scholars and researchers. It was realised that the simplest way to achieve this aim would be to transcribe the manuscripts and publish them in book form. We were fortunate in having on our staff at the time Trevor Hughes Parry who undertook the task of creating a typed version of the manuscripts. The manuscripts are in remarkably good condition, given that many of them are over 200 years old, but the decipherment of the handwriting still presented considerable difficulties and required many hundreds of hours of strenuous effort and painstaking scrutiny. Professor John Pullen of the University of New England accepted my invitation to undertake responsibility for preparing the explanatory editorial notes.

I am also greatly indebted to Professor Donald Winch, of the University of Sussex, through whom we were able to receive the support of the Royal Economic Society in having the collection published by Cambridge University Press. Our thanks are also due to Dr Anne Summers, Curator of the Department of Manuscripts, British Library, for providing us with her invaluable assessment of the collection; and to Mr Colin Hamilton, of K. D. Duval, for his attention and consideration throughout the negotiations.

Patricia James, whose monumental biography has become the major source of reference for all Malthus researchers and whose work on the descriptive catalogue published by Maggs Bros. was so important in facilitating the sale and preservation of the collection, had expressed an ardent wish to be personally involved in the study of the collection when its final location had been settled. Sadly, she did not survive to have that wish fulfilled. But she would surely be happy to know that these manuscripts of her 'dear Malthus' (as she called him) have finally found a safe and secure home. She would also be pleased to know that her own research papers will be preserved here at Kanto Gakuen University alongside those of her 'dear Malthus'. She bequeathed her research papers to Professor Winch who, wishing to ensure their safe keeping, arranged for them to be transferred here. They consist of over ten thousand pages of manuscripts and other documents, representing the accumulated results of her research over more than twenty years. They will be made available in the near future for use by Malthus scholars throughout the world.

The acquisition of the Kanto Gakuen Collection of Malthus Manuscripts has been a major undertaking for our University. Without the foresight of Mr Masatoshi Matsudaira (former President of the Board) and the leadership of

Preface

Professor Yoshindo Chigusa (former President of the University), the acquisition would never have been accomplished.

It is important to remember that this is essentially a collection of original handwritten documents, rather than printed books and articles. They create for anyone who reads them a lasting impression of personal contact with Malthus and his correspondents. Reading Malthus' writing, and holding the papers that he held in his own hands, conveys a vivid sense of the enduring presence and spirit of Malthus himself. Having miraculously survived and been rediscovered after all these years, these manuscripts are a physical symbol of the power of survival of Malthus' ideas, and are a reminder that his ideas are as important and as relevant today as they were 200 years ago.

I am reminded of the lines of Robert Southey:

My thoughts are with the Dead, with them
I live in long-past years,
Their virtues love, their faults condemn,
Partake their hopes and fears,
And from their lessons seek and find
Instruction with an humble mind.

Takeo Satoh
President
Kanto Gakuen University

序文

　ここに関東学園マルサス文書コレクションと呼ぶものの全資料を、わが関東学園大学が入手するに至ったのは、１９９１年３月であった。それまで、文書は、トマス・ロバート・マルサスの長兄、シドナム・マルサスの曽孫あたるロバート・マルサス氏の所有するところとなっていた。英国海峡ワイト島のライドにおいて、ロバート・マルサスは１９７２年に死去されたが、後継者が居なかったため、彼はその屋敷を遺言により、永年自分と妻のメイドとして仕えてくれたキャッチポール（Jane Catchpole）に譲った。しかるに、彼女もまた跡つぎを欠いたまま１９８６年に死去し、これら資料を含めて一切は、１９８６年６月チャリティーのため競売にふされることになった。この時期に至るまで、資料の内容や重要性については、殆んど誰も気づいていた人は居なかった。競売の際には、それらは一つの"古文書籍"として示されているに過ぎなかった。生前のロバート・マルサスは研究者たちに対して、その所有していたさまざまな資料を心安く利用せしめていた。とくに、１９６６年に、パトリシア・ジエームス夫人によって刊行されたマルサスの旅行日記は有名である。しかし、今回発見された資料のあることは忘れていたか、あるいは知っていても、重要なものとは思っていなかったらしいことは明らかである。

　文書は競売に付されたとき、ロンドン、ウィンブルドンの書籍商、コーリン・フロスト氏（Colin Frost）の手に落ちた。彼は、ロンドンの書籍商、マグス・ブロス（Maggs Bros）と提携し、共同事業としてこれを売りに出す計画をもっていた。そこで、マルサス研究家として知られるパトリシア・ジエームス（Patricia James）夫人の手で作成された全般的な説明のカタログを用意して、コレクションは１９８７年に売りに出された。それを買い取ったのは、スコットランド、ピトロッホリの書籍商Ｋ．Ｄ．デュバル（K.D.Duval）であった。そのあとデュバルは、日本での購入者を見つけるべく、日本の書籍商丸善に接触をはかったのである。日本の多くの大学あるいは研究機関との交渉が不成功に終ったあと、丸善は、１９９０年９月になって、関東学園大学との交渉に入るに至った。このとき大学理事会は、このマルサス・コレクションを取得することは、大学にとっての大いなる名誉になるであろうとの判断を下した。そして同時に、コレクションが競売によってバラバラになり世界に散逸してしまうことのないように、一括して大学が購入することは、国際的な学問上の遺産を保護することであり、世界のマルサス研究の発展に大きく寄与することにもなると考えたのであった。

　大学は資料の状況を調査し、購入の交渉を開始すべく、代表団をスコ

ットランドに送ることに決定した。その3人のメンバー、松平正久（理事）、トレバー・ヒューズ・パリー（当時、英語講師）、そして私自身（当時、図書館長）は、1990年12月10日、11日の2日にかけて文書を検討し、 K．D．デュバルとの購入の最終的な調整を行なった。そして、文書は、スコットランドより丸善のオフィスに運ばれ、次いで、1991年3月、大学に到着することとなった。今日、文書は安全に保存するために特別な設計を加えた図書館の貴重本室に納められている。

　文書が大学に到着したのち直ちに、 これを刊行する計画が開始された。文書を公開せずに秘密裡に温存することなく、これを世界のマルサス研究家たちに広く公開することが当初よりの大学の意図する所であったが、この目的に沿うもっとも簡単な方法とは、資料のすべてを写し書きし、書物の形で刊行することに他ならなかった。当時わが大学に、有力なスタッフとして、この大へん困難な仕事の一切を引き受けてくれたトレバー・H・パリー氏が居たことは私どもにとって大いなる幸運であったといえる。 文書は200年以上にわたる年月を経過していたに拘らず、その保存状況はきわめて良好であった。しかしながら、マルサスの手書きの文書を解読するという作業は大変な難事であって、そのためには、パリー氏の何百時間にわたる忍耐づよい困苦に満ちた労働を要求された。そして何よりも私の感謝することは、この出版にさいして、解説のために脚注をつける仕事をお願いした私の懇請を、 オーストラリア・ニューイングランド大学のジョン・プレン教授が心よく御引き受け下さったことである。

　私はまた、英国・サセックス大学のドナルド・ウィンチ教授に対して深く感謝の意を表わさねばならない。ウィンチ教授を通じて、ケンブリッジ大学出版部よりマルサス文書コレクションを出版するに際しての王立経済協会（Royal Economic Society）の協賛をうることが出来たのである。 また私は、この文書の真価に対して貴重なる判断を下さった大英図書館の文書部長アン・サマーズ（Anne Summers）博士、ならびに、文書の購入にさいし幾多の忠言と配慮を頂いたK．D．デュバルのコーリン・ハミルトン（Colin Hamilton）氏に対しても深く感謝の意を表する次第である。

　パトリシア・ジェームス夫人の、手になる不朽のマルサス評伝は、すべてのマルサス研究家が引用参照する所であり、マグス・ブロスより出版されたマルサス文書のカタログは、コレクションの保存と販売の上できわめて重要な役割を果したものであるが、彼女は、この文書がもし将来どこかに安住の棲家を見出すときには、そこに行って研究に従事したいとの熱烈な願望をもらしていたと伝えられる。いま私どもはその期待に答える立場にあるけれども、悲しいことながら、彼女はすでにこの世にはいない。しかし彼女が、彼女の'親愛なるマルサス'（彼女はマルサ

スをこう呼んでいた）が遂に安住の棲家を見出すに至ったことを知った
ならば、パトリシアは心から満足して下さるものと信ずる。そして、彼
女自身が永年かけて行なった調査研究の資料のすべてがまた、’親愛なる
マルサス’と並んで、ここ関東学園大学に保存されていることを知ったな
らば、喜んで頂けることとおもう。彼女は、その調査資料のすべてをウ
ィンチ教授に遺した。　ウィンチ教授は、その安全な保管場所として、
本学を選び、私どもに譲渡されたのである。　パトリシア・ジェームス
夫人の遺した資料は、２０年以上にわたる彼女の研究の蓄積ともいうべ
き、一万頁を越える原稿や文書から成るもので、近い将来、世界中のマ
ルサス研究者たちに利用出来るようになるはずである。

マルサス文書の取得は、わが関東学園大学にとっては、真に巨大なエネ
ルギーを投入しての大事業であった。もしも松平正敏・前理事長の卓越
した洞察力と千種義人・前学長の強力なリーダーシップとがなかったな
らば、この事業は成し遂げられなかったであろう。

　資料のすべては、印刷された書物でも論文でもなく、トマス・ロバー
ト・マルサス自身の肉筆であり、　マルサスの魂の顕現にほかならぬこ
とを確認することはきわめて重要なことと考える。それらを読む人たち
は、なにびとも、マルサスおよび彼の知人たちと個人的に接触している
という印象を受けるであろう。マルサスの書いたものを読み、彼が所有
していた資料を保持することは、私どもに、マルサス自身の魂が永久に
ここに存在することを感ぜしめずにはおかない。今日まで長い年月のあ
いだ、奇跡的に生き残り、発見されたマルサス文書は、マルサスの思想
の生きつづける生命力の具体的な象徴である。それは今日もなお２００
年の前と変らぬ重要な意味を、彼の思想がもち続けていることを我々に
感知せしめるものである。

　私はここに、ロバート・サウジー（Robert Southey, 1774-1843）の詩の
数行を回想する。

わが思想は故人と共にあり、
永い過去の年月、私は彼らと共に生きている。
私は彼らの美徳を愛し、彼らの誤まりを責める。
彼らの希望と不安の心を私も共に分ち合い、
その教えるところより、わが人生の教訓を、
謙虚な心をもって求め、そして学ぶ。

関東学園大学　学長
佐藤　武男

Editorial procedures

Our aim in transcribing the manuscripts has been to create texts which are as accessible and readable as possible while being faithful to the complexity of the originals. Although the University is happy to welcome visits from scholars with an interest in Malthus, it recognises that the relative inaccessibility of Japan will render such visits difficult for many. Their knowledge of the manuscripts will therefore depend upon the accuracy of the transcription, which must be capable of serving as a substitute for a personal visit. For this reason, we decided to record not merely the final intentions of the various writers, but also all their prior deletions and corrections. This has meant a proliferation of footnotes in some instances – especially in the case of draft letters – which might not be of great interest to the general reader, but which will provide for the more specialist reader an authentic account of each writer's process of composition.

The following editorial procedures have been adopted:

- All deletions and insertions in the manuscripts are recorded in footnotes within single inverted commas, followed by the words: *is del.* or *is ins.*

- In the event of additional alterations being superimposed on a prior alteration in the same context, the prior alteration is indicated within brackets; for example, the footnote *'in a different [way] manner' is del.* indicates that initially the word 'way' was replaced by 'manner' and that later the complete phrase 'in a different manner' was deleted.

- As a general rule, the punctuation, spelling, abbreviations and capitalisations have been transcribed exactly as they appear in the manuscripts. Thus, for example, we have not altered the contemporary use of a dash (–) instead of a full stop at the end of a sentence. And missing apostrophes in the manuscripts have not been added – for example, on p. 23 'a quarters allowance', on p. 75 'Dont'. However, diphthongs have been transcribed as separate letters, and capitals have been given to the first words of sentences where they are lacking in MS.

- When the original spelling is either obsolete, or archaic (e.g. 'shewn' for 'shown'), or a misspelling (e.g. 'Heroditus' for 'Herodotus'), or an orthographic error, we have usually added a star (*) to the right of the relevant word to indicate that the transcribed form repeats the original manuscript form and is not a transcription error. The star (*) is equivalent to the more usual '[sic]', but given the large number of spelling errors in the letters (especially those of Malthus), the star (*) was thought to be less visually intrusive and less disturbing for the reader.

- But, in a few instances, in order to avoid confusion and to facilitate the reading of the text, we have corrected the original instead of adding a star (*), showing the correction within brackets – for example, on p. 11, 'W[e]' has been substituted for 'W'; on p. 32, 'a[s]' for 'a'; on p. 33, 'woul[d]' for 'woul', and 'go[o]d' for 'god'; on p. 87, 'ev[er]y' for 'evy'.

- Also, errors in the original punctuation have been corrected in cases where failure to correct would have caused confusion. For example, when a full stop does not appear at the end of a sentence in the manuscript, but when the context clearly indicates that the sentence has ended – because of the sense of the words, and/or because the following word begins with a capital letter indicating the start of a new sentence – then the missing full stop has been added to the transcript. In these cases we have thought it unnecessary and cumbersome to encase the added punctuation in brackets.

- We have not altered abbreviations, or adjusted their punctuation, even though some of the abbreviations are not commonly used today; for example,

  cou'd, cd, c'd
  wou'd, wd, w'd
  yrself
  y^r
  w^{ch} (for 'which')
  y^e (for 'the')
  ser^t (for 'servant')
  D^r, d^r (for 'dear'), as well as the more usual D^r (for 'Doctor')
  Comps (for 'Compliments')

- However, where an uncorrected abbreviation (e.g. 'woud', 'coud') might be interpreted as a proof-reading error in the transcription, a star (*) has been added to indicate that it is thus in the manuscript.

- The manuscript letters are not accompanied by envelopes. Letters of the period were usually not inserted in envelopes, but folded to form a self-closed packet. The address and postmark were placed on sections of the page left free of the written text for that purpose. Thus, when we refer to a postmark being 'on the back', we mean on the back of the folded letter, not on the back of an envelope.

- There are a number of instances where parts of the original text are missing because the manuscript has been damaged, or where a word or words have been obliterated by the seal. The location of the missing word(s) is indicated in the transcript by an ellipsis, and (if possible) by a footnote suggesting what the missing word(s) might have been.

- An ellipsis is also used in situations where decipherment is difficult, with an accompanying footnote suggesting a possible reading.

- The original grammar has been retained, even if it is currently unacceptable – e.g. in letter no. 7, 'Mrs Siddons, you know, don't play this part'; in letter no. 8, 'Mr Wakefield has got a swell'd ankle' and 'had not I just wrote to Maria'. It was not thought necessary to signal these archaic grammatical usages by the insertion of a star (*).

- Watermark dates in the manuscripts have been noted, but they occur only infrequently.

- We have adjusted the layout of the writing to conform to modern practice. For example, all new paragraphs are indented in the transcript despite their sometimes beginning flush with the left margin in the manuscript; and the writer's address at the start of the letter has been positioned on the customary right side.

- An Index to the two volumes will appear in Volume II.

Abbreviations

AT   Latin translations provided by Dr Alan Treloar, Honorary Fellow, Department of Classics and Ancient History, University of New England, Armidale, Australia.

BLG   *Burke's Landed Gentry*, 18th edn, 1972, Burke's Peerage Limited, London.

DNB   *Dictionary of National Biography from the Earliest Times to 1900*, ed. L. Stephen and S. Lee, Oxford University Press, 1937–8.

EB   *Encyclopaedia Britannica*, various editions.

Foster   Joseph Foster, *Alumni Oxonienses: The Members of the University of Oxford, 1715–1886*, Kraus reprint, 1968.

GEC   G. E. C., *The Complete Peerage of England Scotland Ireland Great Britain and the United Kingdom*, St Catherine Press, London, 1910–59.

Malthus   The name 'Malthus' is used when referring to Thomas Robert Malthus. When referring to other persons with the surname 'Malthus', one or more first names are added – e.g. 'Daniel Malthus', 'Sydenham Malthus', 'Marianna Georgina Malthus'.

Malthus Library   The library now housed at Jesus College, Cambridge, consisting of items acquired by Malthus, his father, and other members of the family.

Malthus Library (Dalton Hill)   Items known to have been in the Malthus Library when it was at the house of Malthus' great-nephew, Sydenham Malthus (1831–1916), at Dalton Hill, Albury; but not now in the Malthus Library at Jesus College.

Abbreviations

OCEL   *Oxford Companion to English Literature*, ed. Sir Paul Harvey,
                4th edn, rev. D. Eagle, Clarendon Press, Oxford, 1967.

OED   *Oxford English Dictionary*,   2nd edn, Clarendon Press,
                Oxford, 1989.

Venn   J. A. Venn, *Alumni Cantabrigienses. Part II. From 1752 to
                1900*, Cambridge University Press, 1944.

Bibliography

This bibliography lists works used in the preparation of the editorial notes in this volume. See also the reference works in the Abbreviations above.

Bonar, James 1924. *Malthus and his Work*, 2nd edn, George Allen & Unwin, London.
1941. 'Life of Thomas Malthus', typescript. Rare Book Room, Library of the University of Illinois at Urbana–Champaign.

Bourne, K. and Taylor, W. B., eds. 1994. *The Horner Papers. Selections from the Letters and Miscellaneous Writings of Francis Horner, M. P. 1795-1817*, Edinburgh University Press.

Bray, Louisa 1857. 'Recollections', typescript. Guildford Muniment Room, Guildford.

Danvers, F. C. *et al.* 1894. *Memorials of Old Haileybury College*. Westminster, Archibald Constable and Company.

[Empson, William] 1837. 'Life, Writings and Character of Mr Malthus', *Edinburgh Review*, Vol. 64, pp. 469–506.

Gunning, Henry 1855. *Reminiscences of the University Town, and County of Cambridge from the Year 1780*. 2 vols., 2nd edn, George Bell, London.

Hashimoto, Hitoshi 1990. 'Journal Kept by Harriet Eckersall (afterwards the Wife of T. R. Malthus) during her Trip to France, and Switzerland in 1802', *KSU Economic and Business Review*, Kyoto Sangyo University, No. 17, pp. 25–70.

Hogan, Charles Beecher, ed. 1960–8. *The London Stage 1660–1800. Part 5: 1776–1800*. Southern Illinois University Press.

Hunter, Sir William Wilson 1896. *Life of Brian Houghton Hodgson*, John Murray, London.

Bibliography

James, Patricia 1979. *Population Malthus. His Life and Times*, Routledge & Kegan Paul, London.

James, Patricia, ed. 1966. *The Travel Diaries of T. R. Malthus*, Cambridge University Press.

Jesus College (University of Cambridge) 1983. *The Malthus Library Catalogue*, Pergamon Press, New York.

Lister, Raymond 1970. *Antique Maps and their Cartographers*, London, G. Bell and Sons.

Malthus, T. R.   1966. *First Essay on Population 1798*, London, Macmillan.

1968. *Principles of Political Economy*, 2nd edn, reprinted, Augustus M. Kelley, New York. (first published, 1836).

1989a. *An Essay on the Principle of Population*, ed. Patricia James, Cambridge University Press.

1989b. *Principles of Political Economy*, ed. John Pullen, Cambridge University Press.

Map Collectors' Circle   1964–5. Vol. 2, p. 19, 'Anville'.

1966–7. Vol. 4, p. 124, 'Dunn'.

Masè-Dari, Eugenio 1929. *Tre lettere inedite di R.T. [sic] Malthus*, Presso L'Università degli Studi, Modena.

Nangle, B. C. 1934. *The Monthly Review. First Series 1749–1789.* Clarendon Press, Oxford.

New Palgrave, The. A Dictionary of Economics 1987, ed. John Eatwell *et al.*, 4 vols., Macmillan, London.

[Otter, William] 1968. 'Memoir of Robert Malthus', in Malthus, T. R. 1968.

Paul, C. Kegan 1876. *William Godwin: his Friends and Contemporaries*, 2 vols., Henry S. King, London.

Palgrave's Dictionary of Political Economy 1963. 2nd edn, ed. Henry Higgs, [1925–6], reprinted Augustus M. Kelley, New York.

Pitcher, Roger and Pullen, John 1992. 'Malthus on Classical Languages and Corporal Punishment', *History of Economics Review*, No. 18, pp. 34–45.

Polkinghorn, B. A. 1986. 'An Unpublished Letter from Malthus to Jane Marcet, January 22, 1833', *American Economic Review*, Vol. 76, No. 4, pp. 845–7.

Pullen, J. M. 1981. 'Malthus' Theological Ideas and their Influence on his Principle of Population', *History of Political Economy*, Vol. 13, No. 1, pp. 39–54.

1987a. 'Some New Information on the Rev. T. R. Malthus', *History of Political Economy*, Vol. 19, No. 1, pp. 127–40.

1987b. 'Lord Grenville's Manuscript Notes on Malthus', *History of Political Economy*, Vol. 19, No. 2, pp. 217–37.

Schumpeter, Joseph A. 1954. *History of Economic Analysis*, George Allen & Unwin, London.

Walker, T. A. 1912, *Admissions to Peterhouse or S. Peter's College in the University of Cambridge*, Cambridge University Press.

Zinke, G. W. 1942. 'Six Letters from Malthus to Pierre Prévost', *Journal of Economic History*, Vol. 2, pp. 174–89.

1 Correspondence relating to Malthus' early years

The seventeen letters in this chapter come from three periods in Malthus' pre-university life.

The first three letters are from Richard Graves to Malthus' father, Daniel Malthus, when Malthus was a pupil at a school conducted by Graves at Claverton, near Bath. The letters indicate that Malthus was with Graves for at least three academic years from 1778–9 to 1780–1, between the ages of twelve and fifteen years. They advise Daniel Malthus of his son's academic progress – as well as his love of fighting for fighting's sake – and discuss Graves' literary endeavours and the landscaping interests shared by Graves and Daniel Malthus.

The next two letters were written when Malthus was a student at the Dissenting Academy, at Warrington in the north-west of England. The Academy had been founded in 1757 to cater for the education of the sons of Protestant Nonconformists, i.e. those belonging to Protestant churches other than the Church of England.

At that time, only members of the Church of England were permitted to take degrees at the two English universities, Oxford and Cambridge. Dissenters were thus barred not only from the two universities, but also from the professions which required a university degree. Dissenters were obliged to set up their own schools, and to teach subjects (such as Enfield's lectures on commerce, referred to in letters no. 4 and 5 below) which would prepare the boys for careers in industry and commerce.

As Patricia James has remarked, why Daniel Malthus sent his son to the Dissenting Academy remains a mystery. There is no evidence to suggest that either father or son was a Nonconformist. Malthus was later ordained as a clergyman of the Church of England.

The letters show that Malthus attended the Academy for at least the academic year 1782–3. They deal with his lectures and studies, and refer to the closing down of the Academy, which occurred in 1783.

The remaining twelve letters in this chapter were written in the academic year 1783–4 when Malthus was a student at Bramcote, near Nottingham, at the home of Gilbert Wakefield, who had been a tutor at the Dissenting Academy.

There are seven letters from Malthus to his father, four letters from his father to him, and one letter from Malthus to his mother. They refer to Malthus' studies and leisure activities at Bramcote; they discuss the current state of British politics and London theatre; and conclude with arrangements for Malthus to enrol at Cambridge University.

1. RICHARD GRAVES[1]
TO DANIEL MALTHUS[2]

Claverton, 30 July [1]779

Dear Sir,

30 July 1779   As I observ'd the Bristol Post-mark on y^r Letter, I had some faint hopes, that in the whirl of Surry,* Claverton might rise to your view with some of its former attractions – But probably the Consolation of some friend languishing in the last stage of a Consumption – or some more important business might carry you to the hot-wells – You did not however forget my business as I have yours – I ought immediatly* to have acknowledg'd the Receipt of your Draft for fifteen guineas, as at length I now do – in full for all demands till mid-summer last –

I have got Mr Moreau to come over to Master Bob & another young ...[3] twice a week – who seems to understand the method of teaching French, better than any one I have hitherto employ'd and as he sets them pretty long tasks, their leisure hours will be pretty well taken up –

You may not be satisfied with my little friend's application, but I never saw a boy shew* a quicker sense of the beauties of an author or at least of any humorous & unexpected Strokes – They are reading the Hecyra of Terence,[4] &

---

[1] Revd Richard Graves (1715–1810), poet and novelist, became in 1749 rector of Claverton (near Bath) where he conducted a school (*DNB*). Malthus was sent by his father to reside at Claverton as one of Graves' pupils during at least the three years 1778–9 to 1780–1. Graves was described by William Otter as 'a gentleman of considerable learning and humour' (Malthus 1968, p. xxiii). As these letters show, Graves was a friend of Malthus' father who visited him at Claverton, assisted him with his publications, and joined in landscape-gardening ventures. However, James Bonar's view of the situation was more critical. He said Malthus was sent to Graves 'to be taught Latin and good behaviour' (Bonar 1924, p. 404). He did not regard Graves as a 'commanding intellect', and believed that Malthus' father acted wisely in transferring Malthus to the Dissenting Academy at Warrington (Bonar 1941, Ch. 2, pp. 1–2).

[2] Addressed: 'Daniel Malthus Esqr / Cookham, near / Maidenhead / Berks'. Postmark on the back: 'BATH'.

[3] Word difficult to decipher; possibly 'Gent'. '& another young ...' is ins.

[4] 'of Terence' is ins.

I was willing to see whether any one in the Class was stricken with that 30 July 1779 characteristic stroke of humour, wch Dr Hand[5] lays so great a stress upon –

"Tum tu igitur nihil adduxisti hac plus una sententia"[6]

and tho' there were two boys of 15 years old, Bob was the only one that discover'd a smile of approbation – as he did at Phidippos's* reproach in ye same scene – "Quia paululam vobis accepit pecuniae sublati animi sunt"[7]– Tho' it is not clear, I think, whether Phidippus intended a sneer upon their disappointment, or envied their fancied good luck –

I forget whether I told you that my nephew & my daughter & I made a visit to Hagley & the Leasowes these holidays – and that we were entertain'd by Mr Horne, the present possessor, in a style very different from that which my late friend Mr Shenstone[8] or any Poet, antient* or modern, could have entertain'd us – Mr Horne has built a very elegant house & really, by the force of a superior fortune, greatly improv'd the place. He has enlarg'd & completed the Lake, wch Mr Shenstone could never accomplish, & has rather augmented than diminishd* most of the beauties – He only wants another summer to repair or replace the little pasteboard edifice – which my late friend could not afford to build with any degree of splendor* –

Hagley Park looks rather forlorn – but they are now trying to improve the water – &c – The most beautiful or at least the most agreeable Scene to me, was a pavilion form'd by some lofty Oaks, under w^{ch} (since I was there) the late Lord has put up an Urn, with an elegant, tho' rather stiff, inscription to Mr Shenstone –

The present Lord is now repairing & beautifying the inside of ye house –

---

[5] Ferdinand Gotthelf Hand (1786–1851). His most famous work was *Tursellinus, seu de particulis Latinis commentarii*, 1829–45, an edition of the treatise of Horatius Tursellinus (Orazio Torsellino) (1549–1599) on the Latin particles (AT; *EB*, 14th edn, 1929, Vol. XI).

[6] Terence, *Hecyra*, III. v. 462. Graves was apparently quoting from memory. The original reads: 'Tum tu igitur nil attulisti plus una hac sententia?' ('So you therefore brought back nothing more than this one opinion?': AT.)

[7] Terence, *Hecyra*, III. v. 506–7. Terence's original reads 'paullum', not 'paululam'. ('Because a little sum of money has come to you, you are of cheerful mind': AT.)

[8] William Shenstone (1714–1763) and Richard Graves became friends while students at Oxford University. Of Shenstone's poetry it has been said: 'Most of his verse is artificial and unreal, and has rightly been forgotten, but what remains is of permanent interest.' His achievements as a landscape-gardener appear to have been more significant – he holds 'an important place in the history of landscape-gardening'. In 1745 he took possession of the property 'Leasowes' and made the beautifying of its grounds his life's work. But his limited income did not permit the realisation of all his landscaping plans. Dr Johnson – who had been at Pembroke College, Oxford, with Graves and Shenstone – thought that Shenstone might have written better poetry if he had spent less time and money on his garden (Johnson, *Lives of the Poets*, 1781; cited by Bonar 1941, Ch. 2, p. 2). Graves was one of the executors of Shenstone's will. He composed a poetic inscription for the urn erected in Shenstone's memory in the church at Halesowen (Worcestershire), and wrote *Recollections of Some Particulars in the Life of the Late William Shenstone, Esq. ...*, 1788 (*DNB*).

30 July 1779   The only addition to the Library is a most pompous Sett* of Voltaire's Works in Quarto. Mr Horne seems to have made the same tour thro' the little cantons of Swisse,* which you did – He entertain'd us with a droll anecdote of his treatment by their excellencies, the magistrates of Zug & Lucerne⁹–

My nephew has made me a present of the two N°: of Watts's views of Gent' Seats¹⁰ – in which Ranston, in my opinion, next to Picton Castle, makes the best figure. I fancy the Painter caught a view of my friend Sydenham and Miss Ryves:¹¹ between the two Groupes* of trees – at least his figures are very gentile* – My best Compl^t is due to your good and amiable family. I am Sir y^r oblig'd h.s.

Ric^d Graves

2. RICHARD GRAVES
TO DANIEL MALTHUS¹²

Claverton, 10 Aug.[1780?]¹³

Dear Sir

10 Aug. 1780   Being ignorant of ...¹⁴ Lodging I have taken the liberty to direct a great Coat to you, which they left behind them –

Some fatality certainly attends my projected visit to Clifton hill – I have, in my own imagination, fix'd several days for that purpose; & have as often been disappointed –

---

⁹ The second volume of this *Kanto Gakuen Collection of Malthus Manuscripts* contains a letter from Daniel Malthus to his father written from Marseilles while on a tour of France. It is possible that his tour extended to the cantons of Switzerland. Malthus later made a similar tour of France and Switzerland. Details can be found in the diary of Harriet Eckersall (his future wife) and in Malthus' letters to Giuseppe Acerbi. See Hashimoto 1990 and Masè-Dari 1929.

¹⁰ William Watts, *The Seats of the Nobility and Gentry. In a Collection of the Most Interesting and Picturesque Views Engraved by W. W. ... with Descriptions of each View*, London, 1779–86. Plate VIII shows 'Ranston, in Dorsetshire, the Seat of Thomas Ryves Esqr'. The description accompanying Plate VIII states that Ranston (near Blandford) had been in the possession of the Ryves family for nearly two centuries, and that Thomas Ryves had made 'great Alterations and Improvements'. On Thomas Ryves see the following footnote. Plate II shows 'Picton Castle in Pembrokeshire, the Seat of Lord Milford'.

¹¹ Presumably Sydenham Malthus and Marianna Georgina Ryves. Sydenham Malthus (1754–1821) was Malthus' elder and only brother. Bonar (1941, Ch. 2, p. 1) states that Sydenham had also been a pupil of Graves at Claverton Rectory. Marianna Ryves (born 25 August 1766) was a first cousin of Malthus (and of Sydenham Malthus). She was the daughter of Thomas Ryves (1720–1788), FRS, and Anna Maria Ryves (née Graham) who was the younger sister of Malthus' mother, and would have been only fourteen years old at the time of this letter. In 1783 she married W. L. Symes (1766–1795), and in 1799 married Sydenham Malthus (James 1979). See the letter from Marianna Malthus to Malthus (Ch. 3, letter no. 47 below), and the biography of her brother, Admiral George Frederick Ryves (1758–1826) in Vol. II below.

¹² Addressed: 'To / Daniel Malthus Esq / on Clifton-hill / near / Bristol'. No postmark.

¹³ Internal evidence suggests 1780. See Ch. 1, n. 22 below.

¹⁴ Two words difficult to decipher; probably the names of friends of Daniel Malthus.

4

Don Roberto, who tho' most peaceably inclin'd & who seems rather to   10 Aug. 1780
give up even his just rights, than to dispute with any man, yet (paradox as it
may Seem) loves fighting for fighting's sake – & delights in brusing* – He has
but barely recover'd his Eye-sight & yet I have much ado to keep him from
trying again the Chance of War – And yet he & his antagonist are the best
friends in the world – Learn together – assist each other & I believe, love each
other better than any two boys in the school –

I am as bad a prophet as I am a Poet; I foretold immortality to your Spring
in the Conagre[15] – But alas! not only your ornamental rockwork is destroy'd –
but the Spring itself almost dried up.

'Its ruins ruin'd & its place no more':[16]

I was in hopes however to see some kind of Taste revive amongst us when
last week, I saw the Water dashing from your Spout in the Wall. But upon
surveying the Laurel Grove, I found they had indeed turn'd it into the same
Channel; but had carefully clear'd the Trench from all the *dirty moss, weeds &
perforated* Stones with[17] which Miss Malthus's had so foolishly adorn'd it –
"At est bonus at melior vis – non alius quisquam et tibi amicus –"

I wish you would carry a Fountain-pen,[18] instead of a pencil, in your pocket,
as I should have a chance of more Sketches like what you left at Claverton –
when you were there last – which I shall trace over again, that it may not be
rub'd out –

The Monthly Reviewers have let me off very gently – but have given me
the same hint wch you did – & if [19] my last publication [shou]ld[20] go thro' another
Edition, I shall insist upon your using your Pencil as you did before so much to
my advantage – Tho' I shall reserve a liberty of retaining any whimsical thing
for which I may have a partiality –

Two or three which I intended to omit (as Hymen & Pomona for instance
&c[21]) have been retail'd in two or three news-papers & magazines – as if it had

---

[15] The meaning of 'Conagre' is not obvious. As the letter indicates that Graves and the Malthuses had
been engaged in a landscaping project, 'Conagre' might possibly be an allusion to 'conacre' or 'corn-
acre' – 'In Irish land-system: The letting by a tenant for the season, of small portions of land ploughed
and prepared for a crop' (*OED*).

[16] Cf. Alexander Pope, referring to ancient Rome: 'Their ruins perished, and their place no more!' (*Moral
Essays*, Epistle VII, 'To Mr. Addison Occasioned by His Dialogues on Medals', *Works*, 1881, Vol. III,
p. 204, line 22). Pope's words reflect Caesar's comment on the city of Troy in Lucan, *Pharsalia, or the
Civil Wars*, IX. 969: 'Etiam periere ruinae' ('Even the ruins are destroyed': AT). The Malthus Library
has the *Works* (and other separate publications) of Pope; and Lucan's *De bello civili*.

[17] 'with' is ins. The source of the Latin quotation is not immediately evident and its sense is not clear. A
possible reading is: 'Although he is a good fellow, you would prefer a better one, and a friend to you,
not someone at another time' (AT).

[18] Although the first practical version of the modern fountain pen is often thought to have been produced
by Waterman in 1884 (*EB*, 15th edn, 1992, Vol. IX, p. 253), there are references to working fountain
pens from the eighteenth century, as recorded in the Supplement (1975) to the *OED*.

[19] 'it' is del.   [20] Word partially obscured by seal.   [21] '&c' is ins.

5

10 Aug. 1780   some excellence – So various are the Tastes of Mankind[22] –

I beg my Compl^{ts} to y^r family & Miss Dalton,[23] whom I consider as part of it – From Sir, yr affect humb ser,

Ric^d Graves

3. RICHARD GRAVES
TO DANIEL MALTHUS[24]

Claverton, 20 Oct. 1780

Dear Sir,

20 Oct. 1780   Tho' we are all greatly rejoiced at Mast Malthus's continuing another year with us; yet, I assure you Sir, I shoud* be unwilling to keep him here, if I thought he would not make a greater progress in classical Learning, in his present situation & in the method which he seems now to pursue, with alacrity, than by being remov'd even to a much more capable instructor –

He begins to write tolerable Latin, I think; tho' now & then, thro' inattention, he may be guilty of a solecism. He has finish'd Horace, but is going over an Ode or two in a day, by himself; and has read five Satyrs in Juvenal – with apparent Taste & I never saw a boy of his age enter more instantaneously into

---

[22] A misquotation of 'Such and so various are the tastes of men', Mark Akenside (1721–1770), *The Pleasures of Imagination. A Poem in Three Books*, 1744, Book 3, line 567. Graves' reference to 'Hymen & Pomona' indicates that his 'last publication' was the second edition of his collection of poems entitled *Euphrosyne: or, Amusements on the Road to Life. By the Author of the Spiritual Quixote*, 1780, J. Dodsley, London. (The first edition was published in 1776, and a third in 1783.) This suggests that the (unstated) year of this letter was 1780. The Malthus Library has the first edition of *Euphrosyne*; and the *Poetical Works*, 1781, of Akenside.

'Hymen & Pomona' was a semi-humorous, semi-didactic warning to young people of the dangers of hasty marriages. It compared marriage to the fruits of an orchard. (Hymen was the god of marriage, and Pomona the goddess of orchards.) 'For marriage is an orchard fair, / And various fruits produces, / Of sour and sweet, of joy and care, / Like Autumn's various juices.' Young girls were said to have the characteristics of particular fruits: 'Others, like pears, look sweet, and smile, / On every pretty fellow; / Too early ripe, they please awhile; / But soon they grow too mellow.' And the advice to those contemplating marriage was: 'Look round you well before you wed, / With caution make your choice; / By no fond whim or passion led, / Attend to Reason's voice.' The first edition of *Euphrosyne* was reviewed in the *Monthly Review*, Vol. 55, 1776, p. 71; and the second in Vol. 63, 1780, p. 147. The 'hint' given to Graves by the latter review (and by Daniel Malthus) was probably that the collection contains too many 'trifling performances', although they also contain 'a vein of good-humoured levity and cheerfulness, that will prevent the most captious critic from being much offended by them'.

[23] Jane Dalton (1742–1817) was an orphaned cousin and ward of Daniel Malthus. (He was related to the Dalton family on his mother's side.) 'She became romantically attached to him, and was his constant companion, more than his daughters. She had been handsome until the smallpox spoiled her complexion, was very clever, had an excellent memory, and read much, so that she could converse well on every subject' (Bray 1857). In his will Daniel Malthus left her 'A white Cedar Box ... to be delivered to her unopened.' See James 1979.

[24] Addressed: 'Daniel Malthus Esq' / Cookham – near / Maidenhead / Berks'. No postmark.

the humour of the 5th Satyr which describes so feelingly the efforts &   20 Oct. 1780
mortifications which a Parasite meets with at a great man's Table. He also
reads alternately Virgil's Georgicks* – which with Warton's translation he seems
to understand perfectly well –

He has finish'd Tully's* de Senectute – and is just beginning the Iugurthine
War of Salust* in the afternoon[25] –

As for reading English, by way of amusement, he has almost exhausted
my Library – I think as he is tolerably well acquainted with the Roman history
(for his years) he might read Goldsmith's or any other not too prolix, nor too
concise an English History – Goldsmith's Roman & Greek Histories, I think
excellent in their kind; I mean for a superficial knowledge of them – & I shall
borrow, if not buy [26] his English History –

You must have had great pleasure in *re*viewing the Scenes with your Son
& Daughter, w^{ch}, I suppose you have often seen yrself before.

I beg my best respects to Mrs Malthus – & the rest of y^r amiable family –
from Sir Yr ever-oblig'd humb Ser

Ric^d Graves.

Mr Taylor has advertis'd his two Prints with ruins of Grecian architecture w^{ch}
seem exquisitely finish'd. As they will not be sold in the Shops & no more
taken off than what are subscrib'd for they will be valuable[27] as curiosities, as
well as really beautiful –

---

[25] Joseph Warton, *The Eclogues and Georgics*, in *The Works of Virgil in English Verse*, 1763. Cicero
(Marcus Tullius Cicero), *Cato Major de Senectute* ('Cato Major: or, a Treatise on Old Age'). Sallust
(Gaius Sallustius Crispus), *Bellum Iugurthinum*. The Malthus Library has *Opera omnia* of Cicero in
eight volumes.

[26] 'Gold' is del. Oliver Goldsmith (1728–1774), the poet, wrote *An History of England, in a Series of
Letters from a Nobleman to his Son*, 2 vols., 1764; *The Roman History, from the Foundation of the
City of Rome, to the Destruction of the Western Empire*, 2 vols., 1769; and *The Grecian History, from
the Earliest State to the Death of Alexander the Great*, 2 vols., 1774. The Malthus Library has poetical
and dramatic works by Goldsmith, but not his historical works.

[27] 'valuable as' is ins.

4. MALTHUS
TO DANIEL MALTHUS[28]

April 26 – [1783][29]

Dear Sir,

26 April 1783   I did not receive your letter till the 24th, & the post goes out from hence but three days in the week, so that I am afraid you may not[30] receive this letter while you are at Matlock. The Students seem to drop off rather fast. One went to day,* & two more are to go next thursday. The lectures though are still continued with tolerable alacrity. We are now in the eleventh book of Euclid. I suppose we shall have finish'd the 12th before the end of next month, about which time, D[r] Enfield[31] will have ended his philosophical lectures: he then I beleive* intends to give a few on commerce, till the end of the sessions. In the classics, we read alternately Longinus, & Lucretius.[32] Longinus really "is himself the great sublime he draws".[33] There are many very beautiful passages in Lucretius, though at the

---

[28] Addressed: 'Dan: Malthus Esq[r] / To be lef* at the post office / Matlock, / *Derbyshire*.' Postmark: 'WARRINGTON'. On the back, 'from Warrington Academy' in a different hand.

[29] The year is not stated, but the evidence suggests 1783. Letter no. 4 (of 26 April) and letter no. 5 (of 17 June) are apparently written in the same year. They both refer to the study of Longinus on the sublime, and both appear to have been written to Daniel Malthus when he was on a tour via Matlock to the Lake District. Letter no. 5 refers to the closing down of the Dissenting Academy; this occurred in 1783. Wakefield settled in Bramcote in the autumn of 1783, with a single pupil (see James 1979, p. 21); and Malthus arrived at Wakefield's house in Bramcote in late 1783 (see letter no. 6 below). This letter of 26 April was incorrectly dated '1782' by Bonar 1924 (p. 406, reported in James 1979, p. 21). In Bonar 1941 (Ch. 4, p. 7) it was incorrectly dated '1784'.

[30] 'may not' is ins.

[31] William Enfield, LL D (1741–1797) was tutor in *belles-lettres* and rector of the Dissenting Academy at Warrington from 1770 to its dissolution in 1783. He has been described as 'an amiable and estimable man, an influential writer and persuasive preacher'. He was the author of *The History of Philosophy ... Drawn up from Brucker's Historia Critica Philosophiae*, 1791. Many of his sermons were published, and the Malthus Library (Dalton Hill) contained a copy of Enfield's *Sermons on Practical Subjects. To which are Prefixed, Memoirs of the Author, by J. Aikin*, 3 vols., London, 1798. His other publications include works on natural philosophy and elocution (*DNB*). His many contributions to the *Monthly Review* included reviews of Adam Smith's *Wealth of Nations*, and of *A Letter from Governor Pownall to Adam Smith*. See Nangle 1934, pp. 15–16.

[32] The Malthus Library has Longinus, *De sublimitate commentarius*, and three editions of Lucretius, *De rerum natura libri VI*, including an 1813 edition by Gilbert Wakefield.

[33] Alexander Pope, *An Essay on Criticism*, line 680: 'Thee, bold Longinus! all the Nine inspire, / And bless their Critic with a Poet's fire. / An ardent Judge, who, zealous in his trust, / with warmth gives sentence, yet is always just: / Whose own example strengthens all his laws; / And is himself that great sublime he draws' (*The Works of Alexander Pope*, ed. Joseph Warton, Vol. I, London, 1822, p. 308).

8

same time many (from the nature of his subject) dark & confus'd. Mr Wakefield[34]   26 April 1783
has a very good taste, we therfore* only read those parts, where he in a manner
rises out of his subject. I read another composition in the hall to day.* The best
that we have, come from those of the students, who either cannot, or do not
chuse* to make them themselves. They therefore steal them entire from some
book, or often from a newspaper: however I chuse* rather to make them myself,
though they may not be[35] so good; for the Tutors generally know that they are
not of their own making, though they do not chuse* always to detect them. I am
not an Algebraist, though Mr Wakefield gives lectures on Algebra.[36] When he
first began, I ask'd Dr Enfield if I was to attend; he said, not: only those who
went through mathematics last year. We have had beautiful weather lately. The
trees are almost all in leaf. I am making a little collection of plants. I shall be
glad to see Syd[37] if he calls. He is going to the lakes I suppose.

Your dutiful & affectionate Son
Rob Malthus

5. MALTHUS
TO DANIEL MALTHUS[38]

June 17th [1783][39]

Dear Sir

I have just receiv'd your letter, & am sorry that the weather is so   17 June 1783
unfavourable as not to permit you, to enjoy as you could wish, the beautiful

---

[34] Gilbert Wakefield (1756–1801) obtained a scholarship at Jesus College, Cambridge, in 1772, graduated in 1776, and was a fellow of Jesus College from 1776 until his marriage in 1779. He held the position of classical tutor at the Warrington Dissenting Academy from 1779 to 1783, and later published extensively on classical studies. After the dissolution of the Academy in 1783, he moved to Bramcote, near Nottingham, with the idea of taking private pupils. Malthus was his only pupil in 1783–4. As Wakefield stated in his *Memoirs* (1804): 'The *Warrington-academy*, being now dissolved, I ... removed with my family, and fixt* myself in the *autumn* of 1783, at *Bramcote*, a most pleasant village within *four* miles of *Nottingham*, on the *Derby* road. My wish was to have procured a few pupils for my maintenance; and, in prosecution of this purpose, I wrote to all my friends, real or pretended ... All my applications were answered only by a single pupil, who had been a student under me at *Warrington*' (pp. 234–6). Wakefield's political opinions became extremely radical. He was found guilty of treason and jailed, after declaring that 'the poor and the labouring classes would lose nothing by a French invasion' (*DNB*).

[35] 'not be' is repeated.

[36] At Jesus College, Cambridge, Wakefield 'found Algebra "odious beyond conception", but learned enough of it to graduate B.A. as second wrangler in 1776' (*DNB*).

[37] Sydenham Malthus; see Ch. 1, n. 11 above.

[38] Addressed: 'Danl Malthus Esq' / Kendal / Westmoreland' and annotated: 'To be left at the post office till call'd for.' Postmark: 'WARRINGTON'. On the back, 'from Warrington just before it was dissolved' in a different hand.

[39] The year '1782' is written in a different hand below 'June 17th', but, as explained in Ch. 1, n. 29 above, the year would appear to be 1783.

17 June 1783   spot[40] in which you are at present. I hope the cloud on Soracte[41] may not delay you long after the 26th, as it may perhaps be rather inconvenient to D[r] Enfield that I should remain here after all the rest are gone, for as he would not send commons into the hall for one person he must necessarily have me in his house[42] which might hinder him perhaps from going out. We finish'd yesterday Longinus' sublime treatise, or treatise on the sublime; and tomorrow we shall finish the 12th book of Euclid. I have just been looking over that tremendous proposition (the last but one)[43] the length of which almost discourages one from attempting it. I hope however I shall not quit the field without being master of it. D[r] Enfield is now giving lectures on commerce, as the course of philosophical lectures is finish'd. We are reduced to four in the buildings all of whom I beleive* will be gone before the thurday,* as there is to be no Trustee meeting, on account of the dissolution of the Academy. I receiv'd a letter from Harriet[44] yesterday. She says that in your last letter to Cookham,[45] you did not let them know how they might direct to you. She therefore desired me to tell you the first opportunity, least you should be uneasy at not hearing from them, that they are all pretty well; & that M[r] Ryves has written to M[r] Patten, & that the half year for M[rs] Ryves[46] will be paid into his hands the 17th of this month – my mother will write again to let him know that ten of it was advanced by you.

Give my best respects to Miss Scawen, ...[47] Miss Dalton.

Beleive* me

your dutiful,

and affectionate Son,

Rob[t] Malthus

---

[40] 'spot' is ins.

[41] Soracte is a mountain about twenty-six miles north of Rome. The 'cloud on Soracte' was possibly a reference to Virgil's *Aeneid*, VII. 696. The Malthus Library (Dalton Hill) had Virgil's *Opera*.

[42] *DNB* states that Enfield 'received pupils at his house'. 'Commons' are 'provisions provided for a community or company in common' (*OED*).

[43] Euclid, Book XII, Proposition 17: 'Given two spheres about the same centre, to inscribe in the greater sphere a polyhedral solid which does not touch the lesser sphere at its surface' (tr. Heath, 1956). The Malthus Library has two copies of Euclid's *Elements*.

[44] Probably Malthus' eldest sister, Henrietta (1757–1785). Daniel Malthus' will referred to 'my daughter Harriot'* (James 1979, p. 76).

[45] At this period Malthus' parents lived at Ferry House, Cookham, on the River Thames, in Berkshire. See James 1979, p. 23.

[46] On Mrs Anna Maria Ryves (née Graham) and her daughter Marianna Georgina Ryves, see Ch. 1, n. 11 above.

[47] Word covered by seal; probably '&'. On Jane Dalton, see Ch. 1, n. 23 above. On Louisa Scawen, see Bray 1857, pp. 20–1; they 'were born in the same year and the same month and became intimate friends. In natural abilities and their cultivation they were nearly equal, but their characters were remarkably different.'

6. MALTHUS
TO DANIEL MALTHUS[48]

Bramcot* Nov 20th, –83.

Dear Sir

I suppose you have heard from Harriets letter (to which I am rather   20 Nov. 1783
surprized* that I have received no answer) that I arrived perfectly well at
Bramcot.* M[r] Wakefield as yet has no other pupil, & indeed, for my own part,
I hardly wish it; for unless he was a very pleasant lad, it would not be so agreable*
as at present. M[r] Wakefield acts quite as a companion, & we go out walking or
shooting together – by the by I have bought me a new gun with which I perform
very well, having kill'd three, out of four partridges, that I have shot at.

I mention'd to M[r] Wakefield the Greek Historians: he says, that to read
either of them through seperately* (Thucydides for instance) would take up a
very long time, & after all, make you acquainted only with the style & matter of
one Author; that therefore he thinks, the best way to proceed, is, to select the
most celebrated[49] pieces from each, & work those through well, by which means
you become acquainted with their different styles, & gain a more thorough
knowledge of the languge.*

I am at present reading a funeral eulogy from Thucydides, whose manner
of writing [50] is so short & concise, that I find it [51] very difficult to get on. After
tea I read Horace & Cicero alternately. M[r] Wakefield wishes me to go on a little
in Geometry at the same time as the Algebra, so as to be able to understand
some of Sir Isaac Newtons Principia.[52]

W[e] set down to study about a quarter before seven in the morning,
break[fast][53] at half past eight, dine at one, drink tea at five, sup at eight, & go to
bed at ten.

I went to see a house that was to be let about two miles from Bramcot,*
but I do not think it will [54] suit.[55] I mentioned the price of coals, meat &c in my

---

[48] Addressed: 'Dan! Malthus Esq', / Cookham, near / Maidenhead, Berks'. Postmark on the back: '22 /
NO', and 'Nov 83 / from G. Wakefields' in a different hand.

[49] 'best' is del. and 'most celebrated' is ins.   [50] 'I find' is del.   [51] 'to get on' is del.

[52] The Malthus Library has a copy of Sir Isaac Newton, *Philosophiae naturalis principia mathematica*,
3rd edn, 1726.

[53] Word partially covered by seal.   [54] 'do' is del.

[55] Malthus apparently inspected this house with a view to its being rented by his parents. In 1768 Daniel
Malthus sold the Rookery – the family home near Dorking, in Surrey, which he had built and in which
Malthus had been born – and then appears to have moved about with his family living in rented houses
for nineteen years. In Louisa Bray's words, they 'wandered about for some years before finally settling
in Albury' – so much so that her mother (Malthus' sister) was not aware of her own birthplace. Other
letters in this collection show that at different times they lived at Cookham and Walton-upon-Thames.
Further references to the search for a house occur in letters no. 7, 8, and 33. In 1787 Daniel Malthus
bought a house in the village of Albury, in Surrey. See James 1979, pp. 10, 13, 34–6.

20 Nov. 1783   letter to Harriet. There are no other articles particularly cheap. Love to all. Beleive* me your

dutiful Son

Rob' Malthus.

I see in the papers that [56] M[rs] Crawford has appeard* in the character of Lady Randolph, & intends to drive the usurper M[rs] Siddons from her seat.[57] I suppose Syd has been to see her. I shall like to hear who proves victorious.

7. DANIEL MALTHUS
TO MALTHUS[58]
[Reply to 6]

Nov 27th – 83

My dear Bob,

27 Nov. 1783   I have just received your letter which was sent after me to town.[59] I have been in Hertfordshire, & am here for a day or two in my way back to Cookham. Nothing can give me greater pleasure than the account you send me of your present situation: it is everything I could have desired according to my own tastes & real opinions; & I have no doubt you will find you are laying a foundation for the happiness of your future life. Believe me, my dear boy, that I would not have any part of it disagreeable to you; & therefore it is a double satisfaction to me that you pass your present time as you like to do. I would have the purchase of your acquirements as easy as is possible, tho' it must be acknowledged that

---

[56] 'in the papers that' is repeated, then del.

[57] Lady Randolph is a character in *Douglas*, a romantic tragedy by John Home (1722–1808). The role of Lady Randolph was performed by the two great rival actresses Mrs Sarah Siddons (1755–1831) and Mrs Ann Crawford, formerly Mrs Barry (1734–1801). Opinions differed on their relative merits. Mrs Siddons has been described as 'probably the one great tragedy queen that Britain ever produced' (*OCEL*), and Bonar cited the following extract from the *English Encyclopaedia*: 'In 1783 the celebrated trial of skill took place between the rival Lady Randolphs, Mrs. Crawford at Covent Garden and Mrs. Siddons at Drury Lane, and added laurels to the latter' (1941, Ch. 4, p. 12). In his biography of Mrs Siddons, Boaden said that in the part of Lady Randolph 'there was no question about her superiority' to Mrs Crawford (quoted in Hogan 1960–8, Vol. II, p. 658). But the *DNB* says of Mrs Crawford that 'her Lady Randolph, her great character, was held superior to that of Mrs. Siddons', and that 'Mrs. Siddons owned her fear' of Mrs Crawford. The *Public Advertiser* of 24 December 1783 summed up their respective merits: 'The Siddons, younger and more rich in natural Gifts, certainly offers much to the Mind, and yet much more to the Eye. The Crawford, by some means or other, offers more to the Heart' (quoted in Hogan 1960–8, Vol. II, p. 667). Mrs Crawford appeared as Lady Randolph at Covent Garden on 13, 14, 20, 22 and 25 November 1783. Mrs Siddons' first appearance in London as Lady Randolph was on 22 December 1783 at Drury Lane (Hogan 1960–8, Vol. II, pp. 659–61, 667).

[58] Addressed: 'M[r] Robert Malthus at / the Rev[d] M[r] Wakefields / Bramcot* n[r] / Nottingham'. On the back, 'Nov 83 / while at G. W.' in a different hand.

[59] i.e. London.

12

it is very well worth while to endure some labour, & to go through some difficulties for them. I should however disapprove of so close an attention as prevented active exercise, & you may do all that is necessary, while you are enjoying every real pleasure, & contracting every useful & eligible habit. Your life is so pleasant to me to read that you could not have wrote me a more acceptable letter. I believe you have heard me say that when I was a boy (and I was too much inclined to be an Epicurian) Milton's Allegro[60] appeared to me to unite in it all human delights.

I think M[r] Wakefield has made the best determination with regard to the manner of making yourself acquainted with the Greek Historians; as indeed I have no doubt he will in every plan of study which he may suggest – at the same time perhaps it might not be disagreeable to you to read an English or French translation of them as your amusing[61] books – if a passage occurs which strikes you you may refer to the Greek – it would be proper to begin with Herodotus, & I think I have one.[62]

It[63] will be much for your advantage to go on with your geometry, when you begin to have some notion of algebra. It has been said that even Sir Isaac Newton himself regretted his too great preference of Algebraical solution; but however this be it is certain the flights of Algebra may be better regulated by the sober Geometrician. D[r] Berkeleys father,[64] in the early part of his life, enterd* into a controversy upon this subject.

I congratulate you upon the success of your shooting, tho' I think you will ruin yourself, & that you had better have had my other gun, which you would have been heartily welcome to.

I have not yet seen Kemble. I went to M[rs] Craw[ford][65] in Lady Randolph

---

[60] John Milton's poem 'L'Allegro' (1632) is described as 'an invocation to the goddess Mirth to allow the poet to live with her, first amid the delights of rustic scenes, then amid those of "towered cities" and the "busy hum of men"' (*OCEL*). Milton identified the goddess Mirth with Euphrosyne, one of the Three Graces. (Cf. Richard Graves' collection of poems entitled *Euphrosyne*; see Ch. 1, n. 22 above.) The following lines (for example) from 'L'Allegro' no doubt appealed to the young Epicurean, Daniel Malthus: 'Haste thee Nymph, and bring with thee / Jest, and youthful jollity, / Quips and cranks, and wanton wiles, / Nods, and becks, and wreathed smiles' (lines 25–8). The Malthus Library has the *Poetical Works* of Milton.

[61] 'amusing' is used here in the archaic sense of 'Engaging the mind or attention in a pleasing way; interesting' as distinct from the more modern sense of 'exciting the risible faculty, tickling the fancy' (*OED*).

[62] The Malthus Library has Herodotus, *Historia*, with parallel Latin and Greek texts.

[63] MS has 'I', obviously in error.

[64] 'D[r] Berkeley' was Revd George Berkeley, BA, MA, DCL, son of the philosopher George Berkeley (1685–1753), bishop of Cloyne, in Ireland. Dr George Berkeley and his wife Eliza were at that time neighbours of Daniel Malthus and his family at Cookham. George Monck Berkeley (1763–1793), the son of George and Eliza, wrote an elegy on the death of Malthus' eldest sister, Henrietta. See James 1979, pp. 23–4; Foster.

[65] Word partially covered by seal.

27 Nov. 1783   – Mrs Siddons, you know, don't play this part[66] – the contention is to be in the Grecian Daughter[67] I hear; but you shall know more of this matter. I wonder you have not heard from Harriet. Adieu my dear Boy! My best compliments to Mr Wakefield. Whenever I can do anything for him or you in town, you will give me pleasure in employing me.

D.M.

Dont give up the search for a house. Were the coals 4^d at the pit or brought in? You know we are crazy for a coal mine.

8. MALTHUS
TO HENRIETTA MALTHUS[68]

Bramcot* Decem: 11th 83

Dear –,

11 Dec. 1783   I am quite at a loss how to address you, & though I have considered many, yet I cannot hit upon one superscription that quite pleases me: Dear *Mama*, I think I have outgrown: Dear *Mother*, sounds *uncooth** & *ineligant*:*[69] Dear *Madam*, too distant, & not like an address to a mother: *Honoured Madam* too formal & restrained, & implies no affection. I have therfore* left a *blank*, which you may suppose fill'd up with whatever appellation you most approve of. But to be serious, I am very much obliged to you for your kind letter, which I certainly should have answered before, had not I just wrote to Maria,[70] & given her an

---

[66] As indicated in the next letter from Daniel Malthus (no. 10), he was mistaken in thinking that Mrs Siddons did not play the part of Lady Randolph.

[67] *The Grecian Daughter* is a tragedy by Arthur Murphy (1727–1805), who has been described as having 'more industry than originality' (*OCEL*, p. 566). As recorded in Hogan 1960–8, in the London theatrical season of 1783–4 Mrs Siddons appeared at Drury Lane in the character of Euphrasia on 14 and 19 November 1783, and Mrs Crawford at Covent Garden in that character on 27 November 1783 (the date of this letter from Daniel Malthus). Mrs Crawford played Euphrasia seven more times in 1783–4, but the two further scheduled appearances by Mrs Siddons in February and April 1784 were postponed owing to her illness. The 'contention', in its closest proximity, occurred the following season, when Mrs Siddons played Euphrasia on 27 November 1784 and Mrs Crawford on 29 November 1784. The outcome was described thus: 'Nothing could be more affecting than [Mrs Crawford's] expression of the sorrows in the character; nor anything more languid and undecorous than her level recitation ... Discharge the fire, and she sinks into a tasteless disregard of the business, which injures, if it does not destroy the illusion. It is in this that Mrs Siddons triumphs over her ... But she cannot, so powerfully as Mrs Crawford, assail at intervals the heart' (*Gazetteer*, 30 November; quoted in Hogan 1960–8, Vol. II, p. 755). The Malthus Library has Murphy's *Grecian Daughter*.

[68] Addressed: 'Mrs Malthus / Cookham near / Maidenhead / Berks'. Postmarks: '15 DE' and 'NOTTING / HAM'. On the back, 'Dec. 83 / from G. W.'s' in a different hand. Above the address, the four words: 'surprise, agreeable, Whine,* intelligence' in Daniel Malthus' hand. See his criticism of Malthus' spelling in letter no. 10.

[69] The underlining in the MS suggests deliberate misspelling in jest.

[70] Probably Malthus' sister, Eliza Maria (1761–1832). See James 1979.

14

account of my situation at Bramcot,* which is in every respect very agreable.*
M' Wakefield has got a swell'd ankle which prevents him from going out at present: it has removed from one ankle to the other, & is very painful; which makes[71] him think it must be the gout. If it is, it is a very extraordinary thing, as he hardly ever driks* any whine,* lives very temperately in other respects, & uses a great deal of exercise, & as that disorder has never been in his family.

I received a letter from my father at the same time with yours.[72] He desires me not to give up the search for a house, but I am afraid my endeavours will be unsuccessful that way, as I can hear of none that are to be had. Coals are ¾ & 2ᵈ at the pits. I am rather surprized* to hear that ...[73] is to be had, but if the intellegence* is true, I should think it would suit as well as anything that could be found.

I am glad to hear the Bath waters have agreed with M' Graham:[74] I hope he will still continue to mend.

The air balloon did not come this way.[75] I have seen therfore* nothing of Syd; [76] but take it rather ill, that when he was once launched in that winged vehicle, he would not[77] make me a visit.

Kindest love to all at Cookham; & be assured that though I was at a loss for an address, yet I can truly subscribe myself, Your dutiful,

& ever affectionate Son

Rob' Malthus

---

[71] 'makes' is ins.   [72] See letter no. 7, from Daniel Malthus.   [73] Word unclear; possibly 'Easton'.

[74] Probably Malthus' uncle (his mother's brother), Richard Robert Graham (1735–1816), apothecary. William Hogarth's painting entitled 'The Graham Children' (1742) is in the National Gallery, London. The four children depicted are Henrietta (the future mother of Malthus), Richard Robert, Anna Maria (the future Mrs Ryves, see Ch. 1, n. 11 above), and a baby (name unknown) who died soon after. See James 1979.

[75] If this is to be taken literally, it would seem that Malthus' brother was a pioneering balloonist. The first recorded flight of a manned, untethered balloon occurred on 21 November 1783 (just twenty days before this letter) in Paris in a balloon built by the Montgolfier brothers (*EB*, 15th edn, 1992, Vol. VIII, p. 290). A list of 313 English men and women who had made balloon ascents up to 1838 is contained in Monck Mason, *Aeronautica*, F. C. Westley, London, 1838; but Sydenham Malthus is not on the list. The list may not be complete; the author states it is accurate 'as far as my present information enables me to determine' (p. 245).

[76] 'though' is del.   [77] 'not' is ins.

9. MALTHUS
TO DANIEL MALTHUS[78]

Bramcot* Dec: 25th –83[79]

Dear Sir,

25 Dec. 1783   I write a few lines just to desire you, if you have not yet sent the Heroditus* you mentioned in your last, to put up with it, if you conveniently can, Rutherforth's Propositions.[80]

It is a scarce book, & can only, I beleive,* be got second hand, on which account I was afraid the Bookseller at Nottingham would not take the pains to get it, or I should not have troubled you. I have sent for Vince's Conic Sections,[81] (which Mr Wakefield wished me also to get) as the Bookseller[82] will easily be able to procure them.

The Half quarter of my allowance which I received when I was at home, is, I beleive,* up about this time. When it is convenient I shall be glad of a little money. You need be under no apprehensions of my ruining myself. I shall do nothing in the way [of] expence,* before I have considered whether I can manage it, or not.

I have killed another brace of partridges, but they are so wild, that you can very seldom get a shot, & then at a great distance. Mr Wakefield has still no other pupil. I spend my time very agreeably.* Beleive* me

Your dutiful
& affectionate Son
Robt Malthus

---

[78] Addressed: 'Dan: Malthus Esqr / Cookham near / Maidenhead / Berks'. Postmark: '29 DE'. On the back, 'from G. Wakefield / Dec. 83' in a different hand. Also, in a different hand, some multiplication calculations (with an error).

[79] Malthus remained at Bramcote over Christmas and did not refer to Christmas in this letter.

[80] Probably *A System of Natural Philosophy, Being a Course of Lectures in Mechanics, Optics, Hydrostatics, and Astronomy...*, 2 vols., Cambridge, 1748, by Thomas Rutherforth (1712–1771), DD, Regius professor of divinity at Cambridge.

[81] Samuel Vince (1749–1821), *The Elements of the Conic Sections as Preparatory to the Reading of Sir I. Newton's Principia*, Cambridge, 1781. In 1796 Vince became Plumian professor of astronomy and experimental philosophy in the University of Cambridge.

[82] 'he' is del. and 'the Bookseller' is ins.

10. DANIEL MALTHUS
TO MALTHUS[83]
[Reply to 8 and 9 – Answered by 11]

Cookham Jan.ʸ 5. [1784]

My dear Bob,

    I was return'd to Cookham, when I receiv'd your last letter; but I expect   5 Jan. 1784
soon to be in town for a day or two, & I will then enquire for Rutherforths
propositions. It is a book I have not seen – I have a natural philosophy by Dʳ
Rutherforth in two vol: qᵗᵖ – he was lecturer at Sᵗ John's Cambridge, & the
propositions may possibly be his.

    I sent you, in the parcel, Huntingford's exercises[84] which I thought might
be of some service to you in your Greek.

    I have extracts from the Greek Historians, with the Latin at *the end*, if it
wou'd be more convenient to you – I have no historian all Greek but Diodorus
Siculus.[85]

    I am rather surprised (not surprized) that a Grecian & an Algebraist, &
otherwise very agreeable (not agreable) shou'd have so little intelligence (not
intellegence) as to spell wine *whine*.

    I have not the least doubt of your oeconomy, as I have made you acquainted
with the real state of the family affairs; but you wou'd have been heartily
welcome to my other gun, and that was all I meant.

    I don't know whether I told you that I had seen Mʳˢ Crawford, & Mʳˢ
Syddons,* in Lady Randolph. I thought Mʳˢ C. excellent, & was sorry Mʳˢ S.
undertook the part – it was for her benefit,[86] & to my astonishment (as far as I
can judge) she left Mʳˢ C. ten thousand miles behind her. I never saw a part
better play'd by Garrick,[87] but she has not Garrick's natural powers – It was so
forcible, that I can scarcely conceive her playing it[88] again.

---

[83] Addressed: 'Mʳ Robert Malthus / at the Revᵈ Mʳ Wakefield's / Bramcote / Nottingham'. Postmarks: '5
JA' and 'MAIDENHEAD'. On the back, 'while at G. W. / Jan 5. 83'* in a different hand.

[84] George Isaac Huntingford (1748–1832), bishop (successively) of Gloucester and Hereford. The
'exercises' could have been his *An Introduction to the Writing of Greek, for the Use of Winchester
College*, 2nd edn, 1778.

[85] The Malthus Library has a French edition of Diodorus Siculus, *Histoire Universelle*.

[86] On Mrs Crawford and Mrs Siddons, see letters no. 6 and 7 above. The 'benefit' performance by Mrs
Siddons as Lady Randolph took place on 22 December 1783 at Drury Lane. See Hogan 1960–8, Vol.
II, p. 667.

[87] David Garrick (1717–1779), actor and dramatist.   [88] 'it' is ins.

5 Jan. 1784   I grieve to hear by a letter to Lu[cy][89] just receiv'd that you may possibly go to Nottingham[90] – O what a falling off!

Adieu my dear Bob!

D.M.

I send M[r] Wakefield[91] a note for 30£, & he ...[92] be so kind as to advance you a few guineas.

11. MALTHUS
TO DANIEL MALTHUS[93]
[Reply to 10]

Bramcot* Jan: 14th – 84

Dear Sir,

14 Jan. 1784   I have receiv'd your parcel of books, but do not see in it, the English translation of Heroditus* which you mentioned.[94] I have myself extracts from the Greek Historians, compiled for the use of Eaton* School, which perhaps is the same as yours – I am at present reading some pieces of Heroditus* out of it. When we have no interruption, we divide our day, thus: About two hours & a half in the morning Greek History. After which an hour alternately Euclid and Algebra. After dinner an hour and a half alternately some Greek Poet (at present the Philoctetes of Sophocles) Cicero & verses. After tea till supper, alternately Virgil, Horace, & latin translation to compare with Cicero.

I send you a translation of your Greek inscription, into Latin verse, which I suppose you meant.

Venantes, saltus veriti lustrumque ferarum

Divae, sacratis his procul este locis.

Nympharum hic solus [95] sacrûm respondet agrestûm

Latratus latis vocibus ecce canûm.[96]

---

[89] Word partially covered by seal. Lucy was Malthus' third sister, Anne Catherine Lucy (1762–1823), who married Samuel Man Godschall. See James 1979.

[90] This could possibly refer to a proposal by Wakefield to move from Bramcote to Nottingham in order to attract more students. For Malthus' reaction, see letter no. 11.

[91] 'you' is del. and 'M[r] Wakefield' is ins.   [92] Word unclear; possibly 'will'.

[93] Addressed: 'Dan: Malthus Esq[r] / Cookham near / Maidenhead / Berks'. Postmarks: '16 JA' and 'NOTTING / HAM'. On the back, 'Jan 83 or 84 / from Gilbert Wakefield' in a different hand.

[94] See letter no. 7.   [95] Second 'solus' is del.

[96] 'O hunters, fearing the groves of the goddess and the lairs of the wild beasts, keep away from these consecrated places. Behold, this barking of the sacred dogs is the only reply to the far-flung voices of the nymphs of the fields.' It is probable that 'procul este' was a deliberate reference to Virgil's *Aeneid*, VI. 258 (AT).

Mr Wakefield has alter'd the two last into two very good verses. 14 Jan. 1784

    Hoc solis Dryadum, misto* clamore sacrorum

    Ingeminat latis vocibus umbra canûm.[97]

M^r W: has translated them himself into Sapphics and Alcaics,[98] very well – He is a very capital hand at verses, & makes them without the least trouble to himself. You may have perhaps seen a collection of his, (published while he was at Cambridge) some translations, and some originals, exceedingly well done.[99]

Rutherforts* propositions, which Mr Wakefield wishes me to have, are (he says) [100] the propositions of that Philosophy which you mention, without the proofs.

I have[101] just received Lucy's letter. I am sorry to say there is nobody I know who has a Thermometer near here. The Cold to be sure was excessive that Wednesday before the thaw. We shot a great many fieldfares[102] that day, & the day before – they were grown quite tame by the severity of the cold. I keep a journal of the weather.

Mr Wakefield desires me to tell you, th[at][103] he is much obliged to you for the remittance, but that there was not the least occasion for it before a half year, or a year was up – indeed he had desired me before, to tell you the next time I wrote not to think[104] of such a thing. He told me, to take what I pleased, as it was equally the same to him. I therefore took ten pounds, that we might go on regularly, by the Quarter, as you know I like regularity. I am glad to hear that Mrs Siddons stands her ground so gloriously against Mrs Crawford, who I suppose next season will return to Doublin.* You seem to admire her much more than ever. I should have liked very much to have seen her in Lady Randolph. I am afraid if she exerts herself so much she will not be able to remain long on the stage. It will[105] be a falling off indeed, if we go to Nottingham, but I am in great hopes we shall not. Love to all. Beleive* me

your dutiful & affectionate Son

RM

---

[97] 'The echo repeats the far-flung voices of the Dryads mixed with the clamour of the sacred hounds' (AT).

[98] i.e. lyric metres named after the Greek lyric poets Sappho and Alcaeus who used them about 600 B.C. and are credited with their invention.

[99] 'Wakefield was a graceful writer of Latin verses, and published a small volume of them in his Cambridge days' (*DNB*). See G. Wakefield, *Poemata, Latinè partim scripta, partim reddita: quibus accedunt quaedam in Q. Horatium Flaccum observationes criticae*, Cambridge, 1776 (AT: 'Poems, some composed in Latin, others translated: to which are added certain critical notes on Q[uintus] Horatius Flaccus').

[100] 'are he' is repeated and del.   [101] 'have' is ins.

[102] A 'fieldfare' is a 'species of Thrush (*Turdus pilaris*), well known as a regular and common autumnal visitor throughout the British Islands' (*OED*).

[103] Word partially covered by seal.   [104] 'to think' is ins.   [105] 'will' is repeated.

12. MALTHUS
TO DANIEL MALTHUS[106]
[Answered by 13]

Bramcot* March 16 [84][107]

Dear Sir

16 March 1784   I reciv'd* your parcel of books some time since, & was glad to find that you had at last met with Rutherforths Propositions, for which, & the others, I am much obliged to you, though I was sorry you should have given yourself so much trouble about it. If you should by chance be sending anything else, & could readily meet with Vince's Conic-Sections, I should be glad of them. The bookseller at Nottingham whom I spoke to about them has sent to Town, but cannot get them, at least, has not. I have lately began Aristotles Art of Rhetoric. He is [a] most exact writer, & his ideas of the passions seem very just: though he leaves so much to be understood, & makes such nice distinctions, that it requires a great deal of attention sometimes to comprehend his meaning.

I suppose you have heard that I had no skaiting* all the frost, & as for the wild fowl, they so truly answer'd to their names, that we could never get any tolerable shots.

I suppose by your never having mentioned in any of your letters M' Kemble, that he is nothing very capital, for which indeed I am sorry, as they want a man very much to act with M'' Siddons.

M' Fox,[108] & his party have, it seems, at last given up the struggle, & by the account of the papers M' Pitt is quite elated with his success. I really think he will ruin himself, & will not be able to stand it after all, for the rest of the ministry, I beleive* have but very little ability. He will never be so great a man, as if he had shewn* a little more condescention* & less ambition. It appears almost ridiculous ...[109] young a man should hold the two highest offices in the State.[110]

We have had some very cold weather since the frost, which still continues. Love to all at Cookham. Beleive* me, Your dutiful,

& affectionate Son,

Rob' Malthus

M' Wakefield send[s] his best respects.

---

[106] Addressed: 'Dan: Malthus Esq' / Cookham near / Maidenhead / Berks'. Postmarks: '17 MR' and ' N...G / HAM'. On the back, 'March 83 / from G. W.'s' in a different hand.

[107] Malthus wrote '83' but the contents indicate that this was an error for '84'.

[108] Charles James Fox (1749–1806), statesman.   [109] Word(s) covered by seal; possibly 'that so'.

[110] William Pitt (1759–1806) was appointed first lord of the treasury and chancellor of the exchequer in December 1783 (*DNB*).

20

13. DANIEL MALTHUS
TO MALTHUS[111]
[Reply to 12 – Answered by 14]

Best comps to Mr Wakefield.
April. 7. [1784]

My dear Boy,

I am just come from the West of England, & from passing two or three   7 April 1784
days at Oxford; & I will not lose a post to thank you for your letter. I shall be in
town soon, & will endeavour to get[112] the conic sections – I sent to Cambridge
for the propositions; for you know I don't love to fail in a commission, especially
one of yours Sir. I hope you read Aristotle in the original, & then you will be
sure of getting something by him: not that I mean to undervalue his matter. For
a century or two after the revival of letters, Aristotle made the chief learning of
the schools. Some adventurous men (& it was an adventure of no small peril)
dared to find fault with certain parts of this learning, & with the general effect
of it in promoting vain & useless disputation. By degrees the philosopher was
treated with less reverence, & upon the introduction of experiment, he fell into
such neglect, that except for[113] his Rhetoric, & Poetry, he is seldom taken of*
the shelf of our College libraries, where only he is to be found.

I will send you, when I pack up anything else for Nottingham, the English
Polybius.[114] I would wish you in reading History to follow some method, & you
may as well make this your entertainment as novels or plays – I do assure you
it is only a matter of habit, the liking mutton as well as fricassee, & you will
have ten times a stronger, & a pleasanter digestion for it.

After Thucidides* you shoud* read Xenophon's *history*, & Diodorus
Siculus – if I can meet with these (for I have them[115] not) I will send them to
you. I have the retreat of the ten thousand, which is a very valuable work of
Xenophon's – of the same kind of value that Caesars commentaries are. Have
you read any part of it in the original with Mr Wakefield?[116]

---

¹¹¹ Addressed: 'Mr Malthus at the / Revd Mr Wakefield's / Bramcote / Nottingham'. Postmarks: '9 AP'
and 'MAIDENHEAD'. On the back, 'April 7, while at G. Wakefield's' in a different hand.
¹¹² 'get' is ins.   ¹¹³ 'for' is ins.
¹¹⁴ The Malthus Library has Polybius, *General History*, tr. from the Greek by Mr Hampton. It also has a
three-volume edition in Greek and Latin.
¹¹⁵ 'it' is del. and 'them' is ins.
¹¹⁶ The Malthus Library has Thucydides, *The History of the Grecian War*. It also has five editions of
Xenophon, including two French versions of 'the retreat of the ten thousand'. In letter no. 10 above,
Daniel Malthus states that he does have Diodorus Siculus.

7 April 1784   I have said nothing of Kemble, for after making some promise in one part (Hamlet)[117] he grew worse and worse, & seems to be quite neglected by the managers. He is very far from wanting merit, but I apprehend he has one of the most incorrigible of all faults, con...[118] & is not to be advised, or corrected. He speaks with ...[119] affected emphasis, & wants to give more meaning to a passage than Shakespear,* or anybody else ever intended. He has by no means what Cicero admires in the Catuli "Sine contentione vox – literae neq[ue] expressae neq[ue] oppressae".[120] I have only seen him in King John.

I grieve that you had no skating. I was a good deal upon the ice myself, & was boy enough, or fool enough to learn some of those new tricks.

Thank you for your politicks;* but I am not of your mind with regard to young ministers. They may have a little honesty, & a little of the fine enthusiasm caught from Athens Lacedaemon[121] & Rome, which Sr Robert Walpole used to say cost him a year or two to rid some obstinate boys of. I am afraid that in 'face Romuli'[122] old men[123] buy their political experience with the loss of too many virtues. Adieu my dear Boy – We are all pretty well here, & all send you our love. I fancy Syd will call upon you, or has done it by this time. When shall I send you any money & how?

---

[117] John Philip Kemble (1757–1823), 'a fine actor, with a larger range of characters in which he was excellent than any English tragedian'. His first appearance in London took place at Drury Lane on 30 September 1783, as Hamlet, 'causing some excitement and a keen polemic among the critics'. His first performance in London with his sister, Mrs Siddons, took place at Drury Lane on 22 November 1783. They performed frequently together, but she was generally thought to be superior. His brother Charles Kemble 'thought Kemble a better actor than Mrs Siddons, an opinion shared by Kemble himself, and probably by no one else' (*DNB*; Hogan 1960–8, Vol. II, p. 648).

[118] Word (probably 'conceit') partially obscured by torn MS.   [119] MS torn; word missing?

[120] 'An unlaboured delivery ... the words neither widely separated nor slurred together' (AT): a combination of phrases quoted from *De officiis*, I. 133, in which Cicero praises the oratory of Quintus Lutatius Catulus and his son of the same name.

[121] An alternative name for Sparta, capital city of the province of Laconia in the Peloponnesus.

[122] Bonar (1941, Ch. 4, p. 23) transcribed this as 'pace Romuli' which he believed to be a slip for 'faece Romuli', but Daniel Malthus appears to have written 'face [or faece] Romuli'. Bonar noted that Daniel Malthus was referring to a letter from Cicero to Atticus: viz. 'Dicit enim tamquam in Platonis Politeiai, non tamquam in faece Romuli' (Ad Att. II, i. 8: 'Politeiai' was in Greek in Cicero's original). Cicero was complaining to Atticus that their friend Cato, with the best of intentions and in complete honesty, was causing harm to the Republic by speaking as though he were in Plato's Utopia rather than amongst 'faece Romuli' – 'the lower classes of Rome' (AT).

[123] 'old men' is ins.

14. MALTHUS
TO DANIEL MALTHUS[124]
[Reply to 13 – Answered by 15]

Bramcot,* April 15th [84][125]

Dear Sir,

As Mr Wakefield has thoughts of removing to Richmond,[126] & of taking   15 April 1784
pupils upon a quite different plan from the present, I supposed you would think
of one of the Universities for me. Indeed if Mr Wakfield* had continued in the
situation he is now, though I could not anywhere spend my time[127] more
agreeably, yet I cant say but that before I went into orders, I should have liked
to take a degree either at Oxford or Cambridge. I desired Mr Wakefield to write
to you, which he has done this morning. If you have no preference I am now
clearly myself for Cambridge, & by the accounts Mr Wakefield gives me, I
think his College would be as eligible as any – but that, you will perhaps be
better able to determine from Mr Wakefields letter. With respect to money, if I
am to be entered, when Mr Wakefield goes up to Richmond, which he expects
to take place in about a fortnight or three weeks, he says there will be 15 guineas
necessary for [128] security: I think you had better commission Mr Wakefield to
settle such matters, & at the same time if it is convenient, I should be glad of a
quarters allowance.

[129] It may be as well to defer sending any more books til we know how long
Mr W: intends to stay at Bramcot* after he returns from Richmond, for I think
it is possible that if things turn out in the South according to his wishes, he will
remove his whole family almost immediately, in which case it may be hardly
worth while for me to return from Cambridge.

I have read an extract from the retreat of the ten thousand, with Mr W: I
think I shall never repent of my having been this little time at Bramcot* before
my going to College, for I have (if I am not deceived) got into a more steady, &
regular way of study.

I am by no means against young ministers;[130] but I think that genuine
enthusiasm of You...[131] whi[c]h [132] you mention is seldom found sepera...*[133]

---

[124] Addressed: 'Danl Malthus Esqr, / Cookham, near / Maidenhead / Berks'. Postmarks: '17 AP' and
'NOTTINGHAM'. On the back, 'April 83 / from G. Wakefield' in a different hand.
[125] '–83' in MS, again clearly in error.
[126] Wakefield moved to Richmond, in Surrey, in May 1784. He presumably believed that in a more
populous place where his brother, Thomas Wakefield, was vicar, he would be able to attract more than
the one pupil (Malthus) who had come to him at Bramcote.
[127] 'time' is ins.   [128] 'a' is del.   [129] 'I think' is del.   [130] i.e. Cabinet Ministers.
[131] Word (probably 'Youth') partially covered by seal.
[132] 'of' is del.   [133] Word (probably 'seperate'* or 'seperated'*) partially covered by seal.

23

15 April 1784 from a kind of modesty, & diffidence in their own abilities. This, from the accounts I have always heard, seems to be by no means the case with Mr Pitt, who has taken upon himself the sole management of the State, without one single person of any ability to assist in that arduous undertaking. Love to all. Your dutiful

& affectionate Son

RM.

15. MALTHUS
TO DANIEL MALTHUS[134]
[Answered by 16]

Bramcot,* April 18 [1784][135]

Dear Sir,

18 April 1784   I write a few lines to let you know that Mr Wakefield has received a letter from his brother,[136] & intends to set off for Richmond tomorrow morning. He will stay [137] about a week or ten days, so that if you wish to see him, you can perhaps call upon him at his brother's who has the living of Rich:

If it is your intention that I should go to Cambridge Mr Wakefield will enter me, as he goes up to Richmond to settle, with his family, which will be most likely, about the end of may or beginning of June. Kindest love to all. I hope my mother is better, as I have heard she has been but indifferent lately. Your affectionate Son

RM

M^r W: will put this in the London post office.

---

[134] Addressed: 'Dan: Malthus Esqr / Cookham near / Maidenhead / Berks'. Annotated: 'To be forwarded if he is not at Cookham.' Postmark: '20 AP'. On the back, 'April 83 / from G. Wakefields / from T. R. M' in a different hand.

[135] '–83.' in MS.

[136] Revd Thomas Wakefield (1751–1806), of Richmond, Surrey, matriculated at Jesus College 1775, graduated BA 1779 (Venn).

[137] 'ing' is del.

16. DANIEL MALTHUS
TO MALTHUS[138]
[Reply to 14 and 15 – Answered by 17]

Cookham April. 21. [1784]

My dear Bob,[139]

I receiv'd your first letter the day I came down here from London, where I   21 April 1784
went with your mother. I propos'd to answer it as soon as I coud* return to
consult her upon so unexpected an occasion. I look upon it as a particular
misfortune that we shou'd a second time be obliged to change our plan, & upon
more accounts than one, this matter will want a good deal of consideration. By
your second letter I understand that Mʳ Wakefield is come without you, so that
there will not be so great a hurry. He is come much before the fortnight or 3[140]
weeks you mention'd. I will endeavour to see him at Richmond. I had a letter
from him, in which he offer'd very obligingly to take upon him the entering &
introducing you at Cambridge, but said it wou'd not be advisable for you to go
there to reside till October. Your mother I know has a very great objection to
your going either to Oxford or Cambridge; however I dare say that she wou'd
be induced to trust you there. I have myself a partiality for your taking degrees
& I prefer Cambridge. I think however that if you were obliged to leave Mʳ
Wakefield immediately, your residence at an University might be defer'd upon
account of a scheme we have of going abroad this summer. In short I can
determine nothing so suddenly, or till I have seen your mother. But I cou'd not
help writing a few word[s][141] to you in answer to your two letters: & so, for the
present, adieu my dear Boy. I shall send money by Mʳ Wakefield.

17. MALTHUS
TO DANIEL MALTHUS[142]

May 19 – 84

Dear Sir

Your letter gave me very great pleasure. I write a few lines to let you know   19 May 1784
that I received the note[143] safe, for which I am exceedingly obliged to you. I

---

[138] Addressed: 'Mʳ Robert Malthus / Bramcote / Nottingham'. Annotated: 'at the Revᵈ Mʳ Wakefield's'.
Postmark: '22 AP'. On the back, 'April 84 / while at G. W.' in a different hand.

[139] The words 'my', 'My dear Bob' and 'Malthus' are written again to the right in Malthus' hand with
ornamental scrolls.

[140] Number partially covered by ink.   [141] Word partially covered by ink.

[142] Addressed: 'Daniel Malthus Esq' / Cookham near / Maidenhead / Berks'. Postmark: '21 MY' and
'NOTTING / HAM'. On the back, 'May 84 / from G. Wakefields' in a different hand.

[143] See the last sentence of letter no. 16.

19 May 1784 have employed all my time lately in latin composition, verses, & greek. I have got but very slowly forward in history, as I thought that I had better employ what time I had with Mr Wakefield in matters that more required his assistance. I am sorry you have not been able to enjoy this fine weather. Love to all. Your affectionate

Son
Robert Malthus

2 Correspondence relating to Malthus' years at Cambridge University

The letters in this group begin soon after Malthus arrived at Cambridge University early in November 1784, and end in 1793 with his father congratulating him on his election to a fellowship at Jesus College. There are thirteen letters from Malthus to his father and twelve from his father. They tell of the studies, leisure activities, illnesses and other concerns of Malthus' Cambridge years. Daniel rejoices in his son's successes, encourages his first attempt at publication, assists in promoting his clerical career, and regrets his own lost opportunities. There is tension for a while between father and son over money, and over the content and direction of Malthus' studies, but the lasting impression is one of mutual warmth and affection.

18. MALTHUS
TO DANIEL MALTHUS[1]

Cambridge Nov: 5. 1784[2]

Dear Sir;

I have just time to write a few lines before dinner to let you know that I 5 Nov. 1784
arrived safe at[3] Cambridge, & have got some rooms, the income[4] of which I
believe will be about 15 [5] £ *including* furniture. They are not very elgant* as,
you may suppose, but they will do very well till I have an opportunity of changing
for the better. They are said to smoke at times, when the wind is in certain
quarters, which is certainly rather a disagreeable circumstance, but I hear that it
is a general complaint of almost all the rooms. I have ordered a tin to be made

---

[1] Addressed: 'Dan: Malthus Esq' / Cookham near / Maidenhead / Berks'. Postmark: '8 NO CAMBRIDGE'. On the back, 'Nov 84 just coming / to Cambridge / T. R M' in a different hand.
[2] '1784' in a different hand, with the '7' written over an '8'.
[3] 'at' occurs twice, and the first is del.
[4] In this obsolete meaning, 'income' is 'A fee paid on coming in or entering; entry-money, entrance-fee' (*OED*).
[5] Letters del., possibly 'sh' for shillings.

5 Nov. 1784 which I hope will remedy it.

I was obliged to sleep last night & the night before at the inn, but I purpose being in my own room tonight. The room has been uninhabited only about ten days so that it cannot be very damp. I have borrowed sheets till mine come.

Mr Coppard[6] was not in College when my letter came. He says he answerd* it almost immediately after he got to his rooms. I dare say you will have received it by this time.

It is not usual to pay for the income of the room till the end of the first quarter. I'm in great haste & confusion, so for the present adieu & believe me
your dutiful & affectionate
Robt Malthus

19. MALTHUS
TO DANIEL MALTHUS[7]

Cambridge Nov: 14th – 84[8]

Dear Sir;

14 Nov. 1784 I am now pretty well settled in my rooms, which I find comfortable enough, only they are rather dark & yesterday & the day before troubled me a little with smoak.* I shall in all probability have an opportunity of changing for the better at Xmas when the questionists[9] take their degrees though perhaps it may not be convenient on account of the income, that it will be necessary to advance.

The lectures begin tomorrow; & as I had time last week to look over my mathematics a little, I was upon examination yesterday found prepared to read with the year above me, though I believe I shall attend a few lectures at the same time with those of my own year. We begin with mechanics in Maclaurin's Newton[10] & Keill's physics.[11]

---

[6] Probably William Coppard, BA (fourteenth wrangler) 1774; MA 1777; DD 1816; fellow of Jesus College 1778–85; ordained priest 1777. 'Indicted by the College for neglect of his livings.' Died 1827 (Venn).

[7] Addressed: 'Danl Malthus Esqr / Cookham near / Maidenhead / Berks'. Postmark: '16 NO' and '52 CAMBRIDGE'. On the back, '84 / from Cambridge / just arrived' in a different hand.

[8] Changed from '12th – 83'.

[9] A term formerly used at Cambridge to mean 'an undergraduate in his last term before proceeding to the degree of B.A.' (*OED*).

[10] Colin Maclaurin, *An Account of Sir Isaac Newton's Philosophical Discoveries*, London, 1748; 2nd edn, London, 1750. Maclaurin (1698–1746), mathematician and natural philosopher, was said to be 'the one mathematician of the first rank trained in Great Britain' in the eighteenth century. His other publications included *A Treatise of Fluxions*, 1742, and *A Treatise of Algebra*, 1748. The latter was 'in vogue as a Cambridge text-book for more than half a century' (*DNB*).

[11] John Keill, *Introductio ad veram physicam* ..., 1702; translated as *An Introduction to Natural Philosophy*, 1720. Keill (1671–1721) became professor of astronomy at Oxford in 1712 (*DNB*).

We shall also have lectures on mondays & fridays in Duncans logick,*[12] &   14 Nov. 1784
in Tacitus's life of Agricola[13] on wednesdays & saturdays. I have subscribed to
a bookseller who has supplied me with all the books necessary.

We have some clever men of our college, & I think it seems rather the
fashion to read. The chief study is mathematics, for all honour in taking a degree
depends upon that science & the great aim of most of the men is to take an
honorable* degree. At the same time though I believe we have some good
classics: I am acquainted with two, one of them of this year who is indeed an
exceeding clever man & will stand a very good chance for the classical prize if
he does not[14] neglect himself.

I have read in chapel twice. It seems that it is the custom when the readers
are ab...[15] that the two juniors should read the lessons, & I believe I am the
junior of my year.

I received my trunk last tuesday. Kindest love to all & beleive* me your
dutiful

& affectionate Son
Rob' Malthus [16]

20. MALTHUS
TO DANIEL MALTHUS[17]

Cambridge Dec: 29 – 84.

Dear Sir;

I should have answerd* your letter[18] before but that I waited to receive my   29 Dec. 1784
Tutors bill. I am very sorry that my first quarter at Cambridge should happen at
a time when there is a particular difficulty with regard to money, for there are
many extra expences* then unavoidable, which do not return afterwards. I have
14 guineas remaining of the allowance I received when at home. The bill is 44

---

[12] William Duncan, *The Elements of Logick*,* 1748. The Malthus Library has the 3rd edn. Duncan (1717–
1760) was professor of natural and experimental philosophy in the Marischal College, Aberdeen (*DNB*).
[13] The Malthus Library has *A Treatise on the Situation, Manner, and Inhabitants of Germany; and the
Life of Agricola*. The Malthus Library also has two sets of Tacitus, *Opera*.
[14] 'does not' is ins.   [15] MS torn here; word partially obscured, possibly 'absent'.
[16] Postscript deliberately torn from end. The only letters that remain are 'is' at the end of the first line and
'wn.' at the end of the second.
[17] Addressed: 'Dan Malthus Esq' / Cookham near / Maidenhead / Berks'. Postmark: '31 DE' and '52
CAMBRIDGE'. On the back, 'Dec. 29, 84, / from Cambridge' in a different hand.
[18] Daniel Malthus' letter is wanting.

29 Dec. 1784   pounds, 16 of which is the income of my rooms, & 7, tuition & other articles for the 2 quarters Midsummer, & Michelmas,*[19] which I did not reside.

If you consider that I had 23 pounds when I came from home, out of which I have paid for my journey down, & all the articles necessary in my rooms, such as tea things, teaspoons, bottles, glasses &c:&c: you will see that I have not spent more than was absolutely necessary. If you wish to see the bill I will send it in my next letter. When I am once clear of this quarter I think I shall do very well with my allowance. I certainly will not change my rooms at present.

You surprise me when you talk of the snow about you being 15 inches, for at the most I think it is not above 5 inches any where about Cambridge. I went to Mr Frend[20] our under tutor to enquire how low the thermometer had been in the frost, & he was so good as to give me a little extract of his observations upon the Thermoter* & weather two or three of the coldest days.
Wednesday Decem: 8th

8. Clock. 33. Snow & wind. 12 Cl: 34 Wind high N.
Greatest height in the 24 hours 34. greatest cold 29.
Thursday 9th. 8 Cl: 28¾ wind high. 10 Cl: 27½. 2 Cl: 28½.

4 Cl: 25. wind fallen. 8 Cl: 21½. 12 Cl: 19. Clear. Wind. W.&W.N.W.
Greatest height 29. Cold in the night 16.
Friday 10th. 8 Cl: 18½ very little W. 12 Cl: 24 foggy. 6 Cl: 22.

8 Cl: 18. clear. 12 Cl: 17½. Clear no W. – Wind W.& W. by S.
Greatest height 24. Cold 16¾.
Saturday.11th. Great:hei: 27. Cold 19. Sunday 12th. Gr.H. [21] 31. C: 27.
Monday.13th. Gr:H. 33½. C.27. Tuesday 14th. Gr:H:35 C.31½
Wed: Gr:H:34 C:32. Thursday Gr.H.34 C:27 Friday. Gr:H.32 C.34.[22]
Wednesday 22th* Gr.H:22 C ...[23]

Mr Frend makes use of a thermometer made by a M^r Si[x] (...[24] in the philos: Trans:[25]) upon a very clever ...[26] so as to t[ell][27] the greatest height & cold when you are absent. Farenheite's* scale. M^r F is engaged I beleive* with M^r

---

[19] Michaelmas term is the university term or session beginning soon after Michaelmas, i.e. the feast of St Michael, 29 September. Midsummer Day is 24 June (*OED*).

[20] William Frend (1757–1841) became a fellow and tutor of Jesus College in 1781, but was later dismissed from the office of tutor (1788) and prohibited from residing in the College (1793) because of his radical theological opinions.

[21] '27 C:' is del.

[22] Malthus confused the maximum and minimum for Friday.

[23] Words and numbers covered by seal here and below.

[24] Word obscure, possibly 'discussed' or 'described'.

[25] Royal Society, *Philosophical Transactions*, 'Account of an Improved Thermometer: By Mr. James Six; Communicated by the Rev. Mr. Wollaston, F.R.S.', Vol. 72, Part 1, 1782, X, pp. 72–81.

[26] Word covered by seal; context suggests 'plan'.

[27] Word partially obscured by seal.

Six & some more gentlemen, in trying the local difference of heat & cold in   29 Dec. 1784
different & distant situations. He wishes to get some accurate accounts of the
weather. Mr Six has just published some very curious observations which he
made at Canterbury & which were read at Royal Society June 10th 1784.[28]

It thaws very fast today. The ice has been exceedingly bad except the two
first days before the snow. I have been on my skaits* only 4 times, & have but
just recover'd what I had before. We have a tolerable good College library, &
the publick* library has near 90 thousand volumes in it. We are obliged to have
a master of Arts name to have books out of either. I am glad to hear that the
affair in Town may be settled by one sum: but I am afraid it will not be a very
small one. I do not know how to express my thanks to you for your kindness to
me in this affair. I hope next summer, but I am afraid not before, I shall be able
to return some of the money. I know not what I should have done without your
assistance.

Love to all Believe me, your ever dutiful
& ever affectionate Son
Robt Malthus

21. MALTHUS
TO DANIEL MALTHUS[29]

Cambridge Jan: 29 [1785][30]

Dear Sir;

I beg your pardon for troubling you again; but Mr Newton[31] who receives   29 Jan. 1785
the bills instead of Mr Coppard, (M^r C being out of college) has not got the sum
of my bill, & I do not myself exactly recollect it. I shall be obliged to you
therefore if you will send it down. Pray shall I draw for the bill & my allowance
– that is in the whole, (considering the 14£ which I had left) 55£, that I may pay

---

[28] Royal Society, *Philosophical Transactions*, 'Experiments to Investigate the Variation of Local Heat.
By James Six, Esq.; Communicated by the Rev. Francis Wollaston, LL.B, F.R.S.' Read 10 June 1784.
Vol. 74, Part 2, 1784, XXXII, pp. 428–36. On 29 January 1785 Six sent Frend 'three Thermometer
Indexes' with instructions for fitting them. (Letter held in Cambridge University Library.) In 1794 Six
published *The Construction and Use of a Thermometer, for Shewing* the *Extremes of Temperature in
the Atmosphere, during the Observer's Absence ... with Experiments on the Variation of Local Heat,
and other Metereological Observations.*

[29] Addressed: 'Dan. Malthus Esqr / Cookham near / Maidenhead / Berks.' Postmark: '31 JA' and '52
[CAM]BR[IDGE]'. On the back, 'from Cam. / Jan 85' in a different hand.

[30] The contents show that the year must be 1785.

[31] Presumably Revd Benjamin Newton, matriculated at Jesus College 1780, BA 1783, MA 1786, fellow
1785–7 (Venn).

29 Jan. 1785   as I go on; or for the bill only, & let my accounts run [32] till I receive every quarter. I assure you there cannot be [33] pain to me than applying for money, in the present state of the affairs of the family but as I was conscious to myself that I had not spent more than was really necessary, I thought you would prefer my acting openly & laying before you the state of the case, than concealing it & running in debt.

M[r] Frend says that the index of M[r] Six's Thermometer answers very well in practice. He does[34] not conceive that any inconvenience can arise from the bent tubes. The tube at one end is hermetically sealed, & at the other end the mercury prevents the spirit from evaporating. M[r] F's Thermometer is in a large wood frame with rather a thick back. It is situated just out of his window upon a North wall, & enclosed in a corner by a strip of deal & a wire grate to prevent any mischief from without. It is not above 6 yards from his fire. I think it is very possible that the situation of M[r] Fs Thermometer occasioned the great variation from those with you, though part may perhaps ...[35] to the continual fogs we at ...[36] which certainly make a country warmer. M[r] Frend has had accounts from M[r] Six – his thermometers at Canterbury were as low a[s] 5. All M[r] Six's Themometers* have been compared with Farenheite's* for a long while in the same situations & found not [to] vary above half a degree. M[r] S. has lately publised* some very curious observations which he made at Canterbury in the winter of 82.[37] – You would I think be much entertained with them: Kindest love to all. Believe me your dutiful

& affectionate Son
Rob[t] Malthus

22. MALTHUS
TO DANIEL MALTHUS[38]
[Answered by 23]

Cambridge April 30th – 85

Dear Sir;

30 April 1785   I did not receive your letter[39] till yesterday though I find it dated the 20th. I have entirely recovered the effects of my ague[40] – indeed I think I feel myself better than I did before.

---

[32] 'on' is del.   [33] Malthus probably intended to include 'more' or 'greater' here.

[34] 'does' is ins.   [35] Words partially obscured by seal and torn MS, possibly 'be owing'.

[36] Word(s) partially covered by seal, possibly 'Cambridge have'.   [37] See Ch. 2, n. 28 above.

[38] Addressed: 'Dan: Malthus Esq[r] / Cookham near / Maidenhead / Berks'. Postmark illegible. On the back, 'April / from Cambridge / 85' in a different hand.

[39] Daniel Malthus' letter is wanting.

[40] Malthus' ague and rheumatism are again referred to in letters no. 29, 30, 31, 33 and 34.

I did not mean by what I said in a former letter[41] that I had any intentions of 30 April 1785 going beyond my allowance. I hope by spending the long vacation at home I shall always be able to keep within it. I assure you I should think myself very culpable if I did not. Upon my honour I woul[d] not on any account have my allowance encreased,* as I am very sensible that it is the utmost the family can afford & much more than my share, yet I cannot say but I feel a desire of your being satisfied that a person living *very* moderately at Cambridge will spend a hundred a year & that if he resided constantly he would find it *extremely* difficult to keep within it.

It might be otherwise when you were at Oxford, but from the little knowledge I have gained since I have been at Cambridge I could almost affirm it to be absolutely impossible for a person to live here as a pensioner[42] – (that is pay for his rooms, commons &c:) upon 60£ a year. If you were to consult Mr Wakefield he would satisfy you upon this head. I have heard him say myself that though he lived upon a very frugal plan, & read very hard during his residence at Cambridge, yet he spent above a hundred a year.

All I wish you to understand from what I have said is, that spending my allowance here, I am in the least expensive set, & keeping company with the most agreeable & sensible men I can pick out – such as I think you if you knew them you[43] would not disapprove of.

We are at present reading at lectures Optics, the second part of Maclaurins A...[44] Quintillian* & Lock.*[45] The attending ...[46] lectures closely I assure you takes up a go[o]d deal of time particularly the two first. I have got over my english declamation, but I am much afraid I shall have another latin one, before the division of this term which is 22nd of next month.

I really cannot find one book which I had out of your library the last time I was at home. I remember particularly carrying all I had into the parlour the evening before I went away, & we afterwards put them in their proper places.

---

[41] See letter no. 21.

[42] At Cambridge University, a 'pensioner' is an undergraduate student who pays for his own commons, room, and other expenses; as distinct from a 'sizar' – an undergraduate who receives an allowance from a college to enable him to study – and a 'scholar' – 'a student who receives emoluments, during a fixed period, from the funds of a school, college, or university, towards defraying the cost of his education or studies, and as a reward of merit' (*OED*).

[43] 'you' is ins.

[44] MS torn; word partially missing, probably 'Algebra'. See Ch. 2, n. 10 above.

[45] Possibly John Locke, *Elements of Natural Philosophy*, 1750. The Malthus Library has two works by Quintilian, and the Malthus Library (Dalton Hill) had Locke's *Works*.

[46] Word(s) partially covered by seal, probably 'to these'.

30 April 1785   I will make a catalogue of all the books I have had of you at different times. The post is just going out. Love to all

Beleive* me your dutiful

& affectionate Son

RM.

23. DANIEL MALTHUS

TO MALTHUS[47]

[Reply to 22]

Cookham May 15. [1785]

My dear boy,

15 May 1785   I was extremely pleased with the account of your health, & that you have found the wisdom of our old proverb; which indeed Dr Wathen[48] said you wou'd certainly do. I shall expect to see you fat & fresh colour'd; but it will be difficult for you to take any shape or colour that will hinder you from being welcome to me.

I have no notion, nor ever had that you are likely to distress your family by extravagance or even thoughtlessness. I told you openly & clearly the real state of things, & from that moment placed the most entire confidence in you.

I am sorry you feel a desire of convincing me that nobody can go to our universities without spending 100£ a y^r for you are not likely to succeed. I don't rest the matter upon one time or another, or any knowledge or recollection of my own; but upon the nature of things. If it shoud* be as you represent it, the bishops can no longer expect such an education for the church; nor is it possible that the sons of the clergy in particular shoud* ever go to Oxford or Cambridge, who are most usually bred to the church.

It is notorious that in the universities abroad our young Englishmen spend from 200£ to 2000£ – they are perhaps 8 or 10 & the other 8 hundred live upon 25£ a q^r. This Mr Forster was telling me, t'other day, is the case of Leipsic,* where he was. I don't care a farthing for Mr Wakefield, with his sophas* & papier maché. If he cou'd not go to Cambridge from Nottingham under ten guineas, he was not likely to live upon 50£ a y^r there – 100£ is certainly very little for Robert Malthus Esqr. Another character must be assumed, & I only say there are men of the first learning, & of the first agreeableness that will be

---

[47] Addressed: 'Mr Robert Malthus / Jesus College / Cambridge'. Postmark: '16 MA MAIDENHEAD'. On the back, 'May – / probably 85 / (concerning / expense' in a different hand.

[48] Probably Malthus' uncle by marriage, Samuel Wathen, MD, who married Daniel Malthus' sister, Elizabeth. See James 1979, p. 9.

found under this character. That there may be a few such (but they are a very 15 May 1785 few) who spend large sums at Cambridge I have no doubt. Lord Huntingdon[49] was one of these at Oxford, & the only one I knew there.[50]

I want to know if there is now, at Pembroke,[51] a globe of 20 or 30 feet diameter in the hollow of which a large company may see, as in the concave heaven, the motions of the stars &c.

There are two or three plants I wish you ...[52] about Cambridge – they are in flow'r about ...[53] time.

Erysimum Chinanthoides

Dianthus Deltoides

Hesperis Matronalis

We are all pretty well here,
& all send love.
Ever Y[rs], my dear Bob,
Dan[l] Malthus

The globe was constructed by the direction of D[r] Long.[54] See it if you can.

---

[49] Francis (Hastings), tenth earl of Huntingdon, 1728/9–1789, matriculated at Christ Church College, Oxford, on 22 June 1747 (GEC).

[50] Daniel Malthus matriculated at Queen's College, Oxford, on 18 May 1747, but left without taking a degree (Foster; James 1979).

[51] Pembroke College, Cambridge.   [52] MS torn. Word(s) missing.

[53] MS torn. Context suggests 'this'. The three plants are: (probably) *Erysimum cheiranthoides*, or 'Treacle Mustard'; 'Maiden Pink', of the carnation family; and 'Dames-Violet', of the mustard family. The editors are grateful to Dr Jeremy Bruhl, Botany Department, University of New England, for assistance in identifying these three plants and the trees referred to in letter no. 45 below.

[54] Dr Roger Long (1680–1770). The Malthus Library has his *Astronomy*; Malthus received a copy as a prize at Cambridge. See letter no. 34. Long was master of Pembroke College from 1733 to 1770, and in 1750 was appointed to the Lowndean chair of astronomy and geometry. In 1765 he erected in one of the courts of Pembroke Hall 'a hollow revolving sphere, eighteen feet in diameter; representing on its inner surface the apparent movements of the heavenly bodies. Thirty spectators could be accommodated within it' (*DNB*). Mr A. V. Grimstone, Curator, Pembroke College, has kindly provided the following additional details of Long's 'Great Sphere': The Sphere was an early version of a planetarium. It was made of copper, and was turned by a winch. At the time it was perhaps the largest device of its kind ever constructed. It survived in Pembroke College until at least 1871, the date of some photographs of it held by the College. Malthus would therefore have been able to see it in 1785.

35

24. DANIEL MALTHUS
TO MALTHUS[55]
[Answered by 26]

Dec[r] 19. [1785]

19 Dec. 1785   I receiv'd your letter[56] my dear boy, with the one enclosed from Warring...[57] I had just sent a guinea as usual. I shoud* have imagin'd the letter had come from an uncle or cousin of the family. I dare say you are sensible of a sort of cant[58] in it. I can hardly think the man is a proper person to employ in this business.[59]

You are mistaken if you imagine that I am not well aware of the general taste for reading which you have had for some time; but during the few years which you must devote to a particular course of studies, this might be really inconvenient, & indeed very often turns to a kind of lounge[60] of which, I dare say, you find many examples at Cambridge. I mean, in the first place, that you have very few hours to spare from what is call'd study, & that a great many of them are appropriated to one science. It is possible that the University of Cambridge may be too exclusive with regard to other pursuits, too attach'd to their favourite Mathematicks;* but no person can deny the use & preeminence of this science, & you well know that it is the chief road to honour at the place which you yourself have chosen. I will confess to you that the letter[61] which I wrote to you, was in consequence of one from M[r] Wakefield, who told me that you had in College given as a reason for your sudden relaxation in Mathematicks* my want of esteem for this part of learning. I had very little trouble to justify myself from this charge. There is scarcely any part of learning which I esteem more, & all I have ever said to you which cou'd possibly be misunderstood upon this subject, is that I cou'd always wish to see it applied, & that I desir'd to see you a surveyor, a mechanick,* a navigator, a financier,[62] a natural philosopher, an astronomer, & ...[63] a meer* speculative *algebraist*.

You have a French writer upon Algebra &c in octav: 1st V. which I want – have you not my Glascow* Theocritus. Should you like to have the Greek Euclid.[64]

---

[55] Addressed: 'M[r] Robert Malthus / Jesus College / Cambridge'. Postmark: '19 DE'. On the back, 'Dec 86' in a second and 'Malthus Malthus' in a third hand.

[56] Robert Malthus' letter is wanting.   [57] Several letters, possibly 'ton', are ins.

[58] Daniel Malthus was presumably using 'cant' here in a contemptuous manner to mean the 'special phraseology of a particular class of persons' (*OED*).

[59] See Ch. 2, n. 112 below.

[60] In this context 'to lounge' means 'to pass time indolently or without definite occupation; to idle' (*OED*).

[61] This letter is wanting.   [62] 'a financier' is ins.   [63] Word covered by seal, presumably 'not'.

[64] The Malthus Library has *Theocriti quae extant. Ex editione D. Heinsii expressae* (Greek and Latin), Glasgow, 1746, and two English editions of Euclid's *Elements* (1660 and 1756), but not a Greek edition.

We are at Walton,[65] in a good snug little house, & see the Ryvess[66] often. I   19 Dec. 1785
suppose you know that M[r] Graham[67] has sold Sutton for 1200£, that Georgina[68]
is brought to bed of a boy, & M[rs] Peters of another – both to the great joy of us
all – from particular circumstances. I think it won't be long before I call upon
you at Cambridge. I am ever, my dear boy, with the strongest disposition to
think well & kindly of you upon all occasions,

Your affectionate father

D.M.

25. DANIEL MALTHUS
TO MALTHUS[69]
[Answered by 26]

Walton Jan[y] 13. –86.

My dear Bob,

I find you are not yet in your new rooms. I heartily hope they will prove   13 Jan. 1786
agreeable to you. We shou'd have been truly glad to have seen you here in the
leisure of Xmas, & wou'd have subscribed to your journey – not that I used to[70]
think Oxford the less [71] pleasant, & certainly not the less useful, for being
disburthen'd of some of its society. I imagine you will say the same of
Cambridge.

I have always found that one of my greatest comforts in life, was the delight
I have ever taken in solitude – if indeed one can give that name to anything
which is likely to happen to you, or me. A true hermitage for any length of time
is, I believe, an unnatural state – it woud* be a cruel deprivation of what we
have both of us experienced to be the heart's dearest happiness. But even this at
certain seasons[72] will always strengthen, & refresh the mind, & suffer her wings
to grow, which

– in the various bustle of resort,
Were all too rufled* & sometimes impaird.*[73]

---

[65] Walton-on-Thames is about fifteen miles south-west of London. Daniel Malthus must have moved his
family from Cookham to Walton some time between 15 May 1785 (the date of his letter to Malthus
from Cookham) and 19 December 1785 (the date of this letter from Walton).

[66] See Ch. 1, n. 11 above.

[67] Possibly Richard Robert Graham, the brother of Malthus' mother.

[68] Probably Malthus' cousin, Marianna Georgina Symes (née Ryves). See Ch.1, n. 11 above.

[69] Addressed: 'Mr Robt Malthus / Jesus College / Cambridge'. Postmark: '13 JA'. On the back, 'Jan 13 –
86' in a different hand.

[70] 'to' is ins.   [71] 'agre' is del.   [72] 'times' is del. and 'certain seasons' is ins.

[73] '...Wisdom's self / Oft seeks to sweet retired Solitude, / Where with her best must Contemplation / She
plumes her feathers, and lets grow her wings, / That in the various bustle of resort, / Were all too
ruffl'd, and sometimes impair'd' (John Milton, *Comus*, lines 375–80).

13 Jan. 1786 The skating has been good this y^{r} – did you go to Ely? – by the way have you learnt the heart, & cross roll? All the other tricks, such as skating backwards &c are absurd; but I like these, as they amuse one upon a small piece of ice, & they are very clever in society, either for two, or four – four make this figure °8°. The frost was harder than is usual in England. Jany 2 at Sun rise 14 Farh:* Jany the 3^{d} at 9½ postmerid: 14 again – ask M^{r} _[74] how it was at Cambridge – my Thermometer was upon a north wall at a distance from the house.

Did not I ask you whether you had got [m]y[75] Theocritus[76] with you? Have you got Rutherford's*[77] Philosophy 2 vol: q^{to} I wou'd advise you to read something of that kind, while you are engaged in mathematical studies; & contantly* to use yourself to apply your tools. I hate to see a girl working curious stitches upon a rag. I recommend Sanderson's Opticks*[78] to you, & Emerson's Mechanicks*[79] – Long's Astronomy you certainly have. There are papers of the mathematical kind in the R. Society Trans.[80] which are generally worth reading. How do you manage about books? What good book on mensuration have you met with? Have you seen Bouguer's[81] mensuration of the degree in South America? I suppose S^{r} I's Principia[82] to be your[83] chief classical book, after the elementary ones.

We are all pretty well – but Charlotte[84] will write in a day or two. All send love. Adieu my dear Boy!

D.M.

[74] [Sic]. Daniel apparently could not recall Frend's name. [75] MS torn, word partially missing.

[76] See Daniel Malthus' letter no. 24. [77] Presumably 'Rutherforth'; see Ch. 1, n. 80 above.

[78] The editors have not been able to identify this work.

[79] William Emerson (1701–1782), *The Principles of Mechanicks*,* London, 1758.

[80] Royal Society Transactions.

[81] Pierre Bouguer (1698–1758), French scientist. 'In 1735 he set off on an expedition with C. M. de la Condamine to measure an arc of the meridian near the equator in Peru; he used the results obtained to make a new determination of the Earth's shape. He gave a full account of his researches in *La Figure de la terre*, 1749' (*EB*, 15th edn, 1992, Vol. II, p. 420).

[82] i.e. Sir Isaac Newton's *Principia mathematica*. [83] 'the' is del. and 'your' is ins.

[84] Presumably Malthus' sister, Mary Catherine Charlotte (1764–1821).

26. MALTHUS
TO DANIEL MALTHUS[85]
[Reply to 24 and 25. – Answered by 27]

Cambridge Jan: 18ᵗʰ –86

Dear Sir;

I should certainly have answer'd your former letter,[86] but I expected from   18 Jan. 1786
what you said that I shoud* see you soon at Cambridge.

If I had made you a visit this Xtmas I should not have been able to have
read some things which I wish'd, as they require in parts a little assistance. I
mean Newtons Principia, Fluxions[87] & the second part of Maclaurin.

The 8ᵗʰ & 9ᵗʰ sections of Newton require a great deal of attention &, as we
shall go thro them very quick at Lectures the beginning of next term, I wish to
read them over before. – Besides I find myself very comfortable at Cambridge
– tho few of my friends are in College. I am not much afraid of being left alone;
for tho I enjoy company sometimes, yet I am sure I coud* spend my time very
agreeably to myself in solitude.

The plan of Mathematical & Philosophical reading pursued at Cambridge
is perhaps too much confind* to speculation – The intention seems to be to
ground you well in the principles supposing you to apply them at Leisure after
your degree. In going thro this course of study, if I read popular treatises upon
every branch, it will [88] take up my whole time & absolutely exclude all other
kinds of reading whatever, which I should by no means wish. I think therefore
it will be better for me to pusue* the general course adopted by the University
– seeing the general application of every thing I read, without always descending
to particulars.

I have read nothing of astronomy yet. We shall go to lectures in it I believe
the end of next term – Keil's* & Emerson's are the books read. I have not
you[r][89] Theoc[ri]tus, Rutherfort's* Philosophy, or th[e] french writer upon
Algebra[90] – I think they are all at Cookham.

Mʳ Frend is not in College so that I coud* not get[91] information upon your

[85] Addressed: 'Danˡ Malthus Esqʳ / Walton upon Thames / Surryˣ'. Annotated: 'By Isleworth bag' in a
different hand. Postmark: '20 JA'. On the back, 'Jan, 86 / from Cam–' in a different hand.
[86] Letter no. 24.   [87] Sir Isaac Newton, *Method of Fluxions and Infinite Series*, 1736.
[88] 'abso' is del.   [89] Words partially covered by seal here and below.
[90] Daniel Malthus had enquired about the Theocritus and the French writer on Algebra in his letter no.
24; and about the Theocritus and the Rutherforth books in his letter no. 25. He referred again to
Rutherforth and the French writer on Algebra in letter no. 27, and Malthus referred again to the latter
in letter no. 28.
[91] 'not get' is ins.

18 Jan. 1786   question about the frost. Four of us skaited* down to Ely[92] in about two hours –
the last 14 miles in one. The ice was remarkably fine with the wind in our
backs. We had the greatest difficulty imaginable in getting home again as the
wind blew quite a hurricane in our teeth. Two of our party were obliged to give
up & sleep at an alehouse half way. I & the other walk'd home the last seven
miles in the dark. I shall draw for 35£, 25 the quarter & [the] other ten the
rooms for which I think I shall be able to get into them comfortably. We have
but just received our last quarters bills. Kindest love to all.

Your dutiful & afectionate* son

R Malthus

27. DANIEL MALTHUS
TO MALTHUS[93]
[Reply to 26. – Answered by 28]

Walton Jan[y] 31. [1786][94]

My dear Bob,

31 Jan. 1786   I won't say anything about my calling upon you at Cambridge. It will be
only for a day or two, & I must take my chance. I am glad you amused yourself
so well during the holidays. The skaiting* was fine at Walton, particularly upon
the still part of the Thames near L[d] T.'s wall.[95] I suppose the frost was hardly
long enough for you to learn the heart & the cross roll; but however the thing
most in fashion now is skaiting* backwards. In such a country as Cambridge,
one shou'd think of nothing but journies* upon the ice. Ely Cathedral I believe
is worth seeing – is it Gothick* or Saxon, or a mixture? – I forget – indeed I
never saw it.

I won't dispute with you about your plan of study.

Whate'er is best administer'd is best.[96]

But you must have mistaken me strangely, for it is the very reverse of popular
treatises that[97] I recommended. S[r] I. Newton's Opticks*[98] wou'd hardly be call'd

---

92 Ely is on the river Ouse, and Cambridge is on the river Cam, a tributary of the Ouse. In the cold winters
    at that time, it was possible to skate from Cambridge to Ely along the rivers. Ely is about 15 miles from
    Cambridge in a direct line, but much further by river.
93 Addressed: 'M[r] Robert Malthus / Jesus College / Cambridge'. Postmark: '31 JA'. On the back, in
    different hands, 'Jan 31 / in 86 or 87' and 'Dan Dan'.
94 As this letter is obviously a reply to Malthus' letter of 18 January 1786, the year must be 1786.
95 See Ch. 2, n. 130 below.
96 'For Forms of Government let fools contest; / Whate'er is best administer'd is best' (Alexander Pope,
    An Essay on Man, Epistle iii, lines 303–4).
97 'that' is written over 'which'.
98 Sir Isaac Newton, *Opticks;* * *or a Treatise on the Reflexions, Refractions, Inflexions and Colours of
    Light...*, 1704.

40

a popular treatise, because mathematical processes are applied to their proper   31 Jan. 1786
uses in it: Rutherford* I mention'd as a Cambridge book, & comprising the
whole of this application except Political Arithmetick,* Navigation &
Mensuration[99] – I mean as far as common subjects are concern'd. I can scarcely
conceive that a man wou'd make the worse figure even in taking his degree, if
he were to show the advantages of the differential calculus, by some ingenious
application of it; or that it wou'd be thought vulgar & popular to explain how
the distance of the sun may be best attain'd by a transit of Venus. Fergusons
tracts[100] are popular ones; but I don't mean to say that they have the less merit.

   We are going to dine at the Ryves[101] – every body pretty well, but poor
Maria,[102] who has been out of order for some time – but she is going with us. I
can't find the French Mathematicks* in its place, 1ˢᵗ V. that is. Adieu my dʳ
Bob!

DM

28. MALTHUS
TO DANIEL MALTHUS[103]
[Reply to 27. – Answered by 29]

Cambridge Febʸ: 11ᵗʰ – 86

Dear Sir,
   When I mentioned popular treatises[104] I did not mean to refer to the books   11 Feb. 1786
you recommended in your last letter, but to what you said in a former one,[105]
expressing a wish to see me a practical surveyor, mechanick* & navigator; a
knowledge of which kind woud* be difficult to obtain before I took my degree
while engaged in [106] the plan of mathematical reading adopted by[107] the University.
I am by no means however inclined to get forward without wishing to see the
use & application of what I read – on the contrary am rather remark'd in College
for talking of what actually exists in nature, or may be put to real practical use.

---

[99] 'Navigation & Mensuration' is ins.
[100] James Ferguson (1710–1776), astronomer, wrote a large number of books and tracts on astronomy,
mechanics, electricity and other scientific matters, some in many editions. For example, at the time of
this letter, his *Astronomy Explained upon Sir Isaac Newton's Principles* (1st edn, London, 1756) was in
its seventh edition (1785). The Malthus Library has Ferguson's *A Plain Method of Determining the
Parallax of Venus*.
[101] i.e. Thomas Ryves and Anna Maria Ryves (the sister of Malthus' mother).
[102] Probably Malthus' sister, Eliza Maria (1761–1832).
[103] Addressed: 'Danⁱ Malthus Esqʳ / Walton upon Thames / Surry*'. Next to address, in different hands, 'By
Isleworth bag' and 'Feb 86 / from Cam– / on the studies of the Uni'. Postmark on the back: '13 FE' and
'CAM / BRIDGE'.
[104] Letter no. 26.   [105] Letter no. 24.   [106] 'a' is del.   [107] 'by' is written over 'at'.

41

11 Feb. 1786   With regard to the books you mentioned in your last, – as it is absolutely necessary to read those which our lecturer makes use of, it is difficult to find time to apply to other tracts of the same nature in the regular manner they deserve; particularly as many other books are required to be read during our course of lectures, to be able to understand them as we ought. For instance, we have had no lectures of any consequence in Algebra & fluctions,* & yet a man woud* find himself very deficient in going thro the branches of natural Philosophy & Newtons principia without a decent knowledge of both.

As I attended lectures with the year above me, & the course only continues three years, I shall be entirely my own master after the next summer vacation, & then will be my time to read different authors, make comparisons, & properly digest the knowledge I have taken in.

I believe from what I have let fall at different times, you have conceived the Senate house examination[108] to be more confined to mathematical speculations than it really is. The greatest stress is laid on a thorough knowledge of the branches of natural philosophy; & problems of every kind in these as well as in mathematics are set during the examination; & such a one as the assertaining* the distance of the sun by a transit of Venus is not unlikely sometimes to be among the number.

If you will give me leave to proceed in my own plan of reading for the next two years (I speak with submission to your judgement) I promise you at the expiration of that time to be a decent natural philosopher, & not only to know a few principles, but to be able to apply those principles in a variety of useful problems. I hope you will excuse me for detaining you so long upon this subject, but I thought I had not sufficiently explained myself in my last letter, & that you might possibly conclude from what I there said, that I intended to go on in the beaten track, without once reflecting on the use & application of the study in which I was engaged.

We have had a second wrangler[109] this year which does the college credit.

Our mathematical lectures begin on monday next.

I had just begun the heart & cross roll when the frost broke. I don't know how it comes about, but I have seen no society-skaiting* at Cambridge – We have some good backward skait*[ing][110] but I don't admire [111] it at the best.

---

[108] The Senate House is the building used for meetings of the senate of a university. The Senate House Examination is the examination for degrees in Cambridge University (*OED*).

[109] 'Wrangler' is 'the name for each of the candidates who have been placed in the first class in the mathematical tripos at Cambridge University' (*OED*). The 'second wrangler' is the person ranked second in order of merit amongst the wranglers. Malthus' next letter (no. 31) indicates that he attended the oral examinations in the 'Schools' early in 1786 as a spectator – and contracted rheumatism. Malthus became ninth wrangler at the examinations held in January 1788.

[110] Word partially covered by seal.   [111] 'them' is del.

I see plainly that the man I wrote to at Warrington[112] is not a proper person   11 Feb. 1786
to be employed. The shoemaker I dealt with is a substantial man, & I shoud*
think might do: or I coud* write to the young man who was with Mʳ Aikin,[113] &
is now at Manchester – he is probably sometimes in Warrington.

I hope Maria is better. Kindes* love to all. Believe me your dutiful &

affectionate Son

Robᵗ Malthus

I did not see the french mathematics[114] the last time I was at home, but I am
pretty sure I left it in its place the time before.

29. DANIEL MALTHUS
TO MALTHUS[115]
[Reply to 28]

March 3 [1786].

My dear Bob,

We have all got colds here but are otherwise pretty well. I hope this weather   3 March 1786
gives you no tendency to ague. I write to you in the midst of snows, which may
hinder this letter from getting to you, for our stage coaches stop'd here one day
(Munday* 27. F.) when there fell a snow which by the next morning was 11
inches deep in plano.[116] I have skaited* since [117] upon a kind of 12ᵗʰ cake ice.
Was your snow & the time of it the same. The Th: has not been lower this frost
than 28. What has been the lowest of [118] Mʳ Friend's* this year, or rather winter.
I think you cannot cultivate that acquaintance too much. Selden[119] used to say
that he had learnt more from conversation than from books – he had learnt a
great deal from the latter, so that his company must have been very fortunately
chosen. But the inclination to study, & far above all this, the moral disposition

---

[112] This is first mentioned in letter no. 24. It is possible that Malthus had unfinished business in Warrington
dating from 1783 when he was a pupil at the Dissenting Academy.

[113] John Aikin (1747–1822), MD, son of Revd John Aikin (1713–1780), DD. The latter was a tutor and
later principal of the Dissenting Academy at Warrington. The former received his early education at
the Academy, and was apparently living in Warrington when Malthus was there. See Malthus 1989a,
Vol. II, p. 255.

[114] First mentioned in letter no. 24, then again in 26 and 27.

[115] Addressed: 'Mʳ Robert Malthus / Jesus College / Cambridge' and, in a different hand, '52'. On the
back, 'March – / proby 86' in a different hand.

[116] i.e. on level ground.   [117] First 'upon' is del.   [118] 'my' is del.

[119] Probably John Selden (1584–1654), politician, lawyer and scholar, chiefly remembered for his *Table
Talk*, 1689.

3 March 1786 & character depend so much upon our con[nexions][120] or at least are so strong[ly][121] influenced by them! I have done with our dispute[122] & resign myself with full confidence to you. I respect any reading that is an exercise to the mind, & braces its nerves – & I am likewise a friend to relaxation. "Alternis viget animus"[123] you may write your next epigram upon. Have you taken that opinion we talk'd of with regard to orders?[124] If you have not I am impatient that you shou'd do it. All loves! Adieu my dᵣ Bob!

DM.

30. DANIEL MALTHUS
TO MALTHUS[125]
[Answered by 31]

Sunday [12 March 1786][126]

My dear Boy,

12 March 1786 I am mostly concern'd for your Rheumatism,[127] & the pain you have suffer'd, without thinking of the cause; but it has occur'd to me that you may have taken to fen shooting, which tho' I confess it has no temptations for me, is by some reckon'd a most delightful amusement. As you have been so unfortunate as to get the Rh:[128] by some means or other, I shou'd be better satisfied with such a cause, than with the idea that it was inherent in your constitution. But let me intreat* you to avoid this cause for the future. I am the last person in the world to advise any nice attention to oneself; as such attention by degrees furnishes a kind of employment to the mind, which I have known sometimes to preclude all others. Life is hardly worth accepting upon these terms. All I mean is that you shoud* avoid the things which tend to give you a disorder you are perhaps inclined to, or harden yourself to them by very slow degrees – the latter I shou'd myself prefer. As to fen shooting I shou'd as soon harden myself to the vapour of charcoal, or think myself obliged to spend a month ev'ry year in the

[120] Word partially covered by seal. 'nexions' is ins. in a different hand.
[121] Word partially covered by seal. [122] Letters no. 24 to 28. [123] 'The mind thrives on change' (AT).
[124] Malthus' ordination as a clergyman in the Church of England is further mentioned in letter no. 32.
[125] Addressed: 'Mʳ Robert Malthus / Jesus College / Cambridge' and, in a different hand, '52'. Postmark: 'ISLEWORTH'; on the back, '13 MR'. Also on the back, 'March – probably 86' in a different hand. Beside the address, 'Malthus' is written four times and deleted.
[126] The date of letter no. 30 is given by its postmark and by the fact that it is answered by letter no. 31 of 16 March 1786. In 1786 the thirteenth of March was a Monday.
[127] Malthus had apparently written a letter to his father, or to another member of the family, telling of his 'rhumatism*'. That letter is wanting.
[128] 'the' is written over 'it'. 'Rh:' is ins.

hundreds of Essex.[129] I grieve that you have lost this fine frost – our skaiting*   12 March 1786
has been very good here – a kind of snow ice; but very near, (the part of the
river under L^d ...[130]) & a great range of it. I have taken my morning, noon, &
afternoon walk upon it. My Therm: was only at 32, when the snow fell – at
York it was said to be – 4 March the 4th at 10 p.m. Farh^t*; was at 14 – on the 5th
at Sun R. 7½. I observe in general that the point of Sun R. ...[131] the coldest time,
or about ten min[utes][132] after. When I first got up (about 5½) the Th: on the 5th
March was at 10. I beg you wou'd cultivate as much as possible any attention
Mr Frend may be disposed to shew* you. I wou'd fain have you botanize in
your walks this spring – nothing so fortunate as a botanizing, an experimenting,
or any acquaintance that has a taste for any one thing upon earth but his hair &
his buckles.

As perhaps you may write notes to your Physician, or somebody or other,
don't say *Rhumatism** but consider the derivation,[133] & that no man shou'd
have a disorder which he can't spell, especially a man of Jesus. Adieu my d^r
Boy!

All pretty well here.

31. MALTHUS
TO DANIEL MALTHUS[134]
[Reply to 30]

March 16th – 86

Dear Sir;

My mother mentioned in her last letter[135] to me that you thought I might   16 March 1786
have caught my Rheumatism by shooting in the fens; but I never had any
particular fondness for that kind[136] of shooting – indeed I never tried it but once,

---

[129] A 'hundred' is a subdivision of a county or shire. The low-lying hundreds of Essex were generally regarded as unhealthy.

[130] Word difficult to decipher; possibly 'Tankerv's' or 'Tanckerv's'. See also the reference to 'L^d T's wall' in Daniel Malthus' letter no. 27. Charles (Bennet), earl of Tankerville (1743–1822), had a villa at Walton-on-Thames (GEC, Vol. XII, p. 635).

[131] Word covered by seal, probably 'is'.

[132] Word partially covered by seal.

[133] From the Greek 'rheum' meaning a flow or stream. In English, 'rheum' is the 'watery matter secreted ... from the nose, eyes, and mouth etc. ... which, when abnormal, was supposed to cause disease'. Rheumatism – characterised by inflammation and pain of the joints – was formerly supposed to be caused by a 'defluxion of rheum' (*OED*).

[134] Addressed: 'Danl Malthus Esq' / Walton upon Thames / Surry*'. Annotated: 'By Isleworth bag.' Postmark: '52 CAMBRIDGE'; on the back, '17 MR'. Also on the back, 'March 86– / Cam. / cong Rheumatism, / spelling D.' in a different hand.

[135] His mother's letter is wanting.

[136] Suffix 'est' is del.

45

16 March 1786 & that was last year. I have been only twice out with my gun since I left Walton – neither of the times in the fens.

As I am not in general particularly careful in avoiding things which are apt to give people colds, when I by chance get one, I seldom know how I came by it. The most probable thing that I can recollect to give me a cold & bring on a Rheumatism was the getting my feet wet one day in a walk, & then standing an hour & a half in the Schools[137] the first day they were opened, when the stone floor & walls were exceedingly damp. I felt the first approaches of the disorder very soon after, but it did not occur at all to me at the time [138] to what cause I was to attribute it. By the by I spelt my disorder right[139] when I gave an account of myself in my first letter, but I was afterwards led into an error by seeing Rhumatism* written by a person of whose knowledge in orthography I had a very high opinion, & not having a dictionary at hand I was induced rashly to forego* my own judgement – I confess a man of Jesus, as you call one, ought to be more firm in any thing of that kind than to yield so easily.

There has been no good ice here this last frost, so that I don't so much regret the loss of the skaiting* as I should otherwise. Mr Frend's Thermometer has not at any time been lower than 14, but I am rather inclined to think that either from nature or situation it stands higher than the generality.

At Canterbury where Mr F. was the other frost, that gentlemans[140] Therm: (who sometime ago published an account he kept of three in different situations) at the lowest stood at two degrees below 0.

We had a little fall of snow the night before last, but it rained all yesterday & carried it off.

I have got out of my room again – two or three little walks which I took during the three fine days we had here after the breaking of the frost, have almost recovered my strength.

Kindest love to all. – Believe me your dutiful

& affectionate Son

RM.

---

[137] The 'Schools' is the university building in which most of the examinations are held (*OED*).
[138] 'that' is del.   [139] 'right' is ins.
[140] Mr Six. See letter no. 20.

32. MALTHUS
TO DANIEL MALTHUS[141]

April 19th – 86

Dear Sir,

Waiting for an opportunity of speaking to D[r] Beadon[142] about my taking   19 April 1786
orders, without calling on him expressly for the purpose, I had not receiv'd his
opinion upon the subject when your last letter[143] arrived. D[r] B was not then in
College. I have consulted him since his return, but his answer is not I think
quite satisfactory. He seem'd at first rather to advise against orders upon the
idea that the defect in my speech[144] would be an obstacle to my rising in the
Church, & he thought it a pity that a young man of some abilities should enter
into a profession without, at least, some hope of being at the top of it. When
however I afterwards told him that the utmost of [145] wishes was a retired living
in the country, he said he did not imagine that my speech would be [146] much
objection in that case; that for his own part when I read or declaimed in Chapel
he scarcely ever lost a single word.

As to the business of getting into orders, he did not conceive there was any
legal objection, but the Bishops had it so entirely in their power to ordain whom
they pleased, that it was impossible to say how they would act, he thought there
were some who might refuse but that the generality woud* not.

I was rather mistaken in what I said last year about the bishop of Ely[147] – I
thought D[r] B was very intimate with him, & that he ordained all the Jesus men,
but I find[148] that he has rather been a[t][149] variance with the college lately, &
th[at][150] the men are ordained by any bishop they chuse,* after their testimonials[151]
are sign'd by the College.

---

[141] Addressed: 'Dan! Malthus Esq[r] / Walton upon Thames / Surry*'. Annotated: 'By Isleworth bag.'
Postmark: '52 CAMBRIDGE'; on the back, '22 AP'. Also on the back, 'April, 86 / from Cam' in a
different hand.

[142] Richard Beadon (1737–1824), BA, became master of Jesus College in 1781. He was made bishop of
Gloucester in 1789, and bishop of Bath and Wells in 1802 (*DNB*).

[143] Daniel Malthus referred to taking orders in letter no. 29 of 3 March 1786. Malthus here appears to be
explaining why he had not referred to orders in his reply (letter no. 31 of 16 March) to Daniel Malthus'
'last letter' (no. 30 of 12 March). Alternatively, Daniel Malthus might have written a further letter
(now wanting) after 12 March urging Malthus to enquire about orders.

[144] Malthus was born with a cleft palate and a cleft lip. See James 1979, pp. 2–4 etc.

[145] Malthus presumably intended to write 'my' here.

[146] 'very ob' is del.

[147] Right Revd James Yorke, confirmed 3 September 1781, died 26 August 1808.

[148] 'find' is ins.   [149] Word partially covered by seal.   [150] Word partially covered by seal.

[151] In Malthus' case, a testimonial from the master and fellows of Jesus College was sent to the bishop of
Winchester on 12 May 1789. It stated that Malthus 'hath for these four years last past, in which he
hath been resident amongst us, behaved himself soberly and regularly and been diligent in his Studies,
in which he hath made very good Proficiency; And ... we believe him well qualified for the Order and
Office of a Deacon in the Church.' See Pullen 1987a, p. 127.

19 April 1786   I am most extremely ashamed of the mistake I made in my last letter[152] & have nothing to say in excuse for it.

I'm got into my new rooms & like them very well. I ask'd Mr Frend again about the Thermometer at Canterbury – he says it was[153] Faren.* scale; & that the same night a Ther. upon a steeple 240 feet high stood at 15. I rather think that the reason why Mr Frend's Ther. always stands so high is that it is placed at a window 15 or 16 feet from the ground. Kindest love to all. Your affectionate Son RM.

33. MALTHUS
TO DANIEL MALTHUS[154]

Cambridge June 26th 1786[155]

My dear Sir;

26 June 1786   I had promised myself the pleasure of seeing you the beginning of last week, but was unfortunately prevented by a slight return of my former complaint.[156] I happen'd to be on the water rather late in the evening the week before last, & by playing tricks in a Canoe got myself overturned. Imprudently I remained a considerable time in my wet cloaths* which I imagine gave me cold & occasioned a return of the disorder. I have been laid up as to my hands & wrists this last week, but have now recoverd* their use, & have reason to hope that I shall escape with my feet untouched. I think I shall be able to be in the environs of Guilford* the end of this week or beginning of next.

I am extremely concerned that you have all been in such a disagreeable state of uncertainty with regard to a house, for so long a time;[157] & sincerely wish that you may have now found one that will suit my mother, & yourself – the rest of the family I am pretty sure have very little choice.

I was much vex'd that I coud* not inform myself where those pamphlets were to be had; but Mr Frend left Cambridge before I received your first letter[158] – He intends, I believe, to pass p[art][159] of the summer abroad.

[152] Malthus' previous letter in this collection (no. 31 of 16 March 1786) does not appear to contain any shameful mistake. The 'last letter' referred to here must therefore be wanting, together with a letter from Daniel Malthus admonishing his son for the mistake.

[153] 'was' is written over 'is'.

[154] Addressed: 'Danl Malthus Esqr / at Mr Russel's Stationer / Guilford* / Surry*'. Annotated: 'to be forwarded'. Postmark: '...BRIDGE'; on the back, '27 JU'. Also on the back, 'June 86 / Cambridge' in a different hand. The address suggests that Daniel Malthus and family were in the process of moving from Walton-on-Thames but had not actually settled at Albury. The next letter (no. 34) is addressed to Albury, which is four miles south-east of Guildford, but Daniel Malthus' letter no. 35 of 16 June 1787 indicates that renovations to the house at Albury were still not completed.

[155] The '7' in the date is written over an '8'.   [156] Letter no. 31.   [157] See letter no. 6.

[158] This letter is wanting.   [159] Word partially covered by seal.

I will not be *absolutely* positive, but I think I have made no mistake in the 26 June 1786 account I received from M' F. of the Thermometers at Canterbury. I remember making him repeat once or twice that the Ther. on the ground was 2 degrees below nothing, while that on the top of the tower was 15. – 17 deg. difference. I am extremely sorry to hear of the bad state of your eyes – I hope they are not likely to continue so any time.

Kindest love to all. Believe me
your dutiful
& affectionate Son
R Malthus.

I do not know whether my direction will find you but I thought it the most probable one.

34. MALTHUS
TO DANIEL MALTHUS[160]

Cambridge Febr^y 9th – 1787[161]

Dear Sir;

I have been so hurried lately by the business of the schools, that I have 9 Feb. 1787 hardly had time to look round me, which indeed has been the cause of my long silence. I had to keep the second day of the opening of the schools[162] which was much sooner than I expected. However, I got it over very well, the day before yesterday, & received an *optimè*.[163] I am now very busy making arguments for an opponency[164] which I am to keep next wednesday against the first man of our year. I have attended most of the explanatory part of our course of astronomical lectures, & I like them very well – when the weather grows warmer & finer,[165] we are to begin a regular course of observations.

I have got Longs Astronomy & an edition of Newtons principia without notes for my prize books.

---

[160] Addressed: 'Dan Malthus Esq' / Albury near / Guildford / Surrey'. Postmark: '54 CAMBRIDGE'; on the back, 'FEBY 10 D'. Also on the back, 'fr Cambridge / Feb 87 / preparing for keeping an act in the schools' in a different hand.

[161] The '9' in the date is written over an '8'.

[162] This refers to a public oral examination in which the candidate is required to maintain a thesis. See also letters no. 31 and 36.

[163] 'Optimè', from the Latin, 'optime disputasti', is 'one who has been placed in the second or third division, called respectively senior and junior optimes, in the Mathematical Tripos at Cambridge' (*OED*).

[164] An 'opponency' is 'the action or position of opponent in an academical disputation as an exercise for a degree' (*OED*).

[165] '& finer' is ins.

9 Feb. 1787   I must draw for my quarters allowance, & I am very sorry to say, (to get myself at all clear after having paid the surgeon & apothecary) for fifteen pounds more. I was in great hopes I should have managed with ten, but I received a bill of fourteen pounds for the time I staid* up in the summer beyond the quarter, when[166] I had the Rheumatism, near four of which was for the apothecary. It seems they always charge the college servants &c: for half a quarter tho you only stay a day. Will it be convenient for me to draw now.

I am very well tho a little ...[167] still remains.

I am happy to hear Charlotte[168] is much better. Kindest love to all. Believe me your dutiful

& affectionate Son
R Malthus

35. DANIEL MALTHUS
TO MALTHUS[169]

June 16. [1787]

My dear Boy,

16 June 1787   I wrote to you three or four days since from Albury, but I have some notion I left the letter lock'd up in my desk. I receiv'd yours to Bath,[170] & immediately resolv'd that I wou'd not come to Cambridge at present, as it wou'd be with the utmost reluctance that I shou'd delay the pleasure we shall all have in seeing you at Albury: besides I am far from preferring a publick* time, unless it were to hear the Bishop.

You must find your way to us over bricks & tiles, & meet with five in a bed, & some of us under hedges; but everybody says they will make room for Robert. May I take the liberty of sending my compliments to Mʳ Frend, with my most grateful thanks for the attention he has been so kind as to shew* you. You will guess the pleasure I have in returning thanks for that notice which you wou'd not have had without deserving it. [171] Everything I have heard of you has given me the most heartfelt satisfaction. [172] I have always wish'd, my dear boy, that you shou'd have a love of letters, that you shou'd be made independent of

---

[166] 'at the time' is del. and 'when' is ins.   [167] Word partially covered by seal, possibly 'langour'.
[168] Malthus' sister, Mary Catherine Charlotte (1764–1821).
[169] Addressed: 'Mʳ Robert Malthus / Jesus College / Cambridge'. Postmark on the back: 'JU 16 87' and 'PAID PENNY POST VSM'. Also on the back, 'June 87' in a different hand.
[170] This letter is wanting.
[171] A cross at this point and another at the end of the sentence suggest that Daniel Malthus wished to give the contents particular emphasis.
[172] A second cross here.

mean & trifling amusements, & feel a better support than that of the next man 16 June 1787 who is idle enough to offer you his company. I have no doubt that you will be able to procure any distinction from them you please – I am far from repressing your ambition; but I shall content myself with their adding to your happiness. Ev'ry kind of knowledge, ev'ry acquaintance with nature & art will amuse & strengthen your mind, & I am perfectly pleased that cricket shou'd do the same by your legs & arms. I love to see you excel in exercises of the body; & I think myself that the better half, & much the most agreeable one of the pleasures of the mind is best enjoy'd while one is upon one's legs – this is pretty well for me to say, who have little else left but my bed, & my arm chair. May you long enjoy all the delights of youth, & youthful spirits, of an improving mind, & of a healthful body – but ever and above all, my dear boy, with virtue and its best affections in your heart.

[173] Adieu!
Danl Malthus

We are all pretty well. Your mother & sister send their kindest love. Syd is with us, & sends love, & longs to see you.

36. MALTHUS
TO DANIEL MALTHUS[174]

Cambridge Novr 4th 1787.

Dear Sir;

I suppose you think I am so very busy at Cambridge now, that I cant find 4 Nov. 1787 time even to read much less to write a letter – Having however just got some little part of my business over, I determined to take this opportunity of letting you hear from me, in case I shoud* not find another.

The day before yesterday, I kept an act[175] in the Schools, was two hours & a half in the box, & in high dispute the whole[176] time. I believe it was the longest act that has been known for a good while. I came off with great credit, & got what is call'd a long honour. Upon the whole I was extremely well satisfied with myself as I coud* hardly have expected to have done so well, & coud* not have wishd* to have done much better.

I am much afraid I shall not be near so well satisfied with myself at the

---

[173] An asterisk here.

[174] Addressed: 'Dan Malthus Esqr / Albury near / Guildford / Surrey'. Postmark: 'CAMBRIDGE'; on the back, 'NO 5 87'. Also on the back in a different hand, 'Cam / Nov. 87 / kept an act in ...' (last word unclear, probably 'schools').

[175] An 'act', in the universities, is 'a thesis publicly maintained by a candidate for a degree, or to show a student's proficiency' (*OED*). See Ch. 2, n. 162 above.

[176] 'the whole' is repeated.

51

4 Nov. 1787   Senate house Examination. I find that all the high men (that are to be) have been at Cambridge the whole summer reading hard; so that I can have but a very poor chance among them. I shall think myself fortunate [177] if I get a wrangler, which indeed I shoud* dispair* of but that my keeping in the schools will be much in my favour.

The Tutor has not sent us in, either of our two last quarters bills, so that I have not drawn for my midsu[mmer][178] or last quarters allowance. I suppose you will have no objection to my drawing for both quarters together when the bills do com* in.

I am perfectly well in health. I hope everybody is so at Albury, tho I hear Syd's knee is not yet quite recoverd.* Kindest love to all – Believe me your dutiful &

affectionate Son

R Malthus

37. DANIEL MALTHUS
TO MALTHUS[179]
[Answered by 38]

Albury March 24ᵗʰ. [1788]

Dear Robert,

24 March 1788   I am much obliged to you for your kind enquiries. My blister gave me very little trouble after I saw you, or my cold either. I congratulate you upon your declamation prize. It is agreeable after having excelled in Mathematicks,* to shew* one can do something else. I shall leave the books to your own taste. I beg you wou'd draw for whatever is convenient to you. I will write to Mʳ Elmsly to send you Kirwan's Mineralogy,[180] if he can procure it.

I am,

Dear Robert,

Your affectionate father,

Danˡ Malthus

We are all pretty well here. Your mother has had a very bad cough; but she is now better. Poor Mʳ Ryves[181] has had another attack of an alarming kind!

---

[177] 'I' is del.   [178] Word partially covered by seal.

[179] Addressed: 'Mʳ Robert Malthus / Jesus College / Cambridge'. Postmark: '11 GUILDFORD'; on the back, 'MR 25 88'. Also on the back, 'March –88' in a different hand.

[180] Richard Kirwan, *Elements of Mineralogy*, London, 1784. This was 'the first systematic treatise on the subject in English, and was translated into French, German, and Russian' (*DNB*).

[181] Presumably Thomas Ryves, Malthus' uncle; he died that year (1788). See Ch. 1, n. 11 above.

38. MALTHUS
TO DANIEL MALTHUS[182]
[Reply to 37]

Cambridge April 17th – 88

Dear Sir;

I received the book you were so good as to send me, for which I am very   17 April 1788
much obliged to you.

I have taken for the prize the biographical dictionary[183] which I shoud*
think woud* be a very useful book to have by one, & I believe you have not it
among yours. There is a very extensive work of that kind,[184] I understand, coming
out, but it will be some considerable time before it is perfectly finished, & from
its expence* woud* not come at all within the proposed sum. With regard to
Watsons Theological tracts[185] they are but a guinea & a half in boards, & may
therefore be had at any time.

I have laid aside my chemistry for a while, & am at present endeavouring
to get some little knowledge of general history & geography. I have been lately
reading Gibbon's decline of the Roman Empire. He gives one some useful
information concerning the origin & progress of those nations of barbarians
which now form the polished states of Europe; & throws some light upon the
beginning of that dark period which so long overwhelmed the world, & which
cannot I think but excite one's curiosity. He is a very entertaining writer, in my
opinion; his style is sometimes really sublime, every where interesting &
agreeable, tho perhaps it may in general be call'd rather too florid for history. I
shall like much to see his next[186] volumes.[187]

I have got a history of modern Europe in letters from a nobleman to his

---

[182] Addressed: 'Dan Malthus Esq' / Albury near / Guildford / Surrey'. Postmark: 'CAMBRIDGE'; on the
back, 'AP 19 88'. Also on the back, 'April 88 / from Cam / abt leaving it' in a different hand.

[183] Bonar (1941, Ch. 4, p. 67) suggested that this could be *Biographia Britannica: or, the Lives of the
Most Eminent Persons who Have Flourished in Great Britain and Ireland ...* 6 vols., London, 1747–
66. A copy of this work was in the Malthus Library (Dalton Hill).

[184] Bonar (1941, Ch. 4, p. 67) suggested that the 'very extensive work of that kind' would have been the
second edition of the above, viz. *Biographica Britannica ... The Second Edition with Corrections,
Enlargements, and the Addition of New Lives,* by Andrew Kippis and others, Vols. I–V [Aaron-
Fastolff], London, 1778–93. No more of this second edition was published.

[185] The Malthus Library has *A Collection of Theological Tracts,* 6 vols., 1785, ed. by Richard Watson
(1737–1816), bishop of Llandaff.

[186] 'next' is ins.

[187] Edward Gibbon (1737–1794), *The History of the Decline and Fall of the Roman Empire,* 6 vols.,
London, 1776–88. Vol. I was published in 1776, Vols. II and III in 1781, and Vols. IV, V and VI in
1788. The Malthus Library has an edition in twelve volumes, London, 1783–90.

17 April 1788 s...[188] which seems to be a good thing. I consult Danville's ancient maps[189] & Duns modern Atlas.[190] This kind of reading makes me however lament more the having no prospect of a travelling fellowship.

I have had two or three applications lately for my rooms when I leave College, & the more particular purport of this letter is[191] to know whether you would have me give them up when I leave Cambridge this next time, which I believe will be before the middle of May, – in short whether you design that I shoud* return again to reside, or not. With regard to myself I am perfectly without a choice, & shoud* therefore wish to refer it entirely to you. I shall not I believe be old enough to go into orders this[192] year or more. Thus much perhaps I shoud* say with respect to residing at Cambridge that with a certainty of not exceeding my allowance which I shoud* then think indespensably* necessary, I coud* not live here above five months in the year.[193]

Adieu my dear Sir. I shoud* wish to hear from you soon. Your affectionate Son. R Malthus.

39. DANIEL MALTHUS
TO MALTHUS[194]

Albury. March 20ᵗʰ. [1789][195]

Dear Robert,

20 March 1789   I shou'd have answer'd your letter before, but that I was in hopes of giving you some intelligence about a title which has come in my way. It is Okewood Chapel,[196] which perhaps you may remember to have seen in your walk round Hale, where I think you once was upon some occasion of dining with Mʳ & Mʳˢ

---

[188] Word partially covered by seal. This work was possibly [Oliver Goldsmith], *An History of England, in a Series of Letters from a Nobleman to his Son*, 2 vols., 1764.

[189] Jean-Baptiste Bourguignon d'Anville (1697–1782) compiled over 200 maps. Malthus was possibly referring to his *Atlas Antiquus Major*, 1768. See Lister 1970, p. 49, and *Map Collectors' Circle*, Vol. 2, 1964–5, p. 19.

[190] Samuel Dunn (or Dun), *General Atlas* ('*Dunn's Atlas*'), [1768 etc.]. See *Map Collectors' Circle*, Vol. 4, 1966–7, p. 124.

[191] 'was' is del. and 'is' is ins.   [192] 'for a' is del. and 'this' is ins.

[193] From here onwards, written on the back, but folded under.

[194] Addressed: 'Mʳ Robert Malthus'. No postmark. On the back, in a different hand, 'March / about Oakwood Chapel / probably in 88 or 89' (88 is then del.).

[195] The year 1789 is implied by subsequent detail of letter no. 40, postmarked 1789.

[196] Malthus was ordained deacon on 7 June 1789 and was licensed as the stipendiary curate of Okewood on 8 June 1789 at an annual stipend of £40. See Pullen 1987a, p. 129. Okewood (also spelt Oakwood) is in the parish of Wotton in the county of Surrey. It is in the south of the county, about eight miles in a direct line south-east of Albury. While serving as a curate at Okewood, Malthus presumably resided with his parents at Albury.

Eckersall.[197] You might have a room or two in their farmhouse,[198] (where they   20 March 1789
once lived themselves you know) & you wou'd find your first beginning
extreamly* quiet, with very little duty that cou'd be irksome to you. The living
belongs to S[r] F. Evelyn,[199] & is in the possession of a M[r] Hallam[200] (I may mistake
the name) who is a Cambridge man, & as I understood, resided at Cambridge;
but I since find he is now at least[201] in London. M[r] Duncombe's eldest son[202] has
the curacy; but he proposes to give it up, as he has more duty than he is able to
perform. M[r] Duncombe will see his son next sunday, when he will be able to
give me a more particular account, & a final determination. The business will
then be to apply immediately to M[r] Hallam, who if he shou'd not be engaged,
may have an opportunity of enquiring about you at Cambridge, & might possibly
receive some recommendations from your kind friends there. I beg you wou'd
present my particular compliments to D[r] Beadon, ...[203] my warmest thanks for
his obliging ...ention[204] to you. I cou'd immediately ...[205] such an income upon
you as wou'd be equivalent to a title, & am most willing to do it: I don't know
however if that may be deem'd satisfactory at present, tho' it certainly wou'd
have been accepted [206] some years ago. Okewood is in the Diocese of Winchester.
I don't know that the Bishop of W.[207] is more than ordinarily difficult. I wou'd
not by any means confine you to place: you will therefore consult with intelligent
persons at Cambridge, & I will, as soon as possible, procure you all the

---

197 Probably John Eckersall (1748–1837) and Catherine Eckersall (1755–1837), the parents of Malthus'
future wife, Harriet. See Ch. 2, n. 227 below.

198 Probably Halehouse Farm, situated about half a mile north-west of Okewood.

199 Sir Frederick Evelyn (1734–1812), third baronet of Wotton and Sayes Court (*BLG*, Vol. I, p. 244). As
patrons of the parish of Wotton, the Evelyn family held 'the living', i.e. they could nominate the
rectors and curates of the parish.

200 Revd John Hallam (1753–1824) matriculated at Trinity College, Cambridge 1771; graduated BA
1775, MA 1778; and became perpetual curate of Okewood Chapel (Venn). James notes that Hallam
'seems to have visited Okewood rarely, and in 1820 was living in Westminster' (1979, p. 331).

201 'least' is ins.

202 Revd Thomas Duncumb [sic] (d. 1804) was rector of Shere, Surrey; his son, of the same name, was
rector of Shere from 1805 until his death in 1843. It is probably the latter who held the curacy of
Okewood in 1789. He graduated BA 1783, MA 1786 (Foster).

203 MS torn; probably '&'.   204 Word partially obscured by torn MS; probably 'attention'.

205 Word covered by seal; possibly 'settle'.   206 'as a title' is del.

207 Right Revd Brownlow North (1741–1820).

20 March 1789 information in my[208] power upon the subject of my letter. I wou'd not omit writing by Mr Godschall,[209] tho' I cou'd not do it fully.

I am Dr Robert,

Your affectionate father,

Dan Malthus

Your mother has a very bad cold in her face. Kitty[210] is better I hope. Lucy gone to Mrs Peters.

40. DANIEL MALTHUS
TO MALTHUS[211]

April 25th. [1789]

Dear Robert,

25 April 1789   I have the very great pleasure of telling you that your mother makes an uninterrupted progress in recovery. She has a very free & full enjoyment of sleep, & appetite, & all the sensations of health. The only symptom of consequence that remains, is the swelling of the ancles,* & that within these two days has diminish'd fast.

Everybody will be extreamly* glad to see you here,[212] when you like to come. I am, now that I can leave your mother pretty well, going from the place.

I have been heartily vex'd that this curacy, from one or two unfortunate circumstances in time, but I can truly say from no neglect of mine has fail'd of his purpose. I still expect a letter from Mr Hallam ev'ry day; but I cannot depend upon it. In his last he told me that there was no occasion to write to Dr Beadon. Do you think it wou'd be better to take Harry Ryvess[213] offer (if he shoud* make it again, & I desir'd him to speak to Mr Manning[214] about it), or to try for

---

[208] 'my' is ins.

[209] Probably Samuel Man Godschall (1764–1821), who became Malthus' brother-in-law later in 1789 when he married Malthus' sister, Anne Catherine Lucy (mentioned in Daniel's footnote to this letter). This letter was apparently delivered personally by Samuel Man Godschall to Malthus. Samuel Man Godschall's parents lived in Albury, and he was a contemporary of Malthus at Cambridge. He matriculated at Trinity Hall, Cambridge, and graduated LL B in 1789. See Venn; James 1966.

[210] Presumably Malthus' younger sister, Mary Anne Catherine (1771–1852). See James 1979.

[211] Addressed: 'Mr Robert Malthus / Jesus College / Cambridge'. Postmark: '24 RIPLEY'; on the back, 'AP 28 89'. The letter was apparently written at their home in Albury, but posted at Ripley, which is about 6 miles north of Albury. Next to address, 'April 89' in a different hand.

[212] 'here' is ins.

[213] The context suggests that Harry Ryves was a rector and had offered Malthus a curacy in his parish. This Harry Ryves could therefore have been Malthus' cousin, Revd Henry Pleydell Ryves, a son of Thomas Ryves (1720–1788), of Ranston, Dorset, who married Anna Maria (née Graham), the younger sister of Malthus' mother. Revd Henry Ryves (1759/60–1817) was rector of Chesleborne, Dorset, and prebendary of Chichester (Foster). See Ch. 1, n. 11 above.

[214] Possibly Revd Owen Manning (died 1801), co-author with William Bray (1736–1832) of *History of Surrey*.

something where you are? I don't know what Bishop you wou'd then be ordain'd   25 April 1789
by, or whether he may be prefer...[215] to the B. of Winchester.

Kitty is, I think, something ...[216] amendment seems to be owing to a blister.[217] Everybody else well. I believe I told you Syd was here.

I am Dr Robert, Your affectionate father,
Danl Malthus

41. DANIEL MALTHUS
TO MALTHUS[218]

Sunday [13 June 1790][219]

I find myself anxious to hear from you my dear Bob, & am sorry I did not   13 June 1790
make you promise to write to me. I am at Albury, where Miss D.[220] is the only female inhabitant, of the parlour at least. She was going into Hants;[221] but has been stopt* by her cottage,[222] & another St Anthony.[223] She has been nearly as bad as she was the first time: however she is now recovering. I made a visit to Brighton of a few days, & found your mother pretty well, & Charlotte[224] much

---

[215] MS torn; the missing word is possibly 'preferable' or 'preferred'.

[216] MS torn; the missing words are possibly 'better; her'.

[217] In the sense apparently intended here, a blister, or vesicatory, is a 'sharp irritating ointment, plaster, or other application for causing the formation of a blister or blisters on the skin' in order to reduce inflammation and/or relieve pain (*OED*).

[218] Addressed: 'Revd Robert Malthus / Jesus College / Cambridge'. Postmark on the back: 'JU 15 90'. Also on the back, 'Spring 90 / from Burford' in a different hand. This is the first letter in this correspondence to be addressed to the 'Revd' Robert Malthus. The letter was apparently started at Albury and finished at Burford. There is a Burford in the Cotswolds district of Oxfordshire and another in Shropshire, but the context suggests that Daniel Malthus was here referring to the house called Burford Lodge, near Box Hill in Surrey, about 1½ miles north of Dorking, which is about 7½ miles east of Albury. Burford Lodge was the home of John Eckersall (1748–1837), who was Daniel Malthus' nephew (the son of his sister, Catherine Malthus) and the future father-in-law of Malthus. Later, 'getting tired of the place', John Eckersall moved to Bath (Bray 1857). According to Patricia James, the move from Burford Lodge occurred after the birth at Burford Lodge on 8 April 1790 of the seventh Eckersall child (Anne Eliza), but the Eckersall family did not move directly to Bath. A picture of Burford Lodge is in John Timbs, *A Picturesque Promenade round Dorking, in Surrey*, 2nd edn, 1823, p. 38. According to Timbs, 'Mr. Eckersale* to whom this property belonged in 1786, planted a part of it with choice exotics, and planned several winding walks. Here, also, he erected a votive pedestal and urn, to the memory of the poet Shenstone...'

[219] The Sunday preceding the date of the postmark was Sunday 13 June 1790.

[220] Miss Dalton. See Ch. 1, n. 23.   [221] Hampshire.

[222] Miss Dalton owned a cottage in Albury. According to Louisa Bray, she had a 'remarkable taste in laying out grounds, or doing anything that required a picturesque effect ... Her own Cottage and grounds at Albury were perfection.' In her will she left the 'cottage' (a house with two staircases and about ten acres of ground) to Malthus' brother, Sydenham (James 1979, p. 12).

[223] 'St Anthony's fire', a popular name for erysipelas, arising from the tradition that relief from the disease could be obtained by prayer to St Anthony. Erysipelas is a local febrile disease, accompanied by a diffused inflammation of the skin, producing a deep red colour; often called St Anthony's fire, or 'the rose' (*OED*).

[224] Malthus' sister, Mary Catherine Charlotte (1764–1821).

13 June 1790 about the same, & Katherine[225] in a very agreeable state of health, without being directly cured of the obstruction in her lungs. She goes on bathing, & Charlotte has began* cold bathing. I write this from Burford, poor Burford! for which I feel the affection I am apt to feel for [a] place, which I join in so many scenes with the people I love, while I look back to past days, & which to see utterly seperately* from those people, is a pang to my heart. The Morrisons are here for a few days. Saturday sennight[226] is the last day the Eckersalls will be here. To part with it in all the beauties of spring, & to go to their destination in the month of october is a cruel trial. I hope Mrs E.[227] is led by young & delightful hope – arve Ausoniae semper cedentia retro.[228] My sister Wathen is much better. The Eckersalls for the present, I believe are going to *Paddington*, & she with them, till the journey to Wrington.[229] Let me have a line, with something of your own hopes. The Brighton party returns saturday sennight. The Godschalls[230] are at Pit House. Whoever is at Albury I am sure will be happy to receive you when you return; & none more, believe me my dear Bob, than,

Your truly affectionate

D.M.

I send my letter by the Ms[231] – I coud* not in conscience have made you pay ^{d}6 for it.

---

[225] Despite the spelling 'Katherine', this is presumably Malthus' sister, Mary Anne Catherine (1771–1852), who married Edward Bray a few months later (28 September 1790). They had eleven children. Her daughter, Louisa Bray, recorded that her mother 'at 16 ... was supposed to be going into decline, and for a whole year lived on a vegetable diet, and was bled every month ...' Letters no. 39 and 40 also refer to Catherine's health.

[226] An archaic term meaning 'a period of seven (days and) nights; a week' (*OED*).

[227] Mrs Catherine Eckersall (1755–1837) was a niece of Daniel Malthus – the daughter of his 'sister Wathen', i.e. Elizabeth Wathen (née Malthus). The Mr and Mrs Eckersall of Burford Lodge were thus first cousins to one another, being children of Daniel Malthus' sisters, Catherine and Elizabeth.

Harriet Eckersall (1776–1864), the first of the eleven children of the Eckersalls of Burford Lodge, married Malthus in 1804.

[228] Adapted from Virgil, *Aeneid*, III, 496–7: 'arva neque Ausoniae semper cedentia retro quaerenda'. In the context of the 'cruel trial' about to be faced by Mrs Eckersall – i.e. the leaving of her home at Burford Lodge – the meaning intended by Daniel Malthus in this adaptation of Virgil was probably: 'the fields of Ausonia [i.e. Italy] continually receding into the background' – conveying the sadness aroused by the impending departure (AT).

[229] Another daughter (Anna) of Elizabeth Wathen married (in 1786) Revd William Leeves (1748–1828), poet and composer (*DNB*); rector of Wrington, in Somerset, about nine miles east of Weston-Super-Mare. The letter suggests that Elizabeth Wathen – who was then a widow, her husband having died in 1787 – was to travel with her daughter (Catherine Eckersall) and family to Paddington, and thence to visit her other daughter (Anna Leeves) at Wrington.

[230] Daniel Malthus' daughter, Anne Catherine Lucy (1762–1823), married Samuel Man Godschall on 10 August 1789. See James 1979. Their usual place of residence was Weston House, described at length and with great affection in Louisa Bray's recollections.

[231] Possibly the Morrisons mentioned above. Daniel Malthus apparently believed that they would be passing through Cambridge, and that if they delivered the letter in person, Malthus would avoid having to pay the postage. But the fact that this letter is postmarked implies that this direct delivery did not occur. Daniel Malthus' will (1779) left a legacy of £600 to General George Morrison (1704–1799). See James 1979, p. 76.

42. DANIEL MALTHUS
TO MALTHUS[232]

Manly Bridge[233] Sunday [1793][234]

I heartily congratulate you upon your success – it gives me a sort of pleasure   1793
which arises from my own regrets. The things which I have miss'd in life, I
shou'd the more sensibly wish for you. Alas my dear Bob I have no right to talk
to you of idleness! but when I wrote[235] that letter to you with which you was
displeased, I was deeply impress'd with my own broken purposes, & imperfect
pursuits; I thought I foresaw in you, from the memory of my own youth, the
same tendency to lose the steps you had gain'd, with the same disposition to
self reproach, & I wish'd to make my unfortunate experience of some use to
you. It was indeed but little that you wanted it, which made me the more eager
to give it you: & I wrote to you with more tenderness of heart than I wou'd in
general pretend to, & committed myself in a certain manner, which made your
answer a rough disappointment to me, & it[236] drove me back into myself. You
have, as you say, worn out that impression, & you have a good right to have
done it; for I have seen in you the most unexceptionable character, the sweetest
manners, the most sensible, & the kindest conduct, always above *throwing little
stones into my garden*, which you know I don't well forgive, & uniformly making
ev'rybo[dy][237] easy, & amused about you. Nothing can have been wanting to
what, if I were the most fretful & fastigious,* I cou'd have required in a
companion; & nothing even to my wishes for your [238] happiness, but when they
were either whimsical, or unreasonable, or most likely mistaken. I have often
been ...[239] the point of taking hold of your hand ...[240] bursting into tears, at the
time that ...[241] was refusing you my affections – my approbation I was precipitate
to give you. I hardly know what I say, for I am at Syd's, & talking to him about

---

[232]   Addressed: 'Revd Mr R. Malthus / Jesus College / Cambridge'. Postmark on the back: 'J... 2...' (Second
letter of month, second digit of day, and two digits of year, difficult to decipher). Also on the back,
'from Manly Bridge / about 89 / after he [?had taken] orders' in a different hand.

[233]   Manly (or Manley) Bridge is in Farnham (Surrey), which is about thirteen miles west of Albury. The
Gentleman's Magazine (Vol. 68, 1798, p. 1148), reporting the marriage of Sydenham Malthus, said
he was 'of Manley-bridge, Hants [sic]'.

[234]   Bonar (1941, Ch. 4, p. 65) suggests a '1787' date, and that the 'success' mentioned in the first line was
Malthus' graduation and wranglership. But Malthus did not graduate until 1788. Also, the fact that the
letter was addressed to the 'Revd' Malthus precludes '1787', as Malthus was ordained in 1789. William
Otter (1968, p. xxviii) and William Empson (1837, p. 475) believed that it was written on the occasion
of Malthus' election to a fellowship of Jesus College – which occurred on 10 June 1793. The fact that
the letter was sent to 'Jesus College' suggests that Malthus was exercising his right, as a fellow, to
reside in college.

[235]   'I wrote' appears twice, the first is del. The letter that displeased Malthus is wanting.

[236]   'it' is ins.   [237] MS torn; word partially missing.   [238] 'own' is del.

[239]   MS torn; word missing, probably 'on'.   [240] MS torn; word missing, probably 'and'.

[241]   MS torn; word missing, probably 'I'.

1793 his cottage, which really looks beautifully today. I did not tell you, I believe, that
he went with us to Brighton – he took Maria in the chair with him – but you have
heard from Maria. Write to me, if I cou'd do anything about your church,[242] &
you want anything to be done for you. Such as I am! – believe me, dear Bob,
Yours most affectionately
D.M.
All pretty well. I go for your mother thursday next.

---

[242] This was presumably a reference not to Okewood Chapel, but to Malthus' desire to obtain a church of his own, i.e. to become a rector rather than remain as a curate. He was appointed rector of Walesby, in Lincolnshire, in 1803. See James 1979, pp. 101–2.

3 Later family correspondence

The six letters in this chapter begin with one written in 1796 to Malthus from his father concerning a political pamphlet entitled 'The Crisis...' which Malthus tried unsuccessfully to publish. It shows that Daniel Malthus had supported his son's literary effort and encouraged him to persist in his attempt to have the pamphlet published, even though the radical views expressed in it might have reduced his son's prospects in his ecclesiastical career.

The second letter, from Malthus to his father, was written in 1799, the year following the publication of the first edition of the *Essay on Population*, and provides evidence of the research being undertaken by Malthus for the second edition of the *Essay*.

The third letter was from Malthus to his father in the summer of 1799 when the former was at Stockholm on a tour of Scandinavia and Russia.

The fourth item consists of two drafts of a letter written in February 1800 from Malthus to the editor of the *Monthly Magazine* correcting an obituary of his father that had appeared in the previous issue. The writer of the obituary had stated that Daniel Malthus was the anonymous translator of several French and German works. Malthus replied that his father had indeed published anonymously, but asserted, somewhat indignantly, that his father had not published any translations.

The fifth letter is from Malthus' sister-in-law concerning financial problems arising from the estate of his recently deceased brother, Sydenham. Malthus was an executor of the will. The final letter in this set, dated 1825, is a brief letter to his wife, 'My dearest Harriet'. Inscribed 'Not to be opened till after my death', it discusses the distribution of property between their two surviving children, and concludes with a simple but very moving statement of his affection.

43. DANIEL MALTHUS
TO MALTHUS[1]

Bath April 14th. [1796]

14 April 1796   I am very glad, my dear Bob, that your next week's dinners did not depend upon your pamphlet, as you were so soon discouraged. There is no doubt you might have got it printed, there is still time to do it, & I shou'd be very willing to bear you harmless.[2] The truth is that the market overflows, & if there is not some par[tic]ular[3] abuse, or known name, the booksellers are not willing to risk their money. I wou'd give very little for Debret's* judgement with regard to the pamphlet; but I believe that what he said to you was a pretty true picture of the farce of publick* affairs. If any warning voice can awake us from this apathy, there never was a time when it was more wanted. What you have done appears to me to be extreamly* well done, & to be particularly adapted to the occasion. The bills only make a part of the general subject, & if they are now to be consider'd as puppets that have just passed in the procession, upon my life, it is not worth while to write seriously about anything. Debret,* as I believe I told you before, has seem'd for some time to be turning round to the side where there is most money. I wish you had call'd upon your old friend Mr Wakefield.

Give my love to your mother, & tell her I have found my sister[4] well & in great spirits. She now seems to be feeling the last morning fog or two & I hope I have persuaded her to go to ...,[5] if it be only for a week, till M^r & Mrs Wynne[6]

---

[1] Addressed: 'Revd Robert Malthus / Albury / Guildford / Surrey'. Postmark: 'BATH'; on the back, 'AP 16 96'. Also on the back, in a different hand, '96 / on the pamphlet' and '96 / on the pamphlet / from D. Malthus'. Watermark date: '1795'.

[2] 'bear' is apparently used here in the sense of 'to bear witness ... to testify', and 'harmless' in the archaic sense of 'free from guilt; innocent' (*OED*). In 1796 Malthus wrote a pamphlet entitled 'The Crisis, a View of the Present Interesting State of Great Britain, by a Friend to the Constitution'. As this letter states, he offered his pamphlet to the publisher Debrett, but failed to have it published. It was, however, seen by William Otter and William Empson, both of whom published extracts after Malthus' death. (See Otter 1968, pp. xxxv–xxxvii; Empson 1837, pp. 479–85.) Otter believed that Malthus' father opposed publication of the pamphlet – Malthus 'left [it] in MS. and refrained from printing it at his father's request' (p. xxxv) – but this letter shows that Daniel Malthus in fact encouraged his son to publish it. Mr Charles Kidd, editor, Debrett's Peerage Limited, has advised that their archives do not contain any references to Malthus' proposed pamphlet. See also Bonar 1924, pp. 7, 30–1, 332, 413–14; and Bonar 1941, Ch. 5.

[3] MS torn; word partially missing.

[4] As this letter implies that Daniel Malthus was staying with John Eckersall (1748–1837) at Bath (see Ch. 2, n. 218 above), the sister referred to here was probably Catherine, who married George Eckersall (1715–1770) in 1745, and was the mother of John Eckersall. See James 1979.

[5] Word difficult to decipher, possibly 'Kattern'.

[6] Catherine Eckersall (1777–1821), the daughter of Catherine Eckersall (1755–1837) and John Eckersall (1748–1837) had that year (1796) married the Revd Henry Wynne (1758/9–1828), rector of Killucan, Westmeath, Ireland. This Catherine Eckersall was a great-niece of Daniel Malthus, a first cousin once removed of Malthus, and a younger sister of Malthus' future wife (Harriet). The letter implies that Daniel Malthus (and Malthus) had not previously met the Revd Henry Wynne.

come back again. I saw them pass thro' Bath. Mr W. is an agreeable man, very
like Mr Fullarton of our country. They will be in Orchard Street,[7] or rather, they
are now there, with the Bishop of Ferns N° 22. You must call, if you are in
town. I forgot to say something about the prints in the upper room, which are a
nuisance in their present state. I wish Maria[8] wou'd be so good as to order a
quire of large tea paper, & put them into it. Everybody well here, except the
poor little Ryves,[9] who certainly is very indifferent. By the way, I shou'd except
Mr Eckersall,[10] who has had a smart fit of the gout, but is now recovering from
it.

Adieu my d^r Bob!

Ever most affectionately Yours

D.M.

I can't reconcile myself to your not publishing your pamphlet. I am sure it will
never do you discredit, tho' I can not answer that it will get you a Deanery.

44. MALTHUS
TO DANIEL MALTHUS[11]

Albury Feby. 4th. [1799]

My dear Sir;[12]

As the frost detains you in Town, and me in the country; and as you were
so kind as to make an offer of services to any of us in the way of commissions,
I will mention a few books which if you should hear of at any of the booksellers
where you happen to call, I wish you would get for me.

Susmilch's* Gottliche Ordnung Vol. I, 3rd edition. If it should be in German,

---

[7] The bishop of Ferns and Leighlin (a diocese in the province of Dublin) in 1796 was Euseby Cleaver
(1746–1819), later the archbishop of Dublin (*DNB*). This letter implies that the Wynnes were residing
with him at 22 Orchard St., in the Westminster district, London SW1. Henry Wynne was precentor of
Ferns, 1797–1824. See J. B. Leslie, *Ferns Clergy and Parishes*, 1936; information kindly supplied by
Helen Boothroyd, Assistant Archivist, Lambeth Palace Library.

[8] Malthus's sister, Eliza Maria (1761–1832), who was unmarried, and living at that time with their parents
at Albury.

[9] Presumably a descendant (grandchild?) of Thomas Ryves and Anna Maria Ryves.

[10] John Eckersall (1748–1837).

[11] Addressed: 'Danl Malthus Esqr / at Mr Knight's / Stationer / St James's Street / London'. Postmark:
'[?23] Holborn / Unpaid / Penny Post'; on the back, '... o'clock / ... FE / 99 ...'. Also on the back, in a
different hand, 'from Albury –99 / Feb 4'. Watermark date: '1798'. Also on the back, in another hand,
in pencil, 'Nickson / Duff / I of Fyfe', probably an unrelated note.

[12] Some numbers are written above 'My dear Sir'.

63

4 Feb. 1799   it will be of no use to me. The title seems to indicate that it is; but perhaps there may be a french or english translation.[13]

A memoir of Mr Wargenten,[14] in the Memoires* abregés* de l'academie* Royale de* sciences de Stockholm, printed at Paris in 1772. I should like to see this memoir; but probably there will be no getting it seperate,* & it will by no means be worth while to get the whole colletion.*

Muret's memoir on the state of population in the pais* de Vaud – printed at Berne in 66.[15] This I conceive to be the volume of the Berne transactions which you were[16] looking for & did not find.

Dr Haygarth on the population and diseases of Chester. Printed at Chester 1774.[17]

Kerseboom*[18] on the number of people in Holland.

I think it not impossible that Hookham may have the discourse on Christian union by Dr Styles*[19] which we both inquired for in vain: and perhaps – The

---

[13] Johann Peter Süssmilch (1707–1767), *Die göttliche Ordnung in den Veränderungen des menschlichen Geschlechts, aus der Geburt, dem Tode und der Fortpflanzung desselben erwiesen*, 3rd edn, Berlin, 1765. Malthus quoted extensively from *Die göttliche Ordnung* in his *Essay* and (to a lesser extent) in his *Principles*. There is no record of his having used either an original German edition, or a French or English translation. Patricia James has suggested that, not being able to read German, he must have obtained Süssmilch's statistics indirectly, either from Richard Price's *Observations* (see Ch. 3, n. 23 below) or from other sources. See Malthus 1989a and 1989b; James 1979.

[14] Pierre Wargentin, 'De l'homme; mortalité de l'homme en Suède, comparée à celle de la femme. Du nombre des naissances et des morts dans tous les mois de l'année' in *Mémoires (abrégés) de l'Académie Royale des Sciences de Stockholm*, Paris, 1772, pp. 20–33. Malthus' punctuation and spelling were not entirely accurate. On Per Wilhelm Wargentin (1735–1783), Swedish astronomer and statistician, see Malthus 1989a.

[15] Jean-Louis Muret (1715–1796), 'Mémoire sur l'état de la population dans le pays de Vaud', in *Mémoires et observations recueillies par la Société Oeconomique de Berne*, Berne, 1766. See Malthus 1989a.

[16] 'were' is ins.

[17] John Haygarth (1740–1827), MD. His paper 'Observations on the Population and Diseases of Chester in 1774' was published in the Royal Society's *Philosophical Transactions*, 1778 (*DNB*). In his *Essay* Malthus referred to another publication by Haygarth – *A Sketch of a Plan to Exterminate the Casual Small-pox from Great Britain and to Introduce General Inoculation*. See Malthus 1989a.

[18] Willem Kersseboom, *Eerste (-derde) verhandeling tot een proeve om te weeten de probable menigte des volks in de provintie van Hollandt en Westvrieslandt ... tweede druk*. 3 pt. 's Gravenhage, J. Van den Bergh, 1742. [*First (-third) Discourse in an Attempt to Know the Probable Size of the Population in the Province of Holland and West-Frisia ... Second Printing*. Title translated by F.W. Diehl, University of New England.] There is no known English translation of this work by Kersseboom. Malthus probably knew of it through a reference made by Richard Price in his *Observations on Reversionary Payments*, (1771 and later editions), and incorrectly assumed that Price had used an English translation. Kersseboom wrote several other works on population and the calculation of annuities.

[19] Ezra Stiles (1727–1795), *A Discourse on the Christian Union*, Boston, 1761. Malthus referred to this work in his *Essay*, but appears to have seen only extracts from it. See Malthus 1989a.

interest of great Britain considered with regard to her colonies, together with observations concerning the increase of mankind, peopling of countries &c: 2nd edition London 1761.[20]

I have mentioned these books, not that you give yourself any trouble about them; but merely have them in your recolletion,* if you should happen to be at any booksellers where they are likely to be found. I think I shall be in Town in about a fortnight myself; and have thoughts of calling upon Dr Aikin,[21] who f...[22] being intimate with Dr Price,[23] may perhaps be able to direct me where to find some of the books to which he refers.

Pray tell M^m Dalton how much I am obliged to her for Sr F.M. Eden.[24] I think it is a very useful work, and have been much entertained and informed by the first volume of it. I have got no farther at present. It tends very much to confirm my opinion of the inefficacy of all regular establishments for the poor. My mother has been pretty well upon the whole; though not quite so well these two or three last days. Maria very well. Believe me my dear Sir

Yours most affectionately

RM.

---

[20] [Benjamin Franklin] (1706–1790), *The Interest of Great Britain Considered, with Regard to her Colonies, and the Acquisition of Canada and Guadaloupe.* *To which are Added, Observations Concerning the Increase of Mankind, Peopling of Countries, &c.*, London, 1760; 2nd edn, 1761. Malthus referred to Franklin in several places in his *Essay*. A copy of Franklin's *Works*, 2 vols., 1793, was in the Malthus Library (Dalton Hill). See James 1979; Malthus 1989a.

[21] Dr John Aikin (1747–1822), physician and author. See Ch. 2, n. 126, above. In the *Essay on Population*, Malthus quoted from Aikin's *A Description of the Country from Thirty to Forty Miles round Manchester*, 1795. See Malthus 1989a; *DNB*.

[22] Word partially covered by seal, probably 'formerly'.

[23] Richard Price (1723–1791), DD. The Malthus Library has seven works by Price. Malthus was probably referring here to Price's *Observations on Reversionary Payments*, 1771. (The Malthus Library has the fourth edition, 1783.) He frequently referred to this work in his *Essay on Population* and elsewhere. Price was one of the four authors – the others being Hume, Wallace and Adam Smith – from whose writings Malthus deduced the principle of population.

[24] Sir Frederick Morton Eden (1766–1809). Malthus was obviously referring here to Eden's *The State of the Poor: or, an History of the Labouring Classes in England, from the Conquest to the Present Period...*, London, 3 vols., 1797. He quoted from it frequently in the second and later editions of his *Essay*, and in his *Principles*. The fact that Jane Dalton owned a copy of this three-volume work, and made it available to Malthus, tends to corroborate Louisa Bray's statement in her 'Recollections' that 'Mrs Dalton ... was very clever, and read much, so that she could converse well on every subject.' See *DNB*; James 1979; Malthus 1989a; Malthus 1989b.

45. MALTHUS
TO DANIEL MALTHUS[25]

Stockholm August 18th. [1799][26]

My dear Sir;

18 Aug. 1799   I received your kind letter[27] 2 days after I had written to Lucy. You have already assisted me so much that I cannot think of troubling you any further. I desired Lucy to contrive to get 50£ paid into the hands of S[r] Robert Homes, & as I understood from Otter, that our fellowships[28] would be better this year than we expected, I had no doubt of being able to repay it on my return. I hope however that we shall not have occasion for so much; but it is better to provide against contingencies. Since we left Christiania[29] we have travelled very cheaply, indeed most extraordinarily so, considering that we have regularly gone post;[30] and there was no other way [31] of making the same route in the time that we could allow ourselves. We had travelled expensively as far as[32] Christiania; & our expences* are now beginning again & I understand will not diminish at Petersburgh.* However after all it seems to be a doubtful point whether we shall get there, as the Emperor is so extraordinarily fearful of admitting strangers into his dominions. We hear that the last englishman that went from Stockholm was allowed with some difficulty to pass the frontiers; but his servant & baggage were sent back, & he was only allowed to take a couple of shirts with him. The loss of a wardrobe is of less consequence in entering Russia than anywhere else, as we understand that none of the common fashions of Europe are admitted, & that even in the morning you must wear a coat with a standing collar & long

---

[25] Addressed: 'Dan[l] Malthus Esqr / Albury / Guildford / Surrey / Angleterre'. Postmark: 'STOCKHOLM'; on the back 'SE 9 99' (the English postmark on arrival). Next to address, '99 from Stockholm' in a different hand. Watermark date: '1797'.

[26] This letter was written while Malthus was on a tour of Scandinavia and Russia in the summer of 1799. He left Cambridge on 20 May 1799 with two Cambridge friends, William Otter (see Ch. 5, n. 1 below) and Edward Daniel Clarke (see Ch. 4, n. 1 below), together with a student of Clarke's named John Marten Cripps (see Ch. 4, n. 5 below). They left Cambridge on 20 May 1799, sailed from Yarmouth on 23 May to Cuxhaven, and then proceeded northwards via Hamburg, Kiel and Copenhagen. Malthus kept a diary of the tour, and part of it (ending on 3rd August) has been published by James (1966) with a map of their itinerary, but the rest of the diary was lent to Clarke and is now missing. This letter is the only known record by Malthus of the events contained in the missing part of the diary.

[27] This letter is wanting.

[28] Malthus, Otter and Clarke were fellows of Jesus College, Cambridge, and their fellowships entitled them to a stipend as well as to the right to reside in the College.

[29] The former name for Oslo in Norway.

[30] i.e. travelling with relays of fresh horses obtained at successive places along the route.

[31] Second 'way' is del.   [32] 'far as' is ins.

flaps to your waistcoat.   18 Aug. 1799

We have been highly pleased with our tour upon the whole; but most particularly with the route from Christiania to Drontheim,*[33] which made us not in the least regret the having preferred Norway to Torneo.*[34] In Norway & probably also in the route to Torneo,* it would have been most extremely inconvenient to travel with four in the same party.[35] Otter and I have agreed extremely well & have travelled together very agreeably. I[36] heard from Clarke at Torneo* on my arrival at Stockholm. The date was the 9th of July. He seemed full of enterprise and was just setting off again not only in quest of the Sun but with an intention of penetrating a considerable way into the country, & returning by Drontheim.* This will be a very complete tour if he makes it. I should think he will not be able to get back to Stockholm before the middle or end of September, & in that case if he goes to Petersburgh* he must pass the winter there. The town and environs of Stockholm are very agreeable & in parts beautiful, but we do not find the people very sociable, and consequently have not found it a good place to get information. I enquired of a statistical professor,[37] who ought to know, about the mortality you mentioned, but he had not heard of it. The nibus aretrius was not ripe when we were in our most northern latitude; but we even doubt whether we have seen the plant tho we have looked for it with much care. The white & red deals are the spruce & Scotch, the pinus abies & the pinus sylvestris; but the pinus sylvestris varied much in its colour.[38] Those who talk english in Norway call the pinus sylvestris the fir & the pinus abies the white wood. Adieu my dear Sir. I'm afraid I shall tire your eyes. Kindest love to my mother who I grieve to hear is not so well as usual. RM.

---

[33] Now spelt Trondheim.   [34] Tornio, in Finland.
[35] The party of four split up in Sweden. Malthus and Otter crossed by sea from Stockholm to Finland on their way to Vyborg and St Petersburg, instead of travelling north with Clarke and Cripps to Tornio at the head of the Gulf of Bothnia. Clarke and Cripps undertook an extensive tour of Scandinavia, Russia, Tartary, Turkey, the Holy Land, Egypt and Greece, not returning to England until November 1802, while Malthus and Otter restricted themselves to Scandinavia and Russia.
[36] 'have' is del.   [37] 'about t' is del.
[38] 'redness' is del. and 'colour' is ins. The 'nibus aretrius' is a species of mulberry, possibly the *Morus norwegica*. The 'pinus abies' is probably the *Picea abies*, also known as the Norway Spruce. The 'pinus sylvestris' is known as the Scots Pine.

46. MALTHUS
TO THE EDITOR OF THE *MONTHLY MAGAZINE*[39]

Feby 19th [1800]

To the Editor of the Monthly Magazine

Sir,

19 Feb. 1800   I shall esteem it as a particular favour if you will allow me to correct an erroneous paragraph which appeared in your Obituary [40] for last month. Daniel Malthus Esqr is there [41] mentioned as the translator of some pieces from the French and German. I can say from certain knowledge that he did not translate them; nor was he born to copy the works of others.[42] Whatever he wrote was drawn from the original and copious source of his own fine understanding and genius; but from his character, which was so singularly unostentatious as to shun everything that might attract notice, will probably never be known as his.

I am Sir
yours &c:
Robt Malthus.

Sir,

I shall esteem it as a particular favour if you will allow me to correct an erroneous paragraph which appeared in your obituary for last month. Danl Malthus Esqr is there mentioned as the translator of some pieces from the french and german. I can say from certain knowledge that he did not translate them.

---

[39] Two drafts of his letter to the editor of the *Monthly Magazine* correcting the obituary of his father in the issue of February 1800. Daniel Malthus had died on 5 January 1800. The obituary read: 'At Albury, near Guildford, Daniel Malthus, esq. the admired, though hitherto unknown, translater* of the Sorrows of Werter; of an Essay on Landscape, from the French of the Marquis D'Ermenonville, and of the elegant Translation of Paul et Virginia,* published by Mr. Dodsley, under the title of Paul and Mary. His works evince that Mr. Malthus was a man of taste and learning, and among his friends, he was esteemed for his modesty, liberality, and many amiable qualities.' (A similar obituary appeared in the *Gentleman's Magazine*, Vol. 70, 1800, p. 177, with the final passage 'and among ... amiable qualities' replaced by 'though certainly an eccentric character in the strictest sense of the word'.) Malthus' correction was printed in the March 1800 issue of the *Monthly Magazine*, and is substantially the same as the second of these two drafts. It was his first appearance in print under his own name. See James 1979, p. 77. The first of the two drafts was published (with a few minor variations) by William Otter in his 'Memoir of Robert Malthus' (Otter 1968). In writing his 'Memoir', Otter apparently quoted from Malthus' papers (selecting the first, unpublished draft), not from the version as published in the *Monthly Magazine*.

[40] 'for the month' is del.   [41] Second 'is there' is del.

[42] Malthus' views here on the role of the translator are quite different from those expressed in the Latin essay (dated 1787) for which he received a prize at Cambridge University. See Pitcher and Pullen 1992.

...[43] turn of his mind [44] very little disposed him[45] to imitation, ...[46] the copying in   19 Feb. 1800
any way the works of others. Whatever he wrote, was drawn from the original
and copious source of his own fine understanding and genius; but from his
singularly unostentatious and retired character, and his constant desire to shun
every thing[47] that might attract notice, will probably never be known as his.

I am Sir Yours &c
T. Rob' Malthus.

47. MARIANNA MALTHUS[48]
TO MALTHUS[49]

Albury Jan' 9ᵗʰ 1822[50]

My dear Mʳ R M –

A letter arrived the day before yesterday from Mʳ Swann[51] expressing great   9 Jan. 1822
surprise that an agent in Jamaica is not yet named for the purpose of recieving*
my joimture.*[52] Wou'd you have the gooness* to ask Mʳ Peters[53] to make some
inquiry whether I am under the necessity of relinquishing the payment in
England, after having been so paid for four & twenty years & if so, what are the
necessary steps to be taken, to arange* the business on the best & surest footing.
Mʳ William Robert Harris of Jamaica I imagine will be the proper person to
appoint – if the result makes it necessary to give way to Mʳ Swann's

---

[43] Word obscured by torn MS; probably 'The'.
[44] 'was' is del.   [45] 'him' is ins.   [46] MS torn; word missing, probably 'or'.
[47] 'every thing' changed from 'any thing'.
[48] Malthus' sister-in-law, Marianna Georgina Malthus. Her husband (Malthus' brother, Sydenham) had
died a few weeks earlier, on 21 December 1821. Malthus was an executor of his will. The letter
concerns income from property in Jamaica, and the settlement of Sydenham's outstanding bills. The
Jamaica property had belonged to Marianna's first husband, William Leigh Symes (d. 1795), and
eventually reverted to the Malthuses. The principal part of the property was called the Oxford Plantation.
See James 1979, pp. 39, 125–6, 340–1. Louisa Bray said that William Leigh Symes 'behaved ill' to his
wife and 'spent all his fortune', but from this letter it appears that she had been in receipt of a jointure
from Jamaica for 'four & twenty years' after his death, for the support of herself and her six surviving
children from her first marriage. She also had four children from her second marriage.
[49] Addressed: 'The / Revᵈ T R Malthus / Mʳ Chittington's / West Cliff / Brighton'. Postmark on the back:
'GUILDFORD 30'. Watermark date: '1819'. Some calculations have been written in Malthus' hand
on blank parts of the letter.
[50] Written at the end of the letter.
[51] Henry Swann, Tory MP for Esher. James (1979, pp. 340–1) suggests that he was some sort of trustee
for the estate of William Leigh Symes, and that difficulties arose concerning the distribution of the
estate between the six Symes children on the one hand, and the Malthuses on the other.
[52] A 'jointure' is 'a sole estate limited to the wife, being a competent livelihood or freehold for the wife
of lands and tenements, to take effect upon the death of the husband for the life of the wife at least'
(*OED*).
[53] There is a reference to a 'Mrs Peters' in letters no. 24 and no. 39 above. The context suggests that Mr
Peters was a solicitor.

9 Jan. 1822   determination of altering the mode of payment. Of course all expences* incurred for the purpose of obtaining my jointure fall on the Oxford Estate, it having been so determined by the Island Court of Chanery* on a previous cause.

With regard to the purchase of the Ten Acres – I fear it is a very unprofitable purchase, attended with many inconveniences; – all of which I believe to be magnified from the influence of Mr Drummonds weight of purse – Yesterday Syd^{m54} rode over to see Mr Rudge on the subject – Mr R. appear'd very indifferent about the completion of the purchase, & said we must make our determination for Mr Drummond & others[55] *wanted it*: under all these considerations Syd^m seems to agree with me in the opinion of its being advisable to lay aside all idea of it; – and[56] says cou'd the sidefield be substituted it wou'd be a more advantageous & convenient purchase. Write me word whether you or I shall give the final answer to Mr Rudge –

From the bills already sent in I fear the sum will be much higher than I apprehended – altho' I believe none commence farther back than June. I believe there are five or six bills ...[57] London but I am not in the knowledge of all the addresss.*

Pray give my affectionate love to Lucy[58] & say I hope she feels benefit for her spirits from change of scene & sea air & beg her to accept my thanks for the comfort I have experienced from my removal to her house & the kind & affectionate attentions of Maria.[59] Mary[60] is still there. Jane[61] will take her place next week. Our fireside circle wants its greatest comfort – but they all unite in best wishes to yourself & family with

My dear M^r R M.–

Yours sincerely

M G Malthus

---

[54] Sydenham Malthus (1801–1868), the son of Marianna Georgina Malthus and Sydenham Malthus, and the nephew of Malthus.

[55] '& others' is ins.   [56] MS has 'ands'.

[57] MS torn; word missing, probably 'on'.

[58] Malthus' sister, Anne Catherine Lucy Godschall. Her husband, Samuel Man Godschall, had also recently died, in June 1821. She was apparently on a recuperative holiday with Malthus and his family in Brighton; but died the following year (1823).

[59] Malthus' sister, Eliza Maria.   [60] Another of Malthus' sisters, Mary Anne Catherine.

[61] Jane Malthus (1802–1845), a daughter of Marianna and Sydenham Malthus. She married R. F. Holt in 1828, and had twelve children. It appears that Marianna, Maria, Mary, and Jane stayed successively at the Godschall's home (Weston House, near Albury) while Lucy Godschall was in Brighton.

48. MALTHUS
TO HARRIET MALTHUS[62]

E I Coll[63] Dec[r] 2nd 1825.

My dearest Harriet

Having witnessed the inconveniences[64] which sometimes arise from the want of some discretionary power in the distribution of property, and having the most perfect confidence in you, I have left the whole of my personal property to you.[65] I recommend an equal division between our two dear children,[66] as the kind of distribution which under the actual state of my fortune I think the most just and expedient but which need not be adopted, if any thing should occur to render it decidedly ineligible. I write in great haste, but thought you would like to know my general wishes on the subject of the distribution as a sort of guide to your judgement.

With a deep feeling of the happiness you have spread over my life believe me my dearest Harriet

Your most affectionate Husband

T. Rob[t] Malthus

2 Dec. 1825

---

[62] Addressed: 'M[rs] T. R. Malthus / Not to be opened till after / my death'. Not passed through the post. Watermark date: '1821'.

[63] i.e. East India College, at Haileybury in Hertfordshire.

[64] In referring to these 'inconveniences' Malthus might have had in mind the problems mentioned in the previous letter from his sister-in-law, Marianna Georgina Malthus.

[65] Malthus' very brief will, signed 3 September 1824, contained only this one bequest.

[66] Their third child, Lucy, had died on 23 May 1825. Harriet Malthus duly gave effect to her husband's 'general wishes'; in her will, signed 22 October 1847, she distributed all her property equally between the two surviving children, Henry and Emily (then married to Captain John Watson Pringle). Harriet Malthus died in September 1864.

4 *Themes from the* Essay on Population

The first of these fifteen letters was written by E. D. Clarke to Malthus soon after the publication of the first edition of the *Essay on Population* in 1798 and is concerned with the essay's theological implications. In the last two chapters of the first edition of the *Essay*, Malthus had attempted to reconcile his principle of population with the Divine attributes of omnipotence, omniscience and benevolence. The attempted reconciliation led him to adopt some rather radical, perhaps even heretical, views; and it seems that the criticisms contained in this letter could have influenced his decision to exclude those two chapters from subsequent editions of the *Essay*.

The next two letters, no. 50 and no. 51, were sent by Thomas Beddoes, physician, to Malthus in 1806, objecting to Malthus' statement in the second edition (1803) of the *Essay on Population* that the 'degree of healthiness' had increased. Beddoes agreed that longevity had increased, but argued that, because of the incidence of consumption and scrofula, healthiness had not.

The fourth letter (no. 52) is from Samuel Whitbread to Malthus concerning the Poor Laws, and is a reply to Malthus' published pamphlet, *Letter to Samuel Whitbread*, 1807. The fifth (no. 53) is from Henry Brooke Parnell to Malthus in 1808; it deals with the commutation of tithes in Ireland. The sixth (no. 54), from Alexander Marcet in 1809, advises Malthus of the arrival in London of a copy of Pierre Prévost's French translation (1809) of the fourth edition of the *Essay on Population*. And the eighth letter (no. 56), from Prévost to Malthus in 1821, is concerned with Prévost's plan to translate the fifth edition of the *Essay*.

There are seven letters in this group from Bewick Bridge to Malthus. Bridge had been a mathematical colleague of Malthus at the East India College until resigning for health reasons in 1816. In letter no. 55, dated April 1817, Bridge recounts his efforts to establish a Provident or Savings Bank in Cambridge. In the next six letters (no. 57 to no. 62), written between August and November 1822, Bridge advises Malthus on the correct method of making various demographic calculations – including the rate at which a population will double in size, and life expectancy. Malthus had apparently sought Bridge's assistance on these matters while preparing his article on population for the *Supplement ... to the Encyclopaedia Britannica*, 1824.

The final letter (no. 63) in this set is a draft of a letter sent by Malthus in

February 1830, to R. J. Wilmot-Horton, and discusses the latter's proposal to use emigration as a cure for over-population.

49. EDWARD DANIEL CLARKE[1]
TO MALTHUS[2]

Thrapston,[3] Northampton: August 20th 1798.

Dear Malthus,

Much as I have wished to write to you, I have found no Opportunity till   20 Aug. 1798
this Evening – & am now, after a hot Drive of near 40 Miles, very unfit for Epistolization.

I found Jesus College uninhabited except by two Beings; which, like Bats, one always sees hovering among the Cloisters, about Twilight – Cautley, & Castley. We managed, however, to get Bridge[4] from Peterhouse, to dine with us. He was the Senior Wrangler, of Otter's Year. – With him I enjoyed a couple of Hours, in the most interesting intellectual Discussion, you can imagine. I wish you had been present; because, my poor Memory, which is grown more

---

[1] Edward Daniel Clarke (1769–1822), traveller, antiquary, and mineralogist; BA 1790, MA 1794, LL D 1804; fellow of Jesus College, Cambridge, 1795–1806; ordained 1805; professor of mineralogy, 1808–22; university librarian, 1817–22 (*DNB*; Venn; James 1966).

[2] Addressed: 'London August twenty second 1798. / The Rev⁴ M' Malthus / Albury, near Guildford / Surry*'. Postmark indistinct except for the letters 'A/A'. Below the address, in Clarke's hand, '... J. Tufton' (first word indistinct, possibly 'Hen.'). Clarke became a tutor to the Hon. Henry Tufton in 1790, and made a tour of Great Britain with him in 1791 (*DNB*). On the back, in another hand, 'EDC' and other words indistinct .

[3] Thrapston, in Northamptonshire, is about thirty miles north-west of Cambridge.

[4] Probably Thomas Cautley and Thomas Castley. Thomas Cautley, BA 1786, MA 1789, was ordained deacon in 1785 and priest in 1788, and was vicar of St Clement's Cambridge, 1806–35. He died on 30 November 1835, aged 73. He was 'familiarly known as "His Majesty", having for many years borne the nickname of Og, King of Basan*' (Venn). The *Gentleman's Magazine* (March 1836, p. 328) adds that Cautley was a fellow of Jesus College, and was presented by the College to the vicarage of St Clement's. Og, king of Bashan, was defeated by the Israelites on their journey from Egypt to Canaan. From Cautley's nickname we may conclude that he was of large physical stature – Og's bedstead was nine cubits long and four cubits wide (Deuteronomy, iii, 11).

Thomas Castley, BA (seventh wrangler) 1787, MA 1790; fellow of Jesus College, Cambridge, 1789–1810; rector of Cavendish, Suffolk, 1808–60; author of *Antiquarian Speculations, Consisting of Essays and Dissertations on Various Subjects*, 1817; died 19 May 1860, aged 94 (Venn). Henry Gunning (1855) described Castley as 'a man of most unprepossessing appearance', and added: 'As it was the custom in those days to give some *distinguishing* term to most members of the University, that of *Ghastly* was not inapplicable to Castley' (Vol. II, p. 128).

On Bewick Bridge, see Ch. 4, n. 94 below.

20 Aug. 1798 restive than Cripps's[5] Horse, will afford a very bad Epitome of our Conversation. – You may suppose it was on the subject of your Work. – Cautley had alarmed Bridge the preceding Evening, by his absurd and ignorant Remarks, upon the evil Tendency of your two last Chapters.[6] I entreated that Bridge would suspend his Judgement, till he had read the Work; and when we adjourned to the Combination Room,[7] he thus opened the Debate. –

Bridge/– "Well Cautley, I have examined Malthus's Work with some Degree of Attention; & do not find that any Part of it is calculated to justify your Apprehensions respecting the Tendency of his Writings." –

Cautley./– God bless me! Can you say so, Bridge? – you have been too hasty in your Perusal. I wish you had borrowed my Copy of it, as I have marked several Pages; which would have directed your Attention to the objectionable Passages."

Bridge/ "Pardon me! I did borrow your Copy of it; & I saw all your Marks – but you have very much mistaken the Author's Meaning, or I am grossly deceived myself. – It appears to me full of important Information upon a Subject I was very ignorant of before." –

---

[5] John Marten Cripps (d. 1853), traveller and antiquary; admitted as a fellow-commoner at Jesus College, Cambridge, 1798; travelled extensively with his tutor, Edward Daniel Clarke, throughout Europe and the Near East (*DNB*; Venn; James 1966).

[6] In the last two chapters (XVIII and XIX) of the first edition (1798) of the *Essay on Population*, Malthus discussed the theological implications of his principle of population. His discussion included comments on the 'growth of mind' and on Annihilationism (although he did not use this term), i.e. the doctrine that at death the souls of the wicked, as well as their bodies, cease to exist, and that the immortality of the soul is therefore conditional. These last two chapters were omitted by Malthus from subsequent editions of the *Essay on Population*, and it would appear from this letter that Cautley and Bridge (and possibly others) had influenced their omission. In a letter (dated 1 March 1799) published in the *Monthly Magazine*, April 1799, p. 179, Malthus said: 'It is my intention at a future time to enlarge and illustrate, by a greater number of facts, the principal part of the "Essay on Population;" and, as the subject of the two last chapters is not necessarily connected with it, I shall, in deference to the opinion of some friends whose judgments I respect, omit them in another edition.' And in the Appendix to the fifth edition (1817) of the *Essay* he stated that in deference to the opinion of 'a competent tribunal', he had 'already expunged the passages [of the *Essay*] which have been most objected to' (Vol. III, p. 427). W. Otter, referring to that statement, said that Malthus had 'expunged two whole chapters from his first work, in deference to the opinions of some distinguished persons in our church.' See Otter 1968, p. lii; Pullen 1981.

   Of the four participants in this theological discussion, three (Cautley, Castley, and Bridge) were already ordained, and the fourth (Clarke) was ordained in 1805.

[7] 'Combination-Room' is 'the name given in the university of Cambridge (England) to the college-parlour where the fellows meet after dinner, elsewhere called common-room' (*OED*).

Clarke/ Dont you think he has succeeded in the general Argument; & in particular 20 Aug. 1798 in proving the fallacy of the speculations of Godwin,[8] &c?

Bridge/ From a general View of the Work, I confess I admire it much. It seems to result from deep Thought, & it teaches one to *think* also. Every Page of it convinces me, the Author possesses uncommon Strength of Mind. I could wish he had not added the two last Chapters; not from any Objection to the Sentiments contained in them, but because the Subject of them has not been sufficiently discussed. They have more the Air of a *Syllabus* than a finished Essay; & this View of them strikes more forcibly after reading the very excellent Composition which precedes them; & to which they do not seem a necessary Appendage. That the Author entertained a similar Opinion I am convinced from the Tenour* of his Prefaces, & a Note which he has added.[9] But a Man of his Understanding knows very well that the Public will admit of no Apology, for sending forth Arguments on doctrinal Points, which have not been digested."

I will not fill my Letter by giving you my Answers to these Sentiments of Bridge, because you already know them, & they are of no Importance. I wish to tell accurately what he said, because you will value it. The Conversation continued & Bridge afterwards made the following Observation.–

Bridge/ "It is evident he would not give himself the Trouble to bestow sufficient Consideration upon a Subject he was amply calculated to discuss. A casual Reader, would swear he is a *Materialist*; & yet I can gather sufficient Evidence from his own Writings, to prove that he rejects the Doctrine of *Materialism*. The same Person might also think he admitted the Doctrine of *Annihilation* – and yet I firmly believe he has no Intention to excite such an Opinion."–

---

[8]   William Godwin (1756–1836), author of *An Enquiry Concerning Political Justice* (1793), *The Enquirer* (1797), etc. Malthus' *Essay on Population* was specifically conceived as a reply to the speculations of Godwin (and others). Six chapters of the first edition of the *Essay* (Chs. X–XV) were devoted to Godwin. Godwin replied to Malthus in *Thoughts Occasioned by the Perusal of Dr. Parr's Spital Sermon* (1801), and *Of Population* (1820). They corresponded in 1798; and the last paragraph of this letter indicates that they also met in 1798. See *DNB*; Malthus 1989a. The Malthus Library has *Political Justice, The Enquirer,* and *Of Population.*

[9]   Bridge was presumably referring here not only to the main Preface at the front of the *Essay on Population,* but also to the brief Prefaces which precede each chapter. In the Prefaces to Chs. XVIII and XIX, Malthus' use of words such as 'probably' and 'seems to' implies (as Bridge suggested) that his ideas on these theological matters were not 'finished'. The 'Note' to which Bridge referred occurs in Ch. XIX and explicitly indicates the unfinished state of his views at that time: 'It was my intention to have entered at some length into this subject, as a kind of second part to the essay. A long interruption, from particular business, has obliged me to lay aside this intention, at least for the present. I shall now, therefore, only give a sketch of a few of the leading circumstances that appear to me to favour the general supposition that I have advanced' (Malthus 1966, p. 382).
A line was drawn by Clarke across the page at the conclusion of this paragraph.

20 Aug. 1798   Clarke/– "We will speak to one Point first. What induces you to suppose[10] that any Part of his Work savours of *Materialism*

Bridge/– "He speaks of Intellect, as produced by the Operation of Matter upon Mind; not considering, what he knows as well as every body else, that all our Knowledge, all the Ideas we have, or ever shall obtain, is produced by Sensation.

Clarke/ Admitting, for a Moment, your own Statement: how can Sensation be produced without the Interference of Matter? –

Bridge/ As a Source of Knowledge I grant you, the Interference of Matter is necessary to Sensation; but the formation of Intellect is produced by Reflection in consequence of Sensation; & therefore by the Operation of Mind upon Matter; not of Matter upon Mind."–

(If I am writing Nonsense, all this time, in justice to Bridge I must beg that you will impute it to the *Secretary* & not to the Disputant.)

We then spoke on the Subject of Annihilation; Cautley & Bridge, both declared, any Tenet contrary to the Doctrine taught by the Scriptures, which induced Men to believe that a *bad Mind* would be annihilated.

I cited several Passages from the New Testament in Defence of the Argument. Among others brought by them on the contrary Side, were some calculated to prove that evil Minds were destined to a State of future Misery.

[11] Clarke/– "I grant it! –

Bridge/ "You grant it! And can you for a Moment maintain that a State of Annihilation is a State of Misery? –

Clarke/– "I think I can! I am sure Malthus could; but until you see him you must be contented with my whimsical Mode of Proof – & not attribute Want of Strength to his Arguments, from the Weakness of mine.–

Our Saviour teaches that *"in his Father's House are many Mansions"*; which at once proves that there is a Gradation in the State of Souls after Death.–

For a Moment, let me suppose the highest Point in that Gradation to equal a certain Number – suppose seventy. [12] The Point of Annihilation I will suppose to be *0*, or nothing; that is to say that when the Gradation of Happiness ends the State of Annihilation begins.

---

[10] 'suspect' is del. and 'suppose' is ins.
[11] 'Bridge' is del.   [12] Words del. and indecipherable.

76

Abstracting all Idea of *Matter*, or *Corporealism*, which has nothing to do   20 Aug. 1798
with the soul after death – we may be allowed sufficient latitude of Language to
say of Souls condemned to a State of Annihilation, that *they exist in a State of
Annihilation.*
Therefore they exist in a State deprived of all Pain.
Therefore they exist in a State of *negative Happiness.*
Therefore they exist in a State of *positive Misery*; as *negative Happiness* is
positive Misery.

Q.E.D. –

How do you suppose they took off this Argument? – By saying that we are
not to abstract Corporealism from the State of Souls after Death – as we are
taught to believe we shall answer in the Body, for the Sin committed in the
Flesh.– And soon we received *a Message from the Lords*, after which Parliament
was adjourned.–

Oh, for the Love of A...,[13] write a few Lines to Whitehaven Post Office – to
dispel this more than *Combination-Room Darkness*; which envelopes* in thick
Clouds, all the Visions of my Soul! –

Y^r ever sincere Friend,

E. D. Clarke.

I thank you very much for the Letter you wrote after your Interview with
Godwin.[14] How I longed to sit snug in a Corner & witness the Meeting of two
such Adepts in Speculative Policy! I perfectly agree with you in thinking
Godwin's Notions, respecting the Prudence of Mankind in avoiding [15] Marriage,
inadequate to any Effect in favor* of Population. – I believe I told you I sent
your Work to Mr Pitt, by means of Mr Heale.–

---

[13] Word difficult to decipher, possibly 'Aeolus', the god of the winds in Greek mythology.

[14] A letter dated 20 August [1798] from Malthus to Godwin indicates that his interview with Godwin
took place on 'Wednesday morning'. As 20 August 1798 was a Monday, the interview must have
occurred on Wednesday 15 August 1798. Malthus' letter of 20 August was a reply to one that Godwin
had written after the interview, but Godwin's is wanting. Malthus' letter written to Clarke after the
interview with Godwin is also wanting. See C. Kegan Paul 1876, Vol. I, pp. 321–5; reprinted by J.
Bonar in Malthus 1966, Notes, pp. iii–viii.

[15] Word del.

50. THOMAS BEDDOES[16]
TO MALTHUS[17]

24 Feb. 1806

Sir/

24 Feb. 1806   I beg leave to trouble you with a query,[18] relative to a Subject touched upon in your Essay & to which I am about to advert in a medical work, which is to contain extensive observations on chronic patients. What I have to say will seem to be in opposition to certain opinions *or* expressions of yours. This makes me anxious, because it must create distrust of my own ideas & because the first impression will be unfavourable to me. [19] I suspect that ...[20] whole difference between us is reducible to words; & I shd be extremely glad if it appear so to you, provided you choose to give a few moments' attention to the subject.

Every thing seems to prove the increase of consumption. It is probable from this that scrophula*[21] increases too – My observations here & those which I have been able to make on families from all parts of the kingdom go to prove the excessive (I dare not positively say the increased) frequency of scrophulous disorders. Of these some besides consumption are fatal – as Tabes mensenteria – lumbar abscess – some only produce protracted indisposition. Were these causes not balanced by the cessation of other diseases productive of death in infancy & early life, ...[22] births cd not have been gaining upon the deaths. But if it be true that the proportion of deaths has decreased from 1 in 35 to 1 in 40, do you think it absolutely follows that the healthiness has increased. If the people of any country taken together live longer than formerly, it may be said that they must be deemed more healthy than formerly, till the contrary is proved. But I suppose you will not affirm that longevity & healthiness are absolutely convertible terms. And if it were true that the diminution of deaths were owing to the diminution of acute disorders, longevity and unhealthiness might very well go on increasing together. And if you in your work p. 308 1. 13[23] & in

---

[16] Thomas Beddoes (1760–1808), MD, the celebrated physician, published a number of medical works, political pamphlets, and moral tales. In 1798 he established at Clifton a 'Pneumatic Institute' for the treatment of disease by inhalation. (*DNB*; James 1979, p. 225).

[17] Addressed: 'The Revd T. R. Malthus / Hertford'. Postmark: 'FREE / Feb 25 / 1806'. Above the address, in a different hand, 'London February the twenty / fifth 1806'. Below the address, 'From Davies Giddy'. Watermark date: '1804'.

[18] 'few' is del. and 'query' changed from 'queries'.   [19] 'As' is del.

[20] MS scorched; word partially obscured, probably 'the'.

[21] 'scrophula' (now 'scrofula') is 'a constitutional disease characterized mainly by chronic enlargement and degeneration of the lymphatic glands' (*OED*).

[22] MS scorched and word obscured, probably 'the'.

[23] 'And the returns pursuant to the population act, even after allowing for great omissions in the burials, exhibit in all our provincial towns, and in the country, a degree of healthiness much greater than had before been calculated': *Essay on Population*, 2nd edn, p. 308. Despite Beddoes' letter, Malthus did not alter this passage in later editions of the *Essay*.

similar passages w^d consent to read "greater length of life" in place of "a degree   24 Feb. 1806
of healthiness much greater" all my distress w^d cease. And till the fact be made
out by medical researches I have some hopes that you will consent to leave that
point open.

    If you do me the favour of an answer, will you be so good as [to] say
whether you will allow me to send you a couple of sheets of my book,[24] when
the printer comes to that part. It will be easy to make a few cancels – & you may
save me from errors in toto, or the partial error of too great generalization or
being too positive where the data are insufficient. If you w^d enclose to my friend
Davies Giddy Esq[25] MP H. of Commons he w^d forward y^r answer – I am Sir
                                   very respectfully
                                   your obt Sert
                                   Thomas Beddoes

                        51. THOMAS BEDDOES
                             TO MALTHUS[26]

                                                          6 March 1806

Sir/

    Allow me just to thank you for the explanation with which you have   6 March 1806
favoured me[27] – I entirely agree with you, if that be of any consequence. Indeed
I have committed the same reflections in Substance to the printer – I was only
fearful lest any of y^r expressions should be misinterpreted[28] into a false security
ag^t scrophula* & consumption, for the progressive increase of which last[29] we
have every medical, physiological & I think statistical reason.

    Indelicate as it may be to intrude on you, I intend to trouble you soon to

---

[24] In 1806 Beddoes published *Manual of Health; or, The Invalid Conducted Safely through the Seasons*,
London, 419p.; and in 1807 *Researches Anatomical and Practical concerning Fever, as Connected
with Inflammation*, London, 256p.
[25] Davies Giddy, afterwards Davies Gilbert (1767–1839), MP, was the author of *A Plain Statement on
the Bullion Question, in a Letter to a Friend*, 1811, one of the publications reviewed by Malthus in his
article 'Pamphlets on the Bullion Question', *Edinburgh Review*, Vol. 18, 1811, pp. 448–70. Giddy
married the only daughter and heiress of Thomas Gilbert in 1808, and changed his name to Gilbert in
1817. His friendship with Thomas Beddoes began at Oxford, where he graduated MA in 1789 and
DCL in 1832. At the death of Beddoes in 1808, his son, Thomas Lovell Beddoes (1803–1849), poet
and physiologist, was left in the guardianship of Giddy. Giddy as a member of the Royal Society
supported Malthus' nomination in 1817. He was president of the Royal Society from 1827 to 1830
(*DNB*; James 1979, pp. 357–8).
[26] Addressed: 'The Reverend / Mr Professor Malthus / Hertford'. Not passed through the post. Watermark
date: '18[0]4' (MS torn by seal, third digit missing).
[27] Malthus' letter is wanting.   [28] 'misinterpreted' changed from 'interpreted'.   [29] 'last' is ins.

6 March 1806 read over two or three 8vo pages – which I hope will require no observation & of course no answer to the enclosing letter will be wanted – I am Sr

with great respects

Y^r obed^t Ser^t

Thomas Beddoes

52. SAMUEL WHITBREAD[30]
TO MALTHUS[31]

[5 April 1807][32]

Sir

5 April 1807   I have received the Copy of your printed Letter;[33] and I have read it with attention. I beg[34] in the first place, to return you my thanks for the honourable mention you have thought proper to make of me personally; for the credit you give to my motives; and for the approbation you are pleased to bestow upon many parts of my Labours. – I have two motives for troubling you with this letter. The one is to assure you, that you have totally misunderstood my meaning, when you suppose that I have[35] imputed to you any thing like "hardness of heart". If you will have the goodness to refer to Page 10 of the printed Speech, you will find that I not only pay the tribute due to your understanding; but that I state my persuasion of the most benevolent intentions, in[36] the Author [37] of the Essay on the Principles* of Population; which Intentions also I collect from his

---

[30] Samuel Whitbread (1758–1815), BA (Cambridge) 1784, whig politician. Whitbread entered Parliament in 1790 and became a constant and leading advocate of liberal causes. In 1807 he introduced a poor-law bill. His speech, which made a number of references to Malthus' views, was published as a pamphlet, *Substance of a Speech on the Poor Laws: Delivered in the House of Commons, on Thursday, February 19, 1807*, London, 1807. A second edition was also published in 1807. A copy of the pamphlet is in the Malthus Library. Whitbread's bill has been described as 'of the most elaborate and unwieldy character'; it comprised 'the establishment of a free educational system, the alteration of the law of settlement, the equalisation of county rates, and a peculiar proposal for distinguishing between the deserving and undeserving poor by the wearing of badges. It excited considerable public interest and was keenly criticised in the press by Malthus ... and others' (*DNB*).

[31] Written in the regular hand of a secretary or amanuensis, with all insertions in a different, less precise hand, probably that of Whitbread himself.

[32] Date written at the end of the letter. No address or postmark.

[33] Malthus, Rev. T. R., *A Letter to Samuel Whitbread, Esq., M.P. on his Proposed Bill for the Amendment of the Poor Laws*, J. Johnson and J. Hatchard, London, 1807. A second edition was also published in 1807. The first edition must have been published after 19 February 1807 (the date of Whitbread's speech) and before 5 April 1807 (the date of this letter). For a discussion of Whitbread's *Substance of a Speech* and Malthus' *Letter to Samuel Whitbread*, see James 1979, pp. 136–41.

[34] 'beg' changed from 'begin'.   [35] 'have' is ins.   [36] 'of' is del. and 'in' is ins.

[37] 'of' occurs twice, with the first del.

80

writings.[38] I had observed the effect of the Work[39] upon some who have 5 April 1807 considered it superficially; (an effect far different from that which it is calculated to produce on Persons of deep reflection) and thence I was led to say that a strict guard ought to be placed upon the Heart of the Reader lest it should become hardened in the Study:[40] but I was far from apprehending that my meaning could have been so misconstrued, as to induce any one to imagine I attributed hardness of Heart to the Author.[41] I am anxious therefore thus to assure you that I had no such Intention.

My second Motive for addressing You, is for the sake of canvassing some of the Provisions of the Poor Bill to which you state strong Objections. We agree it seems as to the principle of discriminating between the Idle and Industrious Poor: nor do we differ very materially as to the difficulty of reducing that principle to practice. I doubt more about the possibility of convicting and badging Criminal Paupers than of any other of the Provisions of the Bill, but I thought proper to take the Sense of Parl[i] and the Country upon the Enactment. As to the rewarding of Meritorious Labourers under certain very limited circumstances; if it does no good, at least it can do no harm, and I shall be glad to see the Experiment tried, for the chance of it's* success.[42]

I come to the more weighty Objections you have expressed to two Clauses of the Bill from the combined result of which you apprehend great mischief. It had not before struck me that they could be considered in one point of view.[43] Nor have you yet persuaded me that there is any necessary or probable connexion* between them for the Operation of Evil. But there may also[44] be

---

[38] 'I am desirous of doing the utmost ample justice to his [Malthus'] patient and profound research; to the inimitable clearness of his demonstration, and to the soundness of the principles upon which he proceeds. I believe them to be incontrovertible ... I believe the design and intention of the author to be most benevolent...' (Whitbread, *Substance of a Speech*, p. 10).

[39] 'of the Work' is ins.

[40] 'I think any man who reads them [Malthus' writings], ought to place a strict guard over his heart, lest it become hardened against the distresses of his fellow creatures; lest in learning that misery and vice must of necessity maintain a footing in the world, he give up all attempt at their subjugation' (Whitbread, *Substance of a Speech*, p. 10).

[41] 'To those who know me personally, I feel that I have no occasion to defend my character from the imputation of hardness of heart' (Malthus, *Letter to Samuel Whitbread*, p. 10; see also p. 13).

[42] 'I doubt the practicability of making the criminal poor wear marks; though it is certainly true that a man who has brought himself and family on the parish by his own idleness and vices, deserves to be thus distinguished from those who have been only unfortunate' (Malthus, *Letter to Samuel Whitbread*, pp. 14–15).

[43] Malthus said that the 'principal object' of his apprehensions was 'the operation of the clause which empowers parishes to build cottages, combined with that which determines every property to be rateable' (Malthus, *Letter to Samuel Whitbread*, p. 15). He added: 'I should most earnestly recommend, that, at all events, one or other of the two Clauses which I have particularly noticed should be given up' (p. 31).

[44] 'also' is ins.

5 April 1807 separate Objections to each; And if you please I will first consider them separately. First as to the rating of Personal Property.[45] To say that it is now the acknowledged Law of the Land is no defence of the Principle; although it affords an Answer to those who call it an Innovation. But I maintain that it is equitable. Almost all Capital is rendered productive by the Operation of Labour. Such Capital therefore creates a Population, and should be taxed for the relief of the exigencies of that Population, in the same degree, as the Land is taxed, in relief of the exigencies of the Population required to render the Capital employed upon it productive.[46] Such Capital alone would be taxed; for it would only be the visible productive Capital within each Parish. All Capital rendered profitable without the assistance of Labour as Money in the Funds, &c. is invisible; and would therefore escape taxation. I have a Capital in the Brewing Trade rendered productive by Labour, and therefore creating a population. I have a large Lime Work under the same circumstances. Is it reasonable that I should not pay my just proportion towards the relief of the exigencies of the population so increased, by the Operation of the Capital which produces an extraordinary profit to me? I confess I cannot so deem it. I am conscious that there may be great difficulties in collecting[47] the Rate upon personal Property; and such as it will be very odious if not impossible to overcome; and therefore I do not pledge myself[48] to adhere to the Clause; but I am sure that it is founded in justice.[49] Secondly as to the power proposed to be given to the Parishes to build Cottages, will you here allow me to say, that you reason as if I had proposed to compell* all Parishes, to build fresh Cottages, as often as a fresh demand for them shall[50] arise; rather than as if I only proposed to[51] empower[52] Parishes to build Cottages to a very limited amount: a Power which would never be exercised except under the influence of a strong necessity? Will you also allow me to remark to you, that you speak much more decidedly of the preventive effect arising out of the Scarcity of Habitations in your letter; than in your Essay. You seem to me to have made up your mind much more completely upon its Operation now; than you had done when you published the last Edition of your Work.[53] But must it not be admitted that a situation of things may possibly exist, where the means of Subsistence may be sufficient for[54] a much larger population than can be lodged with decency or comfort? May not that be the case generally? Much more is it[55] not likely to be the case locally? That such is the case in England

---

[45] 'I should think that very considerable difficulties would occur in rating personal property in the mode expressed by the bill' (Malthus, *Letter to Samuel Whitbread*, p. 19).
[46] 'it productive' changed from 'its production'.   [47] 'the collection of' is changed to 'collecting'.
[48] 'particularly' is del.   [49] 'in contending' is del.   [50] 'shall' changed from 'should'.
[51] 'propose to' is ins.   [52] 'empower' changed from 'empowered'.
[53] T. R. Malthus, *An Essay on the Principle of Population; or, a View of its Past and Present Effects on Human Happiness...* 3rd edn, 2 vols., J. Johnson, London, 1806.
[54] 'from' is del. and 'for' is ins.   [55] 'it' is ins.

generally I believe; that such is the case locally I know: and it is for the sake of
providing more space for the habitation of those who do exist, and for whom[56]
the means of Subsistence are ample, (and without fear of calling others into
existence for whom there would not be sufficient means of Subsistence) that I
wish[57] to legislate. I will take the instance of a neighbouring Village, where the
Population has not increased at all in proportion to the means of Subsistence;
but some Houses have been destroyed, and the wholesome increase of population
has been such as added to the demolition of some Cottages produces great
inconvenience; great indecency is the necessary consequence: by adding a few
Cottages I should hope to produce the moral and physical[58] good effects which
are obvious; & to excite an ambition amongst the Labourers to obtain these
more comfortable Habitations; but I do not think [59] one creature would thereby
be added[60] to the population of the Parish. I trust upon reconsideration of this
Clause separately; you will find that it may be very useful, and cannot be
dangerous. In combining the Clauses I think you labour under an error. If I
understand your proposition, it is this. The number of Cottages added to the
existing Habitations in consequence of this Bill will soon produce a great increase
of Population; Labour from the increased supply will of course become cheaper,
which will force all persons with families upon parochial Relief, and the Farmer
will add his Assistance to expedite this effect for the purpose of obtaining the
work of his Labourers, or a large proportion of it, out of the Parish Rate to
which the temptation will be excessive in consequence of the great Capitalist
paying a part[61] of the Rate, from which he cannot derive the same sort of benefit.
First of all, the Capitalist assessed might appeal against the Rate so misapplied;
but I beg you to consider that the agricultural Parishes are those wherein generally
speaking, very little productive personal Property is to be found; I would instance
the Parish where I am now writing. Productive Capital is for the most part
confined to Towns; & where the Cottages could be built very little of such
Capital exists. Where there is a combination of Agricultural and Mercantile
Property, there is a confluence of Population resulting from the Labour employed
in each. The inequality now existing, would thus be diminished; and neither of
the two descriptions of Capitalists could take advantage of the other in the way
you have suggested.

These Sir are the reasons which prevent my feeling the alarm with which
you are impressed in considering certain parts of my Bill. I have stated them;
not for purpose of refuting your arguments, but with the more laudable view I
trust, of obtaining from you [62] such private communications & observations[63] as

---

[56] 'whom' changed from 'who'.   [57] 'Parish' is del. and 'I wish' is ins.
[58] 'physical' is ins.   [59] 'I would add' is del.   [60] 'would thereby be added' is ins.
[61] 'large proportion' is del. and 'part' is ins.   [62] 'by' is del.
[63] '& observations' is ins.

5 April 1807 you may have the leisure or inclination[64] to make to me. I am consciously desirous of doing as much good as I can, and of obtaining all the information possible for the guidance of my own judgment. I need not add that from you I esteem it most valuable. Upon that part of the Bill which allows relief to be granted to Parishes heavily burthened,* out of the County Stocks,[65] I would beg leave to call your attention to the guards I have placed against the Evil you appear to apprehend. The Court is not to take into their consideration the circumstances of any Parish, the Average rate upon which raised for the relief of the Poor, does not exceed double the Average rate raised thro'out the County. An Examination is to be made upon oath into the Management of the Overseers of the Parishes making application; no assistance can be claimed of Right; no Relief can be given so as to reduce the Rate below double the Average of the County: And unquestionably if such facts were to appear as are stated in the Note quoted from Mr. Rose's Pamphlet,[66] namely that the labour of the Parish was in part paid out of the Poors* Rate; all Relief would be witheld,* but the Exposure of such a Practice would be very advantageous, & tend very much to the correction of the Evil. I [67] expect great good from the general publicity of parochial Transactions. It would also be ascertained whether the Rate of each Parish was raised upon the Rack Rental,[68] or upon what proportion thereof. Taking all these circumstances into consideration perhaps you may think the good to be derived is positive, and the discretionary power vested in the justices sufficient to check any possible Evil. I am very happy to find that you approve of the plan laid down for general Education;[69] & feel confident that it may be

---

[64] 'inclination' is changed from 'inclinations'.

[65] See Malthus, *Letter to Samuel Whitbread*, pp. 32–4.

[66] George Rose (1744–1818), MP, *Observations on the Poor Laws, and on the Management of the Poor in Great Britain...*, London, 1805. In a footnote on p. 33 of his *Letter to Samuel Whitbread* Malthus argued that 'the farmers, although they bear themselves a large portion of the assessments, have already learned in some places to prefer low wages and high rates, to low rates and high wages'. He supported this argument by quoting the following footnote from Rose's *Observations on the Poor Laws* (p. 14): 'There is but too much reason to believe that in many parts of England the cultivators of the land are more solicitous to restrain the price of labour than to keep down the poor's rate; in which case the latter in fact becomes a part of the former ...' On George Rose, see *DNB*; and Malthus 1989a, Vol. I, p. 287; Vol. II, pp. 183, 330–1. Malthus referred to Rose's *Observations on the Poor Laws* in the third edition of the *Essay on Population* (see Malthus 1989a, Vol. II, p. 287); and in his *Principles of Political Economy* he referred to Rose's *Speech ... on ... the Corn Laws*, 1814 (see Malthus 1989b, Vol. I, p. 280; Vol. II, pp. 410, 472). The Malthus Library has a copy of Rose's *Observations on the Poor Laws*. Rose published a number of other works on economic and financial matters.

[67] 'should' is del.

[68] 'rack-rent' is 'a very high, excessive, or extortionate rent; a rent equal (or nearly equal) to the full value of the land' (*OED*).

[69] 'The plan of general education, which you have proposed, is admirably calculated to ... elevate as much as possible the general character of the lower classes of the community' (Malthus, *Letter to Samuel Whitbread*, p. 14; see also pp. 34–6).

carried into execution at an expence* comparatively small.[70] I have only to   5 April 1807
repeat, that it was to some of your [71] Admirers, & not to yourself, I meant to
address myself & really my words appear to me to do justice to my feelings. I
am much concerned if I have wounded yours; it was unintentionally; & I shall
be happy of[72] an opportunity of assuring you personally how much I am

Your faithful h^{ble} Servt

Samuel Whitbread

Southill[73] Apr. 5. 1807
I go to London tomorrow & the Bill stands our Commitment[74] on Wednesday
Sennight.[75]

53. HENRY BROOKE PARNELL[76]
TO MALTHUS[77]

Baker St   May 9: 1808

Dear Sir

I feel extremely obliged to you for your observations[78] on the Irish Tythe*   9 May 1808
system & plan for reforming it. I perceive, however, that both you & Smythe*[79]
have not been aware that I have presented a distinct petition from the freeholders

---

[70] With several deletions and insertions, 'an expence* comparatively small' is changed from 'a very
small comparative expence*'.

[71] 'superficial' is del.

[72] 'of' is changed from 'an'.

[73] Southill is in Bedfordshire, about eight miles south-east of Bedford. Whitbread's father, after realising
a large fortune in the brewing industry, purchased Lord Torrington's Southill estate in 1795 (*DNB*).

[74] In this context 'commitment' is 'the action of referring or entrusting (a bill, etc.) to a committee'
(*OED*).

[75] 'Wednesday Sennight' means a week from Wednesday. As 5 April 1807 (the date of this letter) was a
Sunday, Wednesday Sennight would have been Wednesday, 15 April.

[76] Henry Brooke Parnell (1776–1842), later (1841) first Baron Congleton, prominent whig MP, supported
reform of the Irish tithe system, Catholic emancipation, resumption of cash payments, abolition of the
corn laws, etc. He published a number of books and speeches on these issues, and was a member of the
Bullion Committee (1810) and the Emigration Committee (1827). Malthus gave evidence to the latter.

[77] Addressed: 'London May nine / The Rev T. R. Malthus / Hertford / H. Parnell'. Postmark: 'FREE 9
MY 9 1808'.

[78] See Malthus' letter to Parnell of 4 May 1808, to which this letter of 9 May 1808 from Parnell is a reply.
Malthus replied to Parnell on 12 May 1808. Malthus' two letters are quoted in James 1979, pp. 157–
9, 318–9. His views on the problems of Ireland are presented more fully in two articles in the *Edinburgh
Review*: 'Newenham and Others on the State of Ireland', Vol. 12, July 1808, pp. 336–55; and 'Newenham
on the State of Ireland', Vol. 14, April 1809, pp. 151–70.

[79] William Smyth (1765–1849), a lifelong friend of Malthus from their undergraduate days at Cambridge.
Smyth graduated eighth wrangler in 1787; Malthus was ninth wrangler in 1788. From 1807 to his
death, Smyth was professor of modern history at Cambridge. He was the author of *Lectures on Modern
History, from the Irruption of the Northern Nations to the Close of the American Revolution*, 1840, and
Lectures on History. Second and Concluding Series. On the French Revolution, 3 vols., 1840.

9 May 1808 of my County praying for a commutation,[80] & that my constituents expect that I should propose a plan to the house for that purpose. The question will be confined in the debate wholly to tithes, & this debate will not take place till after the discussion of the Catholic question. My motion will be to refer[81] the Queen* County[82] petition for a commutation to a committee of the whole house, a committee being the proper place to take any question concerning the church, for the first time, into consideration; it would not be necessary for me to propose any plan, but it is expected that I should do so & my own inclination is to propose one in the shape of resolutions, stating at the time I explain them to the house that if my motion is carried for its going into the Committee on the petition, that I shall propose these resolutions to the committee as my plan of commutation.

From this explanation you will perceive that I ought to make up my mind to a plan.

I did not say anything concerning a substitution of a portion of the neat rent,[83] because I know it would be impossible to carry any plan of much detail into execution in Ireland. The people of all ranks are unaccustomed to habits of buisness* or detail, & besides it would be nearly impracticable to secure anything like an honest applotment[84] of the quantity of rent to be paid. For these reasons, & for those which I have already suggested against a modus[85] or tax on land; I am inclined to think my choice must lie between the substitution of land & payment by the Treasury. I do not think that the estates to be purchased should necessarily lie in the respective Parishes, or even in the Counties in which the parishes are situated. I think the province would be a more suitable limit. My idea being to give the Clergy their incomes from rents, & not from profits by farming land.

As you say that the principal objection to the payment of the Clergy by the Treasury[86] arises from the depreciation of money, might not this difficulty be

---

[80] A 'commutation of tithes' meant the substitution of a single payment for the periodic payments which landholders were required to make for the support of the Church.

[81] 'send' is del. and 'refer' is ins.

[82] Queen's County, now known as Laoighis County, is in the province of Leinster, in Central Ireland. Parnell succeeded to the family estates in Queen's County on the death of his father in 1801. He represented Queen's County in the parliament of the United Kingdom in 1802, and from 1806 to 1832 (*DNB*).

[83] 'Would it be possible to get over the difficulty [of objections to a system of registering leases] by valuing the estates (which must in fact be done when tithes are valued) and assigning a certain portion of the neat rents of the whole in lieu of tithes?' Malthus to Parnell, 4 May 1808. See James 1979, p. 157.

[84] An applotment is a 'division into plots: apportionment' (*OED*).

[85] A 'modus' is a 'money payment in lieu of tithe. In full, *modus decimandi* [a method of tithing]' (*OED*).

[86] 'by the Treasury' is ins.

met by giving the Clergy security as far as a vote of Parliament can give it, that   9 May 180
at ev[er]y period of 7 years the actual value of their stipends should be
reconsidered? A resolution to this effect agreed to by both Houses of parliament
would secure such a revision, & a committee of the House of Commons would
probably be as good a tribunal to ascertain the quantity of depreciation as any
other. From what I know of the Irish Clergy I do not think they would be
dissatisfied with such an arrangement.

There would be no great difficulty in raising the funds out of which the
Treasury would have to pay the Clergy. I do not believe the annual amount of
tithes in Ireland exceeds £300,000. The people would readily acquiesce in any
new taxes, in consideration of a relief from tythes,* & the only point to be
attended to would be to take care, not to have the system of taxation quite new,
but rather an augmentation of old taxes.

I am the more inclined to this plan in preference to buying land for the
Clergy, if the means of purchasing it are to [be] derived from the sale of the
tithes now chargeable, which is Mr Dudley's plan,[87] because our Landholders
& farmers have not capital to enable them to become purchasers – nor is there
that superfluity of capital in the Country, or [88] so easy a process to recover
money when due in Ireland, as would [89] secure purchasers, not being the
landholders or farmers.

If I can possibly get out of town for a day I should feel very much obliged
to you if you would permit me to see you in the County for half an hour to
explain more fully this important question. At present I am confined in the
Downpatrick[90] Election committee but have hopes of getting free from it in a
week or ten days

I have the Honor* to be
Yr very obliged faithful Ser^t
H Parnell

---

[87] Revd Sir Henry Bate Dudley, formerly Henry Bate, *A Short Address to the Most Reverend and Honourable William, Lord Primate of All Ireland, Recommendatory of some Commutation or Modification of the Tithes of that Country...*, London and Dublin, 1808. This publication by Dudley was one of the three reviewed by Malthus in his article in the *Edinburgh Review* of July 1808. The third edition is in the Malthus Library.

[88] 'that' is del.   [89] 'induce' is del.

[90] Downpatrick is a town in the Down district (formerly in County Down), Northern Ireland, about 21 miles south-east of Belfast.

54. ALEXANDER MARCET[91]
TO MALTHUS[92]

London 23 Dec[r] 1809

Dear Sir

23 Dec. 1809   I received the other day from Geneva a Copy of Mr. Prevost's translation of your 'Essay on Population', which the translator desires me to transmit to you with his best Compliments.[93] As I suppose it not unlikely that you may pay a visit to the Metropolis at this period of the year, I do not send you the book to Hertford; but I shall keep it at your disposal till I have the pleasure of hearing from you. If you should favour us with a call when you come to London, you will find us in Russell square (N°23), a place far less remote from your usual residence than that in which you did us the honor* of visiting us 2 or 3 years ago –

Believe me very sincerely
Dear Sir, your obd[t] h[ble] Servant,
Alex[r] Marcet

---

[91] Alexander John Gaspard Marcet (1770–1822), MD; physician and chemist of Guy's Hospital, London. In 1799 he married Jane Haldimand (1769–1858) who, as Mrs Marcet, became the author of *Conversations on Political Economy* (1816) and many other popular scientific works for young readers. See *DNB*; James 1979.
       Two letters from Malthus to Alexander Marcet (2 July 1807 and 29 October 1809) have been published in James 1979, pp. 363–4. A letter of 22 January 1833 from Malthus to Mrs Jane Marcet has been published in the *American Economic Review*, 1986. See Polkinghorn 1986.
       Patricia James, who in 1979 had not seen this letter from Alexander Marcet, suspected that he 'seems to have been instrumental' in providing Malthus with a copy of Prévost's French translation of the *Essay on Population* (James 1979, p. 362). This letter confirms her suspicion.
[92] Address leaf torn away.
[93] Pierre Prévost (1751–1839), professor of philosophy and physics at Geneva. His French translation of the fourth edition (1807) of Malthus' *Essay on Population* was published in 1809: *Essai sur le principe de population*, 3 vols., J. J. Paschoud, Paris. Pierre Prévost was the brother-in-law of Alexander Marcet. See James 1989, Vol. II, p. 324; Zinke 1942. The Malthus Library has Prévost's translation.

55. BEWICK BRIDGE[94]
TO MALTHUS[95]

Pet: Coll: Camb: April 2nd 1817

My dear Malthus,

I send you a Copy of our Regulations for the "Provident Bank",[96] which do   2 April 1817
not differ very materially, & certainly not as to their *Machinery* from the Hertford
ones.

You will observe that it is our intention to buy stock[97] at the price it bears
at the *time of investment*; & this will be done from a table calculated for the
price of a pound Stock at the nearest price in *pence* above the market price. Our
benefactions have been so *liberal* that we are at present disposed to give 6½ pr
Annum on a pound Stock, instead of[d]*6* as it stands in the 5th regulation. But we
do not intend to alter that regulation till the passing of M[r] Rose's bill,[98] for
which we are most anxiously waiting.

By the bye, you would do me a great favor,* if you would be so good as to
inform me by Letter, what is the object of the *Hertford petition* to Parliament,
or the subject of that bill. If you should, moreover, be disposed to make any
observations upon the Code of Regulations, they would be extremely acceptable,

---

[94] Bewick Bridge (1767–1833), BA (Senior Wrangler) 1780; MA 1793; BD 1811; FRS; fellow of
Peterhouse, Cambridge; professor of mathematics and natural philosophy, East India College, 1805–
16, resigned for health reasons; vicar of Cherry Hinton, 1816–33, where he founded the village school
in 1832: 'He was an admirable man of business, and was a ready and effective member of several
charitable institutions. The Cambridge Savings' Bank is mainly indebted for its existence to his exertions
and skill ... The great character, indeed, of his life, was usefulness' (*Gentleman's Magazine*, July
1833, p. 88). See also Venn; James 1979; Walker 1912.

[95] Addressed: 'Revd T. R. Malthus / ...' (word unclear). Not passed through the post. Presumably delivered
as stated in the letter itself by William Smyth. Watermark date: '1815'.

[96] Malthus was a 'manager' of 'The Provident Institution for Savings, established in the western part of
the metropolis' in 1816. See James 1979, pp. 222–3; Malthus 1989a, Vol. II, pp. 182–3, 331. This
letter implies that he was also involved with a similar institution in Hertford.

   Edward Christian, a former colleague of Malthus at the East India College and one of the founders
of a Provident Bank at Cambridge, also assisted in the formation of a Savings Bank at Hertford. He
described the aim of Provident Banks as follows: 'it is to enable every one, who can save something
out of his earnings, or income, to deposit it where it will be carefully preserved; and where it may
accumulate, till the possessor obtains such a degree of affluence, that he may give his children the best
education, by the effects of which, aided by their own honorable conduct, they may rise to a higher,
even to the highest, scale in society' (*General Observations on Provident Banks; with a Plan of the
Unlimited Provident Bank at Cambridge*, London, 1820, p. 277).

[97] 'it bears' is del.

[98] George Rose, MP (see Ch. 4, n. 66 above). On 5 February 1817 Rose introduced in the House of
Commons a Bill designed to encourage the establishment of savings banks. The Bill was passed by the
Commons on 23 May 1817. Malthus objected to a clause in the Bill which allowed people to receive
parish assistance even though they had up to £30 in a Savings Bank. This particular clause was rejected
by the House of Lords on 1 July 1817, but the rest of the Bill received the Royal Assent on 12 July
1817. See Malthus 1989a, Vol. II, p. 331. In 1816 Rose published *Observations on Banks for Savings*;
a fourth edition with additions was published in 1817.

2 April 1817   as the press is still open, and they will not be finally sealed & settled till the passing of that Bill.

The Bank has now been opened for *two Saturdays*, & the *number & nature* of the depositors has been such as to give us the fairest promise of success. But a most *unnatural* view has been taken of the subject in this place, & therefore I ought not to be too sanguine. When you read over our list of Patron, President, Vice-President, Trustees & Manag' Committee, however, I trust you will see that we are not entirely devoid of strength or protection.

You will receive this Letter by Smyth,[99] & lest he should forget to deliver my Message, I beg my kindest Compts to Mrs Malthus (not forgetting Emily and Lucy), and to the Principal,[100] Le Bas,[101] Luton*[102] & the collected Body; congratulatg* you all most heartily that you are now released from the persecution of Messrs Jackson, Lowndes[103] &c &c.

I am in hopes that before six weeks are elapsed from this time, I shall have the pleasure of spending a day amongst you, but at present my notions are very uncertain, although I have some urgent calls both to Bath & London.

I remain, my dear Malthus Yours most faithfuly*

B. Bridge

56. PIERRE PRÉVOST
TO MALTHUS[104]

à Genève, 13 avril 1821.

Monsieur

13 April 1821   Votre lettre du 27 mars,[105] que j'ai sous les yeux contient des explications que je vous remercie de m'avoir données, et quelques expressions d'estime auxquelles je suis fort sensible.

---

[99]   William Smyth. See Ch. 4, n. 79 above.   [100] Revd Joseph Hallet Batten.

[101] Revd Charles Webb le Bas.

[102] Probably Revd Edward Lewton (1769–1830), registrar and professor of classics and general literature at the East India College, 1805–30. See James 1979.

[103] Some members of the Court of Proprietors of the East India Company had made attempts to have the East India College abolished. Malthus wrote two pamphlets in its defence: *A Letter to the Rt. Hon. Lord Grenville...*, 1813, and *Statements Respecting the East India College...*, 1817. One of the main opponents of the College was Randle Jackson (1757–1837), barrister, and parliamentary counsel to the Corporation of the City of London, the Bank of England, and the East India Company. A colourful and vehement speech by a Mr Lowndes described the College as 'a ricketty, squint-eyed, stupid brat'. Their attempts to abolish the College were finally defeated at the General Court on 4 March 1817. See James 1979, pp. 234–44.

[104] Addressed: 'Mr. T. R. Malthus / prof' Hist. & Pol. Econ. in the / E. I. C. Hertfordshire'. Below the address: 'Prévost / London [del.] / Genève Hertford'. Postmarks: 'AP C 21 1821' and 'SUISSE PAR BERNE'. Obsolete spellings in MS (e.g. 'auroit' for 'aurait') are retained in this transcription without being individually signalled by the addition of a star (*).

[105] See Zinke 1942, pp. 179–81.

J'ai bien réfléchi au moyen d'éviter, non tant les pertes que vous prévoyez, 13 April 1821
que l'inconvenient* de manquer en partie le but de présenter votre ouvrage
dans son état le plus parfait. Mon libraire ne s'effraie pas de la concurrence que
l'on peut lui faire; mais je m'effraie de la pensée que le lendemain du jour où
auroit paru ma traduction, vous donneriez au public une édition qui abrogeroit
en partie le résultat de mon travail.[106]

Là-dessus voici l'idée qui m'est venue et que je vous soumets. Je suppose
la rédaction de vos additions au chapitre de la France achevée,[107] ainsi que toutes
les additions, suppressions et changemens* que vous pourriez avoir dessein de
faire ailleurs. Ne pourriez-vous pas vous prêter à en faire faire une copie pour
moi et à mes frais[108] que vous m'enverriez et que je traduirois; en sorte que ma
traduction se trouveroit réellement faite (par anticipation) sur la nouvelle et
sixième édition? –
– Pour vous éviter toute peine, il suffiroit que vous voulussiez bien confier
cette partie de manuscrit à l'un de mes fils qui sont à Londres, l'un associé de
Mr. Haldimand,[109] et l'autre ayant une maison de commerce, Morris Prevost*
& C.[110] (l'un et l'autre également dignes de cette confiance), pour qu'ils le fissent
copier et me l'envoyassent.

Je ne crois pas que votre libraire s'inquiétât beaucoup de la publication en
françois de ces additions. En tout cas, vous pourriez prendre la précaution de
m'interdire la publication de ma traduction avant un avis préalable de votre
part. Et il seroit entendu que vous me donneriez cet avis de manière que l'ouvrage
(je veux dire, la 6ème* édition) parût en anglois et en traduction précisément au
même moment. L'annonce seule de cette coïncidence suffiroit pour déconcerter
les entreprises rivales. – Cela suppose qu'en effet, dans un espace de temps peu
éloigné vous publierez la nouvelle édition; car si elle devoit tarder indéfiniment,
il vaudroit mieux traduire la 5ème.

Je pars en tout ceci de ce que vous me dites que vous me préférez à

---

[106] Prévost's fears that a new (sixth) edition of the *Essay* would make redundant his proposed translation
of the fifth edition were apparently allayed by Malthus' reply of 26 April 1821: 'I have as yet made no
progress whatever towards another edition of the Essay on Population, and indeed have hardly
determined whether, when another edition is wanted, I should make any further additions to the fifth'
(Zinke 1942, p. 181). A French translation of the fifth edition (1817) was published by Prévost and his
son (G. Prévost) in 1823. The sixth edition of the *Essay on Population* was not published until 1826.

[107] Malthus' publisher, John Murray, had suggested that, in a new edition of the *Essay on Population*,
Malthus 'might make some few additions to the chapter on France, and perhaps a very few elsewhere'
(Zinke 1942, p. 180).

[108] 'et à mes frais' is ins. as a footnote.

[109] Prévost's sister-in-law, Mrs Jane Marcet, was the daughter of A. F. Haldimand, a rich Swiss merchant
established in London (*DNB*).

[110] 'qui sont ... Morris Prevost* & C.' is ins. as a footnote.

13 April 1821 Constancio[111] ou même à tout autre, comme traducteur. Puisque ma précédente traduction a obtenu votre suffrage, il me semble que vous approuverez celle-ci, dans laquelle j'ai adopté le plan de calquer sur l'original, sans aucun changement, ni suppression. J'ai quelque droit d'espérer que je n'ai pas désappris pendant ces 10 ou 12 années des principes dont je me suis souvent occupé et dont en particulier j'ai toujours fait état en donnant des cours d'économie politique. J'ai aussi acquis un aide en mon fils (cadet de ceux de Londres) que je me suis adjoint pour ce nouveau travail de traduction, et qui y met tout le zèle d'un néophyte.

En voilà assez, trop peut-être, sur ma traduction projetée, et déja fort avancée. – Quant à Constancio, j'ai été blessé de ses notes; mais quoique j'aie sa traduction, que mon fils a cru devoir acheter, j'avoue, qu'ayant l'original, j'y ai à peine jeté les yeux. Si je trouve (comparaison faite) qu'il y ait à dire, ce sera l'objet d'une lettre subséquente. Je n'ai pas voulu retarder celle-ci.

Je trouve juste votre réponse[112] sur l'emploi du travail mesuré par la peine de l'ouvrier, et j'en éprouve quelque regret.

Je me suis empressé de profiter de votre avis sur les pages 373, 374 de la 5ᵉ édit.

Quant aux taxes, ce que vous dites est très vrai.[113] Je ne l'avois pas perdu de vues;* mais le chapitre de Say est ingénieux; tandis que dans les autres, ses argumens* et ses sarcasmes font peu d'impression.

Il est bien agréable, dans ces temps d'orage, de trouver dans son cabinet quelque consolation au milieu des paisibles recherches de l'économie politique. La section qui vous est propre et que vous àvez* en partie créée me paroît devoir produire à la longue l'impression desirée* et diminuer sensiblement les souffrances de la partie la plus nombreuse du genre humain.

Mon beau-frère Marcet et sa famille se sont long temps* arrêtés à Florence par suite des circonstances; d'où ils sont enfin partis pour Rome, et doivent en revenir de manière à être ici au mois de mai.

Agréez, Monsieur, la part que je prends à la perte douloureuse que vous

---

[111] F. S. Constancio published (Paris, 1820) a French translation of Malthus' *Principles of Political Economy* (1820), and had expressed an interest in translating the *Essay on Population*. When Malthus was asked for his opinion of Constancio as a translator, he replied: 'I thought a translator ought in the main to agree with his author and that as it appeared from some of the notes to Mr. Constancio's translation that he differed from me entirely on the principles of population, he was certainly not exactly the person whom I should have selected as a translator.' He added (to Prévost): 'I need not say how much I should prefer you as my translator to Mr. Constancio or indeed to anybody that I know' (Zinke 1942, pp. 179–80). Zinke described the notes inserted by Constancio in his translation of Malthus' *Principles of Political Economy* as 'rising from casual disagreement to vigorous dissent' (Zinke 1942, pp. 179–80.)

[112] See Zinke 1942, p. 180.   [113] See Zinke 1942, p. 180.

avez faite d'une soeur,[114] et l'expression de ma haute estime et de mon entier   13 April 1821
dévouement.

P. Prevost*

P.S. Je vous remercie de la remarque ...[115] mot *revolution*,[116] dont déja* je connaissais la valeur.

P.S. Vous m'obligerez beaucoup de vouloir me répondre sans délai.

NB. Voulez-vous bien me donner votre meilleure adresse – Est-ce Hertford ou Londres? J'ai hésité.

57. BEWICK BRIDGE
TO MALTHUS[117]

Pet: Coll: Camb: Aug: 28th 1822

My dear Malthus/

Your Rule for finding the *intermediate* periods of doubling[118] had not   28 Aug. 1822
escaped me, but I abstained from giving it you – I – Because it was not
Mathematically accurate – II. Because it is very far from *true* at the beginning
of the Table.

The fact is this – after the first 10 or 12 lines, the periods of doubling are
very nearly in Arithmetic *Progression* – consequently your Method will apply
to the case you have selected, and to the *rest* of the Table *after* it[119] – but if you
want to know how far it is from being *generally* true, try it[120] within the first 6
N^{os} – but this is a part of the Table which of course is of little practical[121] utility.

I thought it right to give you this hint, for fear you should build any *general*
Rule upon a particular case. Your Rule will be true to the *first* decimal from 14
to 40; it will therefore spare the necessity of having recourse to the Logarithmic
Tables through this *important* interval of the Table – but I think the world

---

[114] In his letter to Prévost of 27 March 1821, Malthus apologised for his delay in replying to Prévost's previous letter, and referred to an 'absence from home for some time occasioned by the melancholy event of the death of a sister' (Zinke 1942, p. 179). This would have been Mary Catherine Charlotte Malthus (1764–1821), the fourth of his five sisters.

[115] Several words indecipherable.   [116] See Zinke 1942, p. 181.

[117] Addressed: 'The Revd T. R. Malthus / East India College / near Hertford'. Postmark on the back: 'CAMBRIDGE / 52'.

[118] Letters no. 57 to 62 from Bridge are principally concerned with how to determine the number of years required for a population to double given that the average annual percentage increase of that population is known. The table which Bridge produced for Malthus (enclosed with letter no. 59 but since lost) became the basis for Table II (p. 333) in Malthus' article on 'Population' in Vol. VI (published separately early in 1823) of the *Supplement to the 4th, 5th and 6th Editions of the Encyclopaedia Britannica*, 1824. Its inclusion in the 6th edition of the *Essay* (1826) on page 498 of Vol. I was one of the only two major changes made to the previous edition.

[119] '*after* it' is ins.   [120] 'it' is ins.   [121] 'practical' changed from 'practically'.

28 Aug. 1822 should be told this in the Encyclopaedia – and also that the *mode* of calculating the Tables should be inserted – but of course I do not pretend to *dictate* upon this point.

I was taken very ill yesterday with a sick Headache – but I have been bled & physicked and am (thank God) better today – I doubt however whether I shall be under the necessity of asking the *Reader* at Whitehall to preach for me on Sunday. It is my intention to set off on Friday & spend the day with a friend in ...,[122] and proceed to London on Saturday. I hope the air & exercise I shall get in my *Chair*[123] will be of service to me. I am much obliged to you for your kind invitation to pay you a visit on my Return from London – but my plans lie in a different direction, & must therefore beg of you to excuse me. With kind Regards to Mrs Malthus & family, Ever yours very faithfuly*

B. Bridge

58. BEWICK BRIDGE
TO MALTHUS[124]

Pet: Coll: Sepr 24th 1822

My dear Malthus/

24 Sep. 1822   I am quite amused at the *grave* way in which you have thought it necessary to answer my very *saucy* Letter. To tell you the honest truth I have calculated the per Centage Table to a much greater extent than has yet appeared in any of my Letters to you, & shall be very ready to send you any part of it which you may think will answer your purpose; but before I proceed with my *observations*, let me tell you that I was quite prepared to hear a very indifferent account of poor Le Bas, but I am taken by surprize* with respect to the *Principal* & am truly concerned to find that he has occasion to apply to Dr Luke.

---

[122] Word difficult to decipher; possibly 'Essex'.

[123] Bridge was presumably referring here to a 'light vehicle drawn by one horse' (*OED*).

[124] Addressed: 'Revd T. R. Malthus / East India College / near Hertford'. Postmark: 'CAMBRIDGE 52'. Also, on blank parts of the letter, there are some calculations in Malthus' hand and 'B. Bridge's letter' in a different hand.

What think you of my sending the Table[125] with the decimal N°s 24 Sep. 1822
correspondg* to the value of ⅒ Log ((100+g) – 2) and the period of doubling to
two places of decimals for the following per Centages.

Per Centage	Per Centage	Per Centage	Per Centage
1	From	41	55
2	10 to 40 to	42	60
3	contain the	43	65
4	intermediate	44	70
5	*halves*	45	75
6		46	80
7		47	85
8		48	90
9		49	95
10		50	99

I am of opinion thus much of it would answer every practical purpose, and
at the same time give a very complete view of the *law of variation* of the period
of doubling whilst the per Centage goes over the whole range from 1 to 99. If
you think this will do and I hear nothing from you, you will be put into possession

[125] Bridge's Table, as reproduced by Malthus in his article on 'Population' in the *Supplement to the ...
Encyclopaedia Britannica*, related the '*Per Centage* Increase in Ten Years' to the 'Period of Doubling'.
For example, it showed that if a population increased by 20% in 10 years, then it would double in
38.01 years. Bridge's expression '⅒ Log ((100+g) – 2)', which today would be written '⅒ {Log
(100+g) – 2}', is derived thus:
  If g = percentage increase in 10 years, P = the initial population, and r = annual rate of increase,
then the new population in 10 years time is given by:
  P(100 + g)/100 = P{(100 + r)/100}^{10}
  whence log{(100 + r) / 100} = ⅒ log {(100 + g) / 100}
                                            = ⅒ {log (100 + g) - 2}
  If the population doubles,
    let A = the new population = 2P
    n   = the period (in years) over which the population doubles.
  Then ,
    A   = P {(100 + r) / 100}^{n}
    A/P   = 2 = {(100 + r) / 100}^{n}
    log 2 = n log {(100 + r) / 100}
    n   = log 2 / log {(100 + r) / 100}
            = log 2 / ⅒ {log (100 + g) - 2}
  Thus, the period over which a population doubles can be found by substituting the appropriate
figure for 'g' in the above equation. The time it takes for the population to treble, quadruple, etc. can
be found by substituting log 3, log 4, etc. for log 2 in the numerator.

24 Sep. 1822 of it in the course of a few days, *headed* by a proper explanation of the mode of calculating the Table, and the principles upon which the calculation is founded.

I believe I ought to mention that in the *next* edition of my Algebra (probably not less than *3* years to come, as a very large edition was published about 15 Months ago)[126] I shall entirely re-model my Chapter on the Mode of calculating [127] the increase of[128] population in [129] any given Country, & accommodate it to the existing Circumstances under which the census may then[130] be made. I think it right to mention this *now*, in order that when that edition is published, containing the Table which I am about to send to you, I may not be considered as a *Plagiarist*.

I will immediately look at the Chapter in[131] your Essay which you have directed my attention to[132] – &[133] if any thing occurs which may require observation; such observations shall be forwarded to you along with the Table.

With kind remembrances to M͏ʳ Malthus & family.

I am truly yours

B. Bridge

59. BEWICK BRIDGE
TO MALTHUS[134]

Pet: Coll: Sep. 28ᵗʰ 1822

My dear Malthus/

28 Sep. 1822 As I have rec͏ᵈ no answer to my letter of the 24ᵗʰ instant, I take for granted that you are satisfied with the arrangement & extent of the Table, and therefore send it you according to promise.[135] With respect to the Method of *approximations* there cannot possibly be a better one than *your own*. I have said a word or two more on the subject in the inclosed* paper – but I have done it so clumsily that I should have written it over again had not the *Table* been at the back of it.

---

[126] The first edition of Bridge's *Lectures on the Elements of Algebra* was published in 1810. Malthus referred to it in his *Essay on Population*, 5th edn, 1817, Vol. II, pp. 84–90; 6th edn, 1826, Vol. I, p. 431. There he explains in detail Bridge's 'general formula for estimating the population of a country at any distance from a certain period, under given circumstances of births and mortality'. A fifth edition of Bridge's *Algebra* was published in 1821 and a sixth in 1826, both with the new title *A Treatise on the Elements of Algebra*. Further editions followed.

[127] 'of' is del. and 'calculation' changed to 'calculating'. [128] 'increase of' is ins. [129] 'the' is del.

[130] 'then' is ins. [131] 'in' is ins. [132] See Ch. 4, n. 146 below. [133] '&' is ins.

[134] Addressed: 'The Rev͏ᵈ T. R. Malthus / East India College / near Hertford'. Postmark on the back: 'CAMBRIDGE 52'. Also, there are some calculations in Malthus' hand on blank parts of the letter.

[135] The 'inclosed* paper' and the 'Table' are wanting.

I have read the Chapter[136] in your Essay (alluded to in your last letter), and   28 Sep. 1822
so far as I can perceive your Arithmetical reasoning is very correct. To tell you
the truth I have no faith whatever in the information derived from registers of
Births, deaths, & Marriages, and consider the Method *per Censum* as the only
one by which we can estimate with the slightest degree of accuracy the tendency
which the whole[137] population of a Country has to increase or decrease at any
given period. I shall be most ready to have such further communication with
you as you may desire, previous to your sending the Article to Mr Napier.[138]
With kind remembrances to M^{rs} M.

Yours most faithfuly*
B. Bridge

60. BEWICK BRIDGE
TO MALTHUS[139]

Pet: Coll: Octr 15th 1822

My dear Malthus/

To tell you the truth I was determined to give you a *surfeit* – more especially   15 Oct. 1822
as, by means of the Theorem, I can calculate the period of doubling or trebling,
or *enning* (I mean *n* times) to any number of decimal places[140] without any
mental effort, just as Ladies do their knotting, knitting, or Patchwork. From one
of your Letters[141] I inferred that you would like to see how Matters went on by
centuries, and therefore gave you the *early* part of the Table; but I have not the
Slightest wish or desire you should insert a single line more than what you
think proper; indeed I am of opinion (as *you* are satisfied with it) that the insertion
of the *halves* for the first ten numbers will be amply sufficient for all practical
purposes. In a word, my wish is that you should consider all the Matter contained
in my several scrawls as your sole and entire property, and make such use of it
as may suit your convenience.

---

[136] Bridge's references in this paragraph to the unreliability of the registers of births, marriages and
deaths, and to the mode of calculation of a more accurate estimate of births and deaths suggest that
Malthus may have directed him to Book II, Ch. IX, 'Of the Checks to Population in England
(continued)', in Vol. II of the 5th edn, 1817, of the *Essay on Population*.

[137] 'whole' is ins.

[138] Macvey Napier (1776–1847) was the editor of the *Supplement to the … Encyclopaedia Britannica*,
1824. He later became editor of the *Edinburgh Review* (*DNB*).

[139] Addressed: 'The Revd T. R. Malthus / East India College / near Hertford'. Postmark: 'CAMBRIDGE
52'.

[140] 'to any number of decimal places' is ins.   [141] Malthus' letters are wanting.

15 Oct. 1822   I have never read either Dr Price or Mr Milne;[142] but I will procure the books (if possible) from the Public Library this Morning, and if I have any observations to make which I may think to be worth your Notice, I will [143] forward them to you.

Pray who is Mr Rikman?*[144] will you be so good as to inform me, what situation he holds in Society, and whether his observations on the Population returns are worth reading – and if they *be*, where I may procure them.

Could you also, without much trouble, put me in possession of the Arithmetical[145] results of all the census's wh[ich][146] have been made in America & the several Countries of Europe, since census's have been established. Of course I only ask for this at your *leisure*, as I am in no sort of hurry whatever. You have already[147] supplied me with the N^{os} for England & Wales, and for North America I beleive.*

With kind regards to Mrs Malthus & family

very truly yours

B. Bridge

61. BEWICK BRIDGE
TO MALTHUS[148]

Pet. Coll. [circa 20 October][149] 1822

My dear Malthus/

c. 20 Oct. 1822   I have looked over several of the Chapters in Dr Price and Mr Milne but have not been able to hit upon the passage in which those Authors assert that the "Expectation of life" is an Arithmetic Mean between the ratios of the births and deaths,[150] and as you have not assigned your reasons for supposing that it is

---

[142] Joshua Milne (1776–1851) was actuary to the Sun Life Assurance Society. In 1815 he published *A Treatise on the Valuation of Annuities and Assurances in Lives and Survivorships; on the Construction of Tables of Mortality; and on the Probabilities and Expectations of Life...*, 2 vols., which is said to have brought about 'a revolution in actuarial science' (*DNB*). In the *Essay*, 6th edn, Vol. I, p. 286 n. and in the *Supplement*, p. 230, Malthus discussed the table that appeared in Milne, Vol. II, p. 569.

[143] 'inform' is del.

[144] John Rickman (1771–1840), BA (Oxford) 1792, FRS 1815, statistician, played a major role in preparing, organising and reporting on the censuses of 1801, 1811, 1821, and 1831. From 1820 till his death he was the Clerk of the House of Commons. A friend of Robert Southey, he 'sympathised with Southey's conservatism, and with his hatred of Malthus and the economists' (*DNB*). Southey, inspired by Coleridge, described Malthus' writings as 'mischievous metaphysics' and Malthus himself as 'a mischievous booby' and a 'mischievous reptile'. See James 1979, pp. 103, 110–11; Malthus 1989a, Vol. II, pp. 328–9.

[145] 'Arithmetical' is ins.   [146] MS torn by seal; word partially missing.

[147] From 'You have already' to the end of the sentence is ins.

[148] Addressed: 'The Revd T. R. Malthus / East India College / near Hertford'. Postmark: 'CAMBRIDGE 52'.

[149] On the probable date of the letter, see n. 158 below.

a *Geometric* mean between those quantities, I must for the present leave this   c. 20 Oct. 1822
Matter *sub judice* as it stands in your Letter.

For my own part I know of no other mode of estimating the "expectation
of life" but by having recourse to the *doctrine of Chances*; upon this principle
Table V, Vol: II, page 569 in Mr Milne's work is calculated, as will appear from
the following investigation.

I ought to premise however that *all* his Tables are calculated upon this
principle, but I have selected Table V to make my observations upon, [151] because
I consider it as the most perfect and best arranged of any one in the book.

You will perceive that in this Table Mr Milne's *hypothesis* is that no person
exceeds the age of 100, and[152] the numbers standing in the *second* column (which
express the number of persons living at the end of 1, 2, 3, 4 &c. years) [153] are of
course[154] considered as *Matters of fact*.

The *object* of the Table is to shew* [155] what portion of these 100 years each
person has the *chance* of attaining to at his birth and at all intermediate periods
between that and 100, under the circumstances of Mortality exhibited in the
third Column of the Table.

It appears then that out of 10000 persons which are *born*, only 7985 are
found to be living at the end of the first year, the chance which any given person
therefore has of living through the *first* year is measured by the fraction $\frac{7985}{10000}$;
for the same reason the chance which this person has of living through the
second year is measured by the fraction $\frac{7441}{10000}$, through the *third* by $\frac{7134}{10000}$, through
the *fourth* by $\frac{6911}{10000}$, and so on; so that the *portion* of the 100 years which any
given person has the chance of attaining to at the time of his *birth*, is measured
by the sum of the fractions $\frac{7985}{10000} + \frac{7441}{10000} + \frac{7134}{10000} + \frac{6911}{10000} +$ &c continued to 99 terms.

Since these fractions have a common denominator we need only add their
Numerators; i.e, we need only add together the Numbers standing in the *second*
Column of the Table, with the exception of the *first* (10000): this sum I make
356154, which being divided by 10000 gives 35.6154 (*say* 35.62) for the
expectation of each person at the time of his birth; the difference between this
number & the number in Mr Milne's Table shall be considered anon.

Reasoning as before, the *portion* of the 100 years which any given person
of *one year* old has the chance of attaining is measured by the sum of the fractions

---

[150] In his article on 'Population' for the *Supplement to the … Encyclopaedia Britannica*, 1824, p. 328,
Malthus explained Price's rule for calculating the expectation of life. For the period 1810 to 1821,
Malthus estimated that the average ratio of births to population was 1:29.9, and the average ratio
of deaths to population was 1:52.17. He then stated that 'according to Dr Price, the mean between them,
which, in this case, is 41, will give the expectation of life'.

[151] 'upon' is ins.   [152] 'and' is ins.   [153] Word del.   [154] 'may' is del. and 'are of course' is ins.

[155] 'the chance' is del.

c. 20 Oct. 1822 $\frac{7441}{7985} + \frac{7134}{7985} + \frac{6911}{7985} + \frac{6747}{7985}+$ &c to 98 terms; now $356154 - 7985 = 348169$ and $\frac{348169}{7985}$ $= 43.6028$ (say 43.61) for the expectation of a person *one year* old.

Proceeding in this manner the Table as it
stands in the Margin is very readily
constructed.
The difference between this Table and
that of Mr Milne must now be accounted
for.

Age	Expectation
0	35.62
1	43.61
2	45.80
3	46.77
4	47.27
5	47.42
&c	&c

You will be pleased to observe that in finding the "Expectation" of persons at their *birth*, we reasoned as if 2015 Children had died on the day they were *born*; but as the census was taken at the *end* of the 1ˢᵗ year, you are aware that each of those persons had an *equal chance* of living or dying in the course of that year; and by the doctrine of Chances this is equal to *half a years life*; we must therefore add .50 to 35.62 which gives 36.12 for the *full* "Expectation" of each person at the time of his birth.

For the same reason .50 must be added to *each* of the Numbers in the foregoing Table, to give the value of the *full* "expectation" of each person at the several periods of life as they stand in the Table. The Table then becomes

Age	Expectation
0	36.12
1	44.11
2	46.30
3	47.27
4	47.77
5	47.92
&c	&c

which is Mr Milne's Table; and I hold (& that pretty sternly) that Mr Milne himself ought to have annexed some such explanation as this to the foot of his Tables.

With respect to your observation at the latter part of your Letter, I have been so unfortunate as *not* to hit upon any passage in the works either of Dʳ Price or Mʳ Milne where they estimate the "expectation of life" by dividing the population by the deaths; there are some passages at pages 423, 426, 427, 434,

&c of Vol. II of Mr Milne where this division is made, but it is there applied to find the *ratio of Mortality* & not the *expectation of life*, and so far he is right.[156]

Since I wrote my letter on Tuesday last (Octr 15th) the hint which you gave me some time since[157] about your having had a slight breeze at the College, has been confirmed by intelligence from other quarters.[158] With kind respects to M^rM.

c. 20 Oct. 1822

Yours very faithfully
B. Bridge

62. BEWICK BRIDGE
TO MALTHUS[159]

Novr 2nd 1822 Saturday Morning/

My dear Malthus/

I have been so occupied for the last 3 or 4 days either with business or engagements that I really have not had time to consider your Letter of the 28th October[160] till this Morning – and I have risen early [161] on purpose that I may send this Letter by our Friend Smyth.

2 Nov. 1822

I have sent back to the Public Library the works of Dr Price, Mr Morgan[162] & Mr Milne (the 4th Ed: of Dr Price I could not procure) and have neither time nor inclination to return to them or their *Errors*. The principle which I still

---

[156] Referring to Price's rule for calculating the expectation of life, Malthus said: 'This rule, however, is only a rough approximation, and in the few cases, where sufficient data have been obtained in progressive countries for calculating the expectation of life more accurately, it has turned out to be nearer to the annual mortality than to the mean referred to here.' And, referring to calculations by Milne, he added: 'from what has been stated, it may safely be concluded, that the expectation of life lies very much nearer the annual mortality, particularly in cases of very rapid increase, than to the mean proposed by Dr Price' (Malthus, *Supplement to the ... Encyclopaedia Britannica*, 1824, p. 328; see Ch. 4, n. 118 above).

In his article on 'Population' for the *Supplement*, the final part of which was sent to Macvey Napier on 7 January 1823, Malthus did not refer to Bridge's view that, to estimate the expectation of life, recourse must be had to the 'doctrine of Chances'. As the following letter indicates, Bridge considered the views of Price and Milne in this matter to be '*Errors*'.

[157] 'some time since' is ins.

[158] The 'slight breeze at the College' was probably a reference to student riots which occurred at the East India College on Sunday, 22 September 1822. For further details of the riots, see James 1979, pp. 326-7. These were not reported in *The Times* until Saturday, 19 October (p. 3, cols. a, b). Thus, this last paragraph was probably added to the letter on or after 19 October. The expression 'Tuesday last (Octr 15th)' indicates that the last paragraph could not have been written later than the following Tuesday, 22 October.

[159] Addressed: 'The Revd T. R. Malthus / East India College / By favor* of / Professor Smyth'. Not passed through the post.

[160] Malthus' letter is wanting.   [161] 'this Morning' is del.

[162] William Morgan (1750–1833), FRS, nephew of Richard Price, chief actuary to the Equitable Assurance Society. His publications included *The Doctrine of Annuities and Assurances on Lives and Survivorships Stated and Explained...*, 1779; and *The Principles and Doctrine of Assurances, Annuities on Lives, and Contingent Reversions, Stated and Explained*, 1821 (*DNB*).

2 Nov. 1822   consider as the *true* one for estimating what is technically called the "Expectation of life" does not rest upon the Authority of either of those Gentlemen. My *Masters* upon this subject have been De Moivre[163] & Halley,[164] and they are[165] Masters upon whose judgement I have very great reliance. At the end of De Moivre's quarto Work on the doctrine of Chances[166] you will find a Table not very unlike that of Table V in Mr Milne,[167] constructed by D^{r}Halley, and in the body of De Moivre's Work you will see how he applies the principle for which I contend to the calculation of Annuities upon lives. I may further add, that in such parts of the Works of the three Authors before mentioned as I have read, the *principle* upon which they go for estimating the "Expectation of life", does not differ essentially from that of De Moivre & Halley.

That there is not a single "*Matter of fact*" in any one of the *five* Authors I have alluded to I am very ready to allow, taking the expression *Matter of fact* in its strictest sense – for I hold that the whole science of Population &c as it at[168] *present* exists has no better foundation than, either *hypothesis* or *Tables which, from the very nature of things must necessarily be very inaccurate.* At the same time there is no doubt that like *Chemistry* &c it is fast approaching towards a scientific shape; and that to this end I am ready to allow your Writing has very much contributed.

With respect to the expression *Matter of fact* as used by me in my last letter I have only to observe, that you certainly will agree with me that when a Table is constructed upon the principle that no person lives beyond the age of 100, this is mere *hypothesis*; but if this Table also contains the Number of persons born on a given day in a given Country, with the Number that die off in each successive year, so far as[169] this Table accords with the real[170] state of things in that given Country it is *Matter of fact*, but certainly *no further*; and this is all I meant.

You have now received from me all that I know about the mode of calculating "the Progress of Population" and "the Expectation of life", and if you squeeze me for ever it will be quite impossible for you to get a drop more. I should recommend you to avail yourself of the opportunity which presents itself of touching up[171] Smyth a little; he is particularly fond of *Arithmetic* and subjects connected with it.

With kind regards to Mrs M. & family

Yours ever

B. Bridge

[163] Abraham de Moivre (1667–1754), *The Doctrine of Chances: or, a Method of Calculating the Probability of Events in Play*, 1718. His other publications included *Annuities upon Lives...*, 1725. De Moivre 'came next to Halley as a founder of a science of life-contingencies' (*DNB*).

[164] Edmund (or Edmond) Halley (1656–1742), astronomer.   [165] 'are' is ins.

[166] 'on the doctrine of Chances' is ins.   [167] 'and in the body of De M' is del.   [168] 'at' is ins.

[169] 'as' is ins.   [170] 'real' is ins.   [171] 'up' is ins.

63. MALTHUS
TO ROBERT JOHN WILMOT-HORTON[172]

[circa 15 February 1830][173]

Dear Sir,

    I saw your correspondence with M[r] P. Thompson*[174] and [175] have received and read your second series with much interest. I had before met with[176] M[r] Duchatel['s] work,[177] and [178] thought it very good. You know that[179] I agree with you in the main [180] on the advantages of emigration, though there have always been a few shades of difference between us. In the present work[181] I cannot but think it rather rash in you[182] to say that nothing can be less true and less philosophical than to suppose[183] that the removal[184] [of] a redundant population would have a tendency to stimulate the increase of the remainder. It is no doubt[185] true [186] that good wages may be employed in two different ways, either so as to increase the comforts, and[187] emprove* the permanent[188] condition of the labouring classes, or to [189] accelerate the rate of their[190] increase; but as it is an acknowledged fact[191] that with very few exceptions population rapidly recovers itself after any great loss which it has sustained, it must be allowed that experience shews* the latter of the two results from emproved* wages to be more probable than the former. It is a very just and philosophical observation of M. Duchatel

c. 15 Feb. 1830

---

[172] Robert John Wilmot-Horton (1784–1841), BA 1806, MA 1815 (Christ Church, Oxford); MP 1818–30; knighted 1831; governor and commander-in-chief of the island of Ceylon 1831–7. The son of Sir Robert Wilmot, he married in 1806 the daughter and heiress of Eusebius Horton, and assumed the additional name Horton in 1823 in compliance with his father-in-law's will. Wilmot-Horton believed that emigration would provide a cure for pauperism, and hence for the many other social problems arising from pauperism. In 1827 he became chairman of a House of Commons Select Committee on Emigration from the United Kingdom. Malthus gave evidence before the Committee. See James 1979.

    In 1830 Wilmot-Horton published *An Inquiry into the Causes and Remedies of Pauperism...* in four parts. The 'First series' contained correspondence with C. Poulett Thomson 'upon the conditions under which colonization would be justifiable as a national measure'. The 'Second series' contained correspondence with M. Duchatel. The 'Third series' contained letters to Sir Francis Burdett 'upon pauperism in Ireland'. The 'Fourth series' contained a discussion with N. W. Senior.

    Malthus' letters to Horton are in the Catton Collection, Derbyshire Record Office.

[173] Draft of a letter sent on 15 February 1830. Watermark date: '1828'. Final version in the Catton Collection.

[174] Charles Edward Poulett Thomson (1799–1841), Baron Sydenham (1840), governor-general of Canada (1839) (*DNB*).

[175] 'I' is del.   [176] 'with' is repeated in MS.

[177] Charles Marie Tanneguy, Comte Duchatel (1803–1867), had published in 1829 *La Charité dans ses rapports avec l'état moral et le bien-être des classes inférieures de la société*, Paris.

[178] 'had been much pleased with it and' is del.   [179] 'You know that' is ins.

[180] 'to [the] your opinions' is del.   [181] 'particular' is del. and 'the present work' is ins.

[182] 'in you' is ins.   [183] 'than to suppose' is ins. over 'that' which should have been del.

[184] 'taking away' is del. and 'removal' is ins.   [185] 'no doubt' is ins.   [186] 'as I have stated' is del.

[187] 'increase the comforts, and' is ins.   [188] 'permanent' is ins.   [189] 'stimulate' is del.

[190] 'their' is ins.   [191] 'truth' is del. and 'fact' is ins.

c. 15 Feb. 1830   that when a population passes rapidly from a very[192] depressed to a much better[193] state, it is to be apprehended, that the power of custom will[194] "not give way immediately to the imfluence*[195] of an emproved* condition and that the moral change will[196] not be accomplished so quickly as the physical one". [197] This would not however weigh with me against a plan of emigration in certain circumstances of a country; but surely the contemplation of the probability of it cannot be called unphilosophical if the conclusions of philosophy are to rest as they ought to do upon large[198] experience.

To go to another subject, I am rather afraid that though you may prove[199] that the Irish paupers are somehow or other supported by the state; yet that those who [200] at present have no perception of[201] the burden, and would have a decided perception of a tax, would be unwilling to pay [202] a tax in order to relieve themselves from an imperceptible[203] expense. [204] As a matter of fact indeed [205] it must be acknowledged, that though it is very easy to shew* that[206] the redundancy of population cruelly[207] impoverishes the labouring classes, and ought on that account to be removed, if possible, [208] but it is not so easy[209] to shew* that there is a large mass of ablebodied men who are actually contributing nothing towards their livelyhood,* and that such a[210] redundancy notwithstanding its effects in lowering[211] generally the price of labour, diminishes the incomes of the higher and middle classes of society who are the principal supporters of labour[212] in *proportion* to the whole support of that part of the population assumed to be redundant.

Though therefore I am a decided friend to[213] emigration myself in the present state of things[214] and would willingly pay my share of any tax necessary to accomplish it[215] yet I can readily understand why a proposition for borrowing a large sum of[216] money for this purpose would be likely to be so unpopular, [217] particularly while there is such a loud call for economy in every department, that few ministers would venture upon it. If you should fail therefore in your laudable effort it will not be your fault, but the result of the nature of the case.

---

[192] 'very' is ins.   [193] 'an improved' is del. and 'a much better' is ins.   [194] 'will' changed from 'would'.
[195] 'imfluence'* is changed from 'imfluences'*.   [196] 'will' changed from 'would'.
[197] 'The [probability] chance of' is del.   [198] 'enlarged' is ins. and changed to 'large'.   [199] 'prove' is ins.
[200] 'do not' is del.   [201] '*feel*' is del. and 'have no perception of' is ins.   [202] '[the] such' is del.
[203] 'imperceptible' is ins.   [204] 'which they are not sensible of' is del.
[205] 'I think' is del.   [206] 'it is very easy to shew* that' is ins.   [207] 'greatly' is del. and 'cruelly' is ins.
[208] 'yet that it does not proportionally diminish the incomes of those who would probably pay a tax imposed to discharge the interest of a loan for the purpose of imigration*' is del.
[209] From 'but it is not so easy' to end of paragraph is ins.
[210] 'the incomes' is del. and 'such' is ins.
[211] 'though it lowers' is del. and 'notwithstanding its effects in lowering' is ins.
[212] 'who are the principal supporters of labour' is ins.   [213] 'for' is del. and 'a decided friend to' is ins.
[214] 'in the present state of things' is ins.   [215] 'for the purpose' is del. and 'to accomplish it' is ins.
[216] 'a large sum of' is ins.   [217] 'wh' is del.

Mr Duchatel is properly cautious in giving an opinion as to the expense; but a c. 15 Feb. 1830 little incautious I think in saying, that nothing would be more easy than to frame such measures as would prevent the recurrence of an excess of population.

Your friend Major Moody[218] called during our vacation when I was absent, and I have not yet had an opportunity of seeing him.

Have you seen Sir John Walsh's pamphlet [219] on Poor Laws in Ireland. I think it a good one, and well worthy of attention. I have always thought it a mistake to suppose that poor laws will prevent[220] the migration of the Irish to England for better wages.

---

[218] There is a Major Thomas Moody of the Royal Engineers in the 1830 *Army List*. He saw war service in Martinique and Guadeloupe, was promoted to the rank of major in 1816, and died in 1849 (Information kindly provided by Michael Ball, National Army Museum).

[219] At this point the date 1830 has been written in pencil in another hand and circled. Sir John Benn Walsh, first Lord Ormathwaite (1798–1881), *Poor Laws in Ireland, Considered in their Probable Effects upon the Capital, the Prosperity & the Progressive Improvement of that Country*, London, 1830 (*DNB*).

[220] 'prevent' is repeated in MS.

5 Miscellaneous correspondence

A. JOURNEY TO NORTHERN EUROPE

64. EDWARD DANIEL CLARKE AND WILLIAM OTTER[1] TO MALTHUS[2]

Jes. Coll. Ap. 6.– [1799]

Dear Malthus,

6 April 1799   I thought I had written. I find you are beating back towards the Cap-a-pee,[3] in Dress. – We have entertained ourselves not a little with your friend Mr Forster's[4] Idea of a Medium between full Dress, & a Frock,[5] resulting from a Sattin* Waistcoat and Breeches. –

I had given up all thoughts of taking any Dress – and even now I think it w^d be the wisest Plan. As the Season will not be open during Summer any where.

You must posit.[6] come down here. I can not make another journey to Town. In great haste,

E.D.C.

Passports not yet procured.
Rich. Gay was at Bath.

---

[1] William Otter (1768–1840) was a student at Jesus College, Cambridge, at about the same time as Malthus, and became a fellow of the College in 1796. They remained lifelong friends. His eldest daughter Sophia (d. 1889) married Malthus' son Henry (1804–1882) in 1836. Otter's 'Memoir of Robert Malthus' was included in the second posthumous edition (1836) of Malthus' *Principles of Political Economy*. In 1836, he was appointed bishop of Chichester (*DNB*).

[2] Addressed: 'Revd Robt Malthus / Albury near / Guildford / Surrey'. Postmarks: 'C AP 8 99' and 'CAMBRIDGE'.

This two-part letter concerns the preparations being made by Clarke, Otter and Malthus for their forthcoming journey (with Cripps) to Northern Europe. See Ch. 3, n. 26 above.

[3] 'Cap-a-pee' or 'Cap-à-pie' means 'From head to foot: in reference to arming or accoutring' (*OED*).

[4] Possibly the same Mr Forster, who was at 'Leipsic', mentioned by Daniel Malthus in letter no. 23.

[5] 'Frock' in this context could refer to either 'an upper garment worn chiefly by men; a long coat, tunic, or mantle'; or a 'frock-coat' – 'a double-breasted coat with skirts extending almost to the knees, which are not cut away but of the same length in front as behind' (*OED*).

[6] i.e. 'positively'.

April 6th – [1799] 6 April 1799

Dear Malthus –

On this important subject of Dress Scarcely know what to think. I should be sorry if we were prevented from seeing any thing new or interesting for want of being properly equipped & on the other hand I am sensible that independent of the Expense any addition to our Baggage will be felt as a very severe Encumbrance. Perhaps however this latter Inconvenience might be in a great measure obviated. Suppose for Instance we should think it right to enter Norway either by the south of Sweden or by Fredrikstadt[7] immediately from Copenhagen we may[8] easily send our superfluous & ...[9] equipage by Sea to Stockholm or Petersburgh* & carry only the needful with us – & the same ...[10] might be done in returning – If you approve of this, Black will be the best court dress for you & me, because, we can convert ...[11] on our return into a good preaching Coat – With regard to the rest, I shall cherish a length of hair ...[12] a new blue Coat with a velvet collar for Gay days. I wear a suit of mix'd [13] Cloth with pantaloons, in Commons. In addition to these a blue Jacket and Trousers for shipboard & other dirty or ...[14] occasions – If in your researches into the History of the North[15] you meet with any Author very full of information on this you must not fail to mention it to me because as I have not much time to employ in that way,[16] I should be glad not to lose any of it in reading stale unprofitable [17] Books – It gives me pleasure to find that you are employing your thoughts and spirits in preparations for the Tour. I begin now to think that we shall go tho' somehow I always feared that something inauspicious would cross upon our Tour. Clarke has just now been with me. I perceive he does not at all like our going into Norway first. Tho he says that you hinted it before. This would depend upon the Seasons, that is whether June and July are better than August and Septr for seeing that Country. If you can make Interest with any Merchants in London, Letters to their Friends or Correspondents in any great Town would be very desireable.* I shall myself try about amongst my Connections in London. Tho I have not much hope from them. Will you come here two or three days before

---

[7] 'either by the south of Sweden or by Fredrikstadt' is ins. Otter probably meant to write 'Fredrikshald' (now known as Halden), the Norwegian coastal town on the Swedish border.

[8] 'may' is ins. [9] Word illegible.

[10] The word appears to be 'think', but Otter probably meant to write 'thing'.

[11] Word indistinct, probably 'them'. [12] Word(s) illegible. [13] Word del. [14] Word illegible.

[15] 'of the North' is ins. [16] 'much' is del and 'in that way' is ins. [17] 'Matter' is del.

6 April 1799   we set out. I believe it will not be much[18] out of your way. I should like to come to London but I fear I shall not be able. Write to me soon & do not be afraid of telling me all you think upon these Matters. [19]

Yr. sincere Friend

Will[m] Otter

When is your letter for the Gentleman's Magazine?[20] –

B. BULLION

65. MALTHUS
TO FRANCIS HORNER[21]

Hertford Feb[y] 5th 1810.

My dear Sir;

5 Feb. 1810   Your letter[22] was sent to the College at Haileybury, and as we have not yet removed from Hertford, I did not receive it till yesterday.[23] I was very glad to hear from you on a subject which has excited my curiosity in a considerable degree without my having been able to satisfy it by any information that I could

---

[18] 'much' is ins.   [19] Several words illegible.

[20] There is (as yet) no report of any letter by Malthus in the *Gentleman's Magazine* around April 1799. Otter was possibly referring to the letter by Malthus, dated 1 March 1799, in the *Monthly Magazine*, April 1799, pp. 178–9. See Ch. 4, n. 6 above.

[21] Francis Horner (1778–1817), MP, one of the founders of the *Edinburgh Review* (1802), chairman of the Bullion Committee (1810), opponent of restrictions on the importation of corn, and advocate of the resumption of cash payments by the Bank of England. Horner and Malthus were close friends and correspondents, despite their differences on the Corn Laws and despite Horner's having said in 1808 that in all Malthus' work there is 'a want of precision in the statement of his principles, and distinct perspicuity in upholding the consequences which he traces from them' (letter to J. A. Murray, quoted in James 1979, p. 150).

   This letter gives Malthus' views on the state of the currency, and commends Horner for his speech in the House of Commons which led to the setting up of the Bullion Committee. However, it is not certain that the letter was ever received by Horner. The absence of an address and a seal suggests it was not sent. Also, if the letter as it stands was in fact sent, it would be difficult to explain why it was returned to Malthus or his descendants or how it came to be in this Malthus archive. Other letters from Malthus to Horner were not returned. Another possibility is that the letter is a copy or draft of another which was actually sent; in this case, the almost complete absence of deletions and additions would suggest a copy rather than a draft. This letter has been published in Bourne and Taylor 1994, pp. 627–30.

[22] Horner's letter is wanting.

[23] When the East India College was opened in February 1806 it was located at Hertford Castle, Hertford, which the East India Company had leased for twenty years. Malthus accepted his position on 10 July 1805, and James (1979, p. 175) suggests that he probably moved to one of the Company's houses in Hertford at the beginning of November 1805. Having decided that Hertford Castle would not in fact be suitable, the Company purchased land about two miles south-east of Hertford and proceeded to construct a new college, known as Haileybury College. The College moved from Hertford Castle to Haileybury College some time in 1809, but this letter indicates that Malthus and his family were still residing in Hertford in February 1810 (Danvers 1894, pp. 16–18; James 1979, pp. 168–89).

108

obtain; and I was quite pleased to see the notice of your motion in the papers, as 5 Feb. 1810 I felt confident that in your hands the question would be put in the best train for solution. I have been looking at the Morning Chronicle[24] of the 2nd, and congratulate you upon the deserved applause which you got for your motion, and the manner in which it was introduced. I conclude that I see but a small part of your speech, but from what I can collect I think it probable that our ideas on the subject may not materially differ. I have no where seen the reasonings of M[r] Riardo* and M[r] Mushet to which you allude.[25] The view which on the whole I am most disposed to take of the subject is the following.

I think that the shock which Mercantile confidence has received from the present disturbed state of Europe, and the proceedings of Buonaparte,* particularly during the last year and a half, or two years, has rendered the use of the precious metals in the transfer of commodities more necessary, and therefore more general than formerly. This increased demand arising from the increased use of the precious metals, has naturally increased their value on the continent; and if our circulation had been in its natural state, that is, if paper had continued exchangeable for gold at the Bank a considerable exportation of guineas and bullion would have taken place which would soon have raised the value of the currency of this country to a level with that of the continent; and then of course things would have gone on as usual. As our currency however, in its present state, consists so much of paper, and that paper not payable in specie, this equalizing process cannot easily take place. The small quantity of gold in circulation, even if it were all exported, would not be sufficient for the purpose; [26] and if the increased issues of the Bank were merely to the extent of filling up the vacancy thus made in the circulation, the restoration of the level would be hopeless. Under these circumstances the value of the currency of this country

---

[24] The *Morning Chronicle* of 2 February 1810 gave a summary of Horner's speech in the House of Commons on 1 February in which he moved 'for a variety of accounts and returns respecting the present state of the circulating medium, and the bullion trade'. According to the report, Horner argued that 'it was necessary for the House to make an enquiry into the causes of the present high price of gold bullion, and the consequent effect upon the value of the paper currency'. Other reported speakers on the motion included Davies Giddy, Henry Thornton, and Spencer Perceval (Chancellor of the Exchequer). The motion was carried, but the *Morning Chronicle* makes no mention of applause. Horner was also reported as stating that he intended to move at an early date for the appointment of a Select Committee to investigate the matter. The Bullion Committee was appointed on 19 February 1810, and its report was presented to the House of Commons on 8 June 1810. (See James 1979, pp. 196–7.)

[25] David Ricardo (1772–1823), *The High Price of Bullion, a Proof of the Depreciation of Bank Notes*, 1810; and Robert Mushet (1782–1828), *An Enquiry into the Effects Produced on the National Currency, and Rates of Exchange, by the Bank Restriction Bill...*, 1810; 2nd edn, 1810; 3rd edn, 1811). Malthus reviewed these two pamphlets (and four others) in his article 'Depreciation of Paper Currency', *Edinburgh Review*, Vol. 17, February 1811, pp. 339–72. Horner's allusion to Ricardo and Mushet must have occurred in his (missing) letter to Malthus; the allusion did not appear in the report in the *Morning Chronicle*. Ricardo's *High Price of Bullion* and Mushet's *Enquiry* are in the Malthus Library.

[26] 'and still less would it accomplish its object if the vacancy occasioned by' is del.

5 Feb. 1810 must remain lower, the[27] currencies of the continent, the exchange be constantly and greatly against us, and a permanent premium continue for the exportation of the precious metals. This state of things you will observe might take place with little or no increased issue of Bank of England paper. It might arise indeed exclusively from the circumstance of a change having taken place in the value of bullion and currency on the continent, which the restriction of payments in Specie at the Bank had prevented from being communicated to our circulation in the ordinary way.

Should it appear by the papers you have called for that no increased issues of Bank paper have taken place, I shall be strongly disposed to attribute the present state of things to the cause I have mentioned. It is highly probable that the new channels of trade which British merchants have opened under the present difficulties have occasioned the necessity of prompter payments, and the consequent use of a greater quantity of the precious metals, than the old channels; but it should be remarked that such an increased use confined exclusively to British trade would not produce the effects observed. It would raise the market price of bullion in this country higher than on the Continent in general; and would tend to occasion a favourable exchange with those countries which were not particularly circumstanced with regard to the necessity of receiving[28] payments in specie. One of the first inquiries which should be made therefore, is, whether the market price of bullion in this country is equal ...[29] the market price on the Continent; and if it be not, which I conceive must be the[30] case, from its continued efflux, it is quite clear that the source of the difficulty could not originate exclusively in the peculiar wants of the British trade as at present carried on, but in some cause of a more general nature affecting the comparative values of British and Continental Currency. This cause may either be an increased issue of Bank paper, which would lower our currency compared with that of the Continent; or an increased use of the precious metals on the continent, which would raise the continental currency compared with ours. The effects on our foreign exchanges and on the market prices of the precious metals compared with their mint prices, would be the same in both cases, though they would imply very different degrees of culpability on the part of the Bank Directors.

It is important, however, to observe, that, though the Bank Directors would not be equally culpable in the two cases, they would not be entirely without blame in either; and whichever supposition turns out to be true, the remedy for the evil complained of, can be no other than a diminution of the issues of Bank paper. In the natural state of things previous to the Bank restriction a rise in the value of continental currency compared with British, from whatever cause

---

[27] MS has 'the', but the sense requires 'than the'.   [28] 'receiving' is ins.
[29] Word obscure, probably 'to'.   [30] 'the' is ins.

arising, would be necessarily remedied by the influx of Bank notes, to be exchanged for gold, and the exportation of the gold so exchanged. And during the restriction, it should be the invariable rule of the Bank Directors so to regulate the issues of their notes as to make their value resemble as nearly as possible the value which they would have if they were exchangeable for specie. The great evil of the present circulation, is, that it does not naturally suit itself as formerly to the necessarily varying value of continental currency, but requires on the part of the Bank Directors great attention, great knowledge, and great disinteredness,* qualities which though they appear on the whole to have possessed in a greater degree than could have been expected, they have not possessed in a sufficient degree. It is not indeed very easy, under the present enormous payments, which the Bank has to make in discharging the half yearly dividends, and in the assistance which it is continually giving to Government, to restrict its issues sufficiently, without narrowing its discounts to private merchants in a degree which might occasion some embarassment* to the trade of the country, and very general complaints: yet still a diminution of notes in some quarter or other appears to me to be the only remedy; and in answer to the complaints to which it might give rise, it might be observed that in the natural state of the currency of any country, its merchants must always be liable to temporary embarasments* arising from the varying value of the precious metals, or the varying state of confidence, although they might not be quite so great as when an unnatural state of things had for some time been persevered in, and required to be remedied. At all events however the diminution should take place gradually.

The increased use of the precious metals in mercantile transactions, which I have supposed above to arise principally from the shock which commercial confidence has received, must undoubtedly have been very much aggravated, and may indeed have been in great part caused, by the number of armies in Europe requiring payments in Specie.

Any questions tending to elucidate the point of the increased use of the precious metals in Europe, from whatever cause arising, will materially facilitate the object of the enquiry.

You will also have an opportunity of ascertaining, whether bullion is frequently exported by the ordinary merchant in payment of the goods which he receives; or whether this export is conducted exclusively by the Bullion merchant according as he sees his advantage in the rate of exchange, selling under such circumstances a bill to the ordinary merchant, which he enables his correspondent to discharge by the transfer of bullion.

If the price of bullion in England has not yet reached the continental price,

5 Feb. 1810 I conceive that very little [31] has of late been imported, whatever M[r] Rose[32] may say to the contrary. Indeed his conclusions are perfectly absurd, and quite contradict the great acknowledged facts which have rendered the inquiry necessary. I don't exactly know how the imports are valued, but I suspect that the rate of exchange is not added to them, in which case with the exchange at 20 or 25 per cent against us, 55 millions of exports would be more than repaid[33] by 45 millions of imports and a balance would remain to be discharged in specie by us, which accords with the actual state of things without rejecting the Custom House Accounts.

These accounts however are not much to be depended on, as they always involve (if not corrected in the way suggested, or some other) the absurdity which you have justly commented upon, of a constant balance in our favour.

All questions elucidating the manner in which our great exportations are paid for will be of considerable use. I don't know how we can receive bullion for any of them, in which case, as it seems to be acknowledged that we make considerable payments in specie, the drain upon our bullion must be considerable. In the present state of things if justly represented, the Bank may import Bullion on account of its double capacity but it can never answer to a private Bullion merchant to do so; he will be rather imployed* in buying up the plate of the silversmiths which he can get cheaper than foreign bullion.

I heard some time ago, but not from very good authority that an unusual rise had taken place on the continent in the value of gold compared with silver – is this so? It would prove that in the extended use of the precious metals, gold was found more convenient for distant remittances.

Excuse this long letter, and the desultory manner in which it is written. You shall hear from me again if I think of more questions. I hope politics go on tolerably. I should like to hear of your proceeding in the inquiry. M[rs] M desires comps. Very sincerely Y[rs] T R Malthus.

---

[31] 'bullion' is del.
[32] In 1811 George Rose published *Substance of the Speech Delivered in the House of Commons by the Right Honorable George Rose, on ... the Sixth of May 1811, ... on the Report of the Bullion Committee.*
[33] 'balanced' is del. and 'repaid' is ins.

NOTES FOR THE LETTER
TO FRANCIS HORNER

[4 or 5 February 1810][34]

[35] Whether on the continent there is any marked change in the comparative   4 or 5 Feb. 1810
values of gold and silver

In what manner the prodigious exportations of British goods are paid for.

Should there be found upon the whole a decided balance of[36] exports, it
would imply a depreciation of currency

In a natural state of things, a considerable and continual exportation of
Bullion, would soon raise its value in the country from which it is exported, but
if this rise of value be prevented by its place being supplied by paper, it cannot
be expected to return.

From whatever cause the high value of gold on the continent may have
arisen, as in the natural couse* of things the level would be soon effected* by
exportation from this country, it is probable that the only remeredy* is the
diminution of paper.

It is possible that the general shock which mercantile confidence has
received from the present state of Europe, may have rendered the use of the
precious metals much more general in all transactions. This would naturally
raise the value of bullion on the continent, and without any increased issues of
paper on our part, would lower the comparative value of our currency.

Agravated*[37] perhaps by the products of the Spanish mines being
interrupted.

An oppertunity* of settling the point whether bullion is exported by the
ordinary[38] merchant to pay for goods which he has ordered or [39]

Not necessary to suppose that the Bank has been culpable. The Bank may
feel quite innocent.

If the exchange is 20 per cent against this country then 55 millions of
exports would be balanced by 45 imports.

Whether the price of bullion in England has nearly reached the continental
price. Till it has, it cannot of course answer to the bullion merchant to purchase
bullion abroad though it may have been necessary for the Bank.

Embarassment* to Commerce from sudden restriction of Bank issues.

---

[34] See the letter above. These notes were presumably written after Malthus had received Horner's letter,
and were used by Malthus in composing his reply. Some of the material in the notes recurs in the reply.
Since Malthus said he received Horner's letter the day before replying, the notes were probably written
on 4 or 5 February 1810.

[35] A large number '1', perhaps indicating that this is the first page, is written here.   [36] 'of' is ins.

[37] From 'Agravated*' to the end of the sentence is ins.   [38] 'ordinary' is ins.

[39] Sentence breaks off here.

4 or 5 Feb. 1810   One of the great objections to such a system of circulation.

A temporary balance against us, notwithstanding an excess of exports, would be producd,* by our merchants giving long credits while [40] in the new channels just opened the merchants may require present payments.

A particular demand for bullion in this country to carry on [41] its trade in the new channels in which it was flowing would not alone produce the effects observed.

One cause of the demand for payments in specie is of course the present state of the exchange and another that we are probably now forced to deal with [42] countries and merchants who do not want [43]

66. FRANCIS JEFFREY[44]
TO MALTHUS[45]

Edin. 2^d April 1811

My dear Malthus –

2 April 1811   This fine weather has been the ruin of me – I cannot sit at home and work, and the habit of idleness gains strength every day – However I still hope to see you about the middle of this month – but I shall meet you with tenfold comfort if I learn first that I may rely on your doing something for me for this N^{o46} – Now do not be alarmed about time for I see now clearly that I shall not be able to get more than a half of it printed before I set out – and that I shall send a full third to be made up after my return – My project for you then is this – You shall do another article upon Bullion and paper – but you shall not do it until after the discussion in the House and I shall carry it down with me when I return here about the 12 of May – I ordered our booksellers to send you two or three *Scotch* pamphlets upon the subject – All seem to me to take a bolder view at least of the matter than most of the Southern – You will see a review too in the New British on the one side of the question – and will consider whether those general

---

[40] 'the' is del.   [41] 'new channels' is del.   [42] 'merchants' is del.   [43] Sentence breaks off here.

[44] Francis Jeffrey (1773–1850), later Lord Jeffrey, editor of the *Edinburgh Review* (1802–29), a friend of Malthus and a frequent visitor at the East India College. His daughter, Charlotte, married William Empson, a colleague of Malthus at the College, who became editor of the *Edinburgh Review* in 1847 (*DNB*). Malthus replied to this letter on 7 April 1811. See James 1979, p. 207. In this letter Jeffrey comments on Malthus' article on paper currency published earlier in 1811 in the *Edinburgh Review*, and urges Malthus – or rather, virtually commands him – to prepare another article for the *Review* on the bullion and currency question.

[45] Addressed: 'To the Rev^d / T. R. Malthus / E. I. College / near / Hertford'. Postmark: 'AP. W2A 1811'.

[46] The forthcoming number of the *Edinburgh Review* was Vol. 18, No. 35, May 1811. An article by Malthus, 'Pamphlets on the Bullion Question', appeared in the following number – Vol. 18, No. 36, August 1811, pp. 448–70.

and very fundamental speculations do not deserve some attention – The only 2 April 1811 fault of your article[47] is that it is addressed almost exclusively to persons in some degree acquainted with the subject and perhaps these, as they are the only competent judges are the only persons to whom a *conscientious* writer could address himself – but with your powers and on a subject which owes no small share of its difficulty to the stupidity of those who have treated of it I think you might have made most of your readers competent judges before you had done with them – if you had condescended first to state the facts and points at issue in a short recapitulation and then to have laid down the arguments generally and without so much express reference to the faults or merits of the particular authors before you – Perhaps you could do something of this sort still – and I am even unprincipled enough to wish that you could say something to gain over the *incapable* also to our side of the question – their views always go for something and if we do not bid for them the enemy will.

I look enough at the bright side of things – I mean habitually – and ...[48] to my own little concerns – so much so that it is really an effort for me to look at anything else – but it is an effort which I start every now and then to think how I can decline, so completely and *theoretically* – I am very much in a state of *Despair* – while I have scarcely any actual anxiety.[49]

I wish you knew the state of intellectual impotence under which I labour – and the necessity and *the shame* of asking aid which it occasions – I hope the lover of Despotism is well – and that he may be long condemned to groan under the harness of a free government – I will write again to ...[50] you when I am able to think clearly of putting myself en route – but do give me some comfort about the Bullion – Ever most Truly Yours

F Jeffrey

---

[47] Jeffrey is no doubt referring here to Malthus' article, 'Depreciation of Paper Currency', *Edinburgh Review*, Vol. 18, No. 34, February 1811, pp. 340–72.

[48] Word(s) difficult to decipher, possibly 'refer only'.

[49] An example of Jeffrey's 'characteristic pessimism'. 'He was at no time an enthusiast. Throughout his life his natural despondency constantly showed itself' (*DNB*).

[50] Word difficult to decipher, possibly 'tell'.

c. BIBLE SOCIETY

67. EDWARD DANIEL CLARKE
TO MALTHUS[51]

[1812]

Dear Malthus

1812   I have sent you my little pamphlet, anxious enough, God knows, to have your opinion of it. Marsh[52] has been so astonished at the Celerity of its march that he actually sent to Hodson's to know if I had seen any of his proof Sheets.

Before it went to Press on Tuesday Morning I read it to the Bishop of Bristol;[53] and to Tyrwhitt,[54] after it was in the Press. Since it was printed, Dean

---

[51] Addressed: 'Revd Professor Malthus / East India College / Hertford / By Ware'. Ware is about three miles north-east of Hertford. Postmark: 'CAMBRIDGE 52'. The letter tells of Clarke's involvement in the setting up of a branch of the Bible Society in Cambridge, and refers to his pamphlet conflict with the Revd Herbert Marsh on the issue.

[52] Herbert Marsh (1757–1839), BA (second wrangler) 1779; MA 1782; BD 1792; DD 1808; fellow of St John's College, Cambridge, 1779–1807; Lady Margaret professor of divinity, 1807–39; bishop (successively) of Llandaff and of Peterborough; 'Regarded as the outstanding man of letters and divine in Cambridge, and the foremost bishop on the Bench'. Marsh opposed the foundation of a Cambridge branch of the Bible Society on the grounds that 'it sanctioned a union with Dissenters and the circulation of the Bible unaccompanied by the Book of Common Prayer' (*DNB*). In 1812 he addressed the Senate on the issue: *An Address to the Senate of the University of Cambridge, Occasioned by the Proposal to Introduce in that Place an Auxiliary Bible Society* – and published a pamphlet: *An Inquiry into the Consequences of Neglecting to Give the Prayer Book with the Bible; ... with ... Other Important Matters Relative to the British and Foreign Bible Society*, Cambridge. Clarke, who was one of the founders of the Cambridge branch, replied with the pamphlet referred to in this letter: *A Letter to Herbert Marsh ... in Reply to Certain Observations in his Pamphlet Relative to the British and Foreign Bible Society*, Francis Hodson, Cambridge, 1812, 13p. Malthus was involved in the publication of Clarke's pamphlet; on 7 August 1812 Clarke wrote to Otter that Malthus 'will read the sheets, and mention anything that strikes him: but he will neither correct nor transpose' (James 1966, p. 19). Otter published two replies to Marsh: *A Vindication of Churchmen Who Become Members of the British and Foreign Bible Society ... Being an Answer to Dr. Marsh's Pamphlet upon this Subject*, Cambridge, 1812, two editions; and *An Examination of Dr Marsh's Answer to All the Arguments in Favour of the British and Foreign Bible Society ... in a Second Letter to a Friend at Cambridge*, 1812.

[53] William Lort Mansel (1753–1820), BA 1774; MA 1777; DD 1798; fellow of Trinity College, Cambridge; ordained 1783; master of Trinity 1798; vice-chancellor of the university 1799–1800; bishop of Bristol 1808 (*DNB*). In 1813 Mansel published *A Sermon Preached before the Incorporated Society for the Propagation of the Gospel in Foreign Parts ...*, London.

[54] Robert Tyrwhitt (1735–1817), BA 1757; MA 1760; fellow of Jesus College, Cambridge, 1759. As a Unitarian, he rejected the Articles of the Anglican Church, and sought to abolish subscription to the Articles on graduation. 'In 1777 he resigned his fellowship, and ceased to attend the college chapel, though still residing in the college' (*DNB*). He published *Two Discourses, on the Creation of all Things by Jesus Christ; and on the Resurrection...*, 1787, which was republished several times.

Milner[55] made me read it through to him; and ended by shaking my hand; saying 1812
if he were to answer Marsh himself he could not add a Syllable. Under this
Caution and Encouragement I ventured to let it come out this morning.

E. D. Clarke

D. CORN LAWS

68. FRANCIS JEFFREY
TO MALTHUS[56]

Edin. 12 May 1814

My Dear Malthus

I am quite ashamed to think that I have never written to you since my 12 May 1814
return to this country altho' I found a kind letter from you I think actually
waiting my arrival – But I have been so harassed with all kinds of arrears and
engagements[57] that I have been able to do very little either of what I ought to do
– or what I should have liked – We have thought and talked of you however a
great deal which you may believe without any great offence to your modesty
when you remember that your family is one of the very few in this country

---

⁵⁵ Isaac Milner (1750–1820), dean of Carlisle (1791), BA; fellow of Queens' College, Cambridge, 1776; FRS 1776; BD 1786; professor of natural philosophy, 1783–92; Lucasian professor of mathematics, 1798–1820; vice-chancellor, 1792, 1809–10; president of Queens' College, 1788 (*DNB*). In 1813 he criticised Marsh's views on the Bible Society in *Strictures on Some of the Publications of ... H. Marsh, Intended as a Reply to his Objections against the British and Foreign Bible Society*, 1813; to which Marsh replied in *A Reply to the Strictures of I. Milner, D.D., Dean of Carlisle ...*, J. Hodson, Cambridge, 1813.

⁵⁶ Addressed: 'To the Rev^d / T. R. Malthus / E. I. Coy's College / near Hertford'. Postmark: 'MA 13 A 1814'. In this letter Jeffrey commends Malthus for his 1814 pamphlet *Observations on ... the Corn Laws*, while at the same time expressing his regret that Malthus did not publish it in Jeffrey's *Edinburgh Review*. The letter was partially reproduced by Lord Cockburn in his *Life of Lord Jeffrey with a Selection from his Correspondence*, 2 vols., 1852, Vol. II, pp. 145–6. Jeffrey's handwriting is not easy to decipher. The editors have benefited from the readings given by Cockburn, but disagree with some of them. The editors also acknowledge the help of a typed transcript of the letter (by an unknown transcriber) included with the original manuscripts.

⁵⁷ The first paragraph of Cockburn's version ends here.

12 May 1814 which are equally known to me and Mrs J.[58] and as to which we entirely agree –
She desires to be very kindly remembered both to you and Mrs Malthus and if
you will not make a pilgrimage to Scotland to see us – which we think it is your
turn to do we shall certainly be down upon you at Haileybury before you know
where you are –

Will you be very angry if I tell you that it was none of those good feelings
that forced me to write to you at present – but a mixture of regret and admiration
which I have just experienced in reading your pamphlet on the Corn Trade?[59] –
admiration for the clearness, soundness and inimitable candour of your
observations – and regret that you did not let me put them into the Review –
you know they would be read there by twice as many people as ever see
pamphlets – and for your glory and credit it might have been ...[60] all those that
you care about as if your name had been on the title. It cannot be helped now
however – and I must just aggravate my admiration till it altogether stems my
regret – I trust however that you will not ...[61] me a review as well as tantalise me
by having missed one so excellent – Horner had promised to give me some
remarks on the subject – but I am half afraid your pamphlett* will put him in
despair – In my opinion indeed it leaves nothing to be added – tho' I must add
that you have the great advantage of being very much of my way of thinking on
the subject. Horner is much more Smithish – and I had written him two long
letters to ...[62] his confidence when I had the felicity of finding all my lame
arguments set on their legs – and my dark glimpses of reason brought into full
day in your pages.

---

[58] Jeffrey had left Liverpool on 29 August 1813 for New York to marry his second wife, Charlotte
Wilkes, a relative of John Wilkes (1727-1797), politician and radical advocate of political reform.
They returned to England on 10 February 1814 (*DNB*). He had met her in 1810 when she was travelling
in England in the company of her aunt (her father's sister) and uncle, Louis Simond, a French refugee.
In 1815 Simond published *Journal of a Tour and Residence in Great Britain during the Years 1810
and 1811*, 2 vols., Edinburgh. In it he states that he was at Albury, in Surrey, in the summer of 1811.
Patricia James suggests it was likely that Simond met Malthus in Albury at that time. This would
explain why Jeffrey says that Malthus and his family 'are equally known to me and Mrs J.', and why
she desired to be remembered to them, even though as Mrs Jeffrey she had arrived back in England
only three months earlier and had not (as this letter implies) met the Malthuses since then.
  Malthus referred to Simond's views in the fifth edition (1817) of the *Essay on Population*. He used
Simond's observations on English life to support his view that the condition of the labouring classes
depends on their ability to obtain conveniences and comforts, as well as food (*DNB*; Malthus 1989a,
Vol. II, pp. 25, 335–6).

[59] T. R. Malthus, *Observations on the Effects of the Corn Laws, and of a Rise or Fall in the Price of Corn
on the Agriculture and General Wealth of the Country*, 1814; 2nd edn, 1814; 3rd edn, 1815. The
Cockburn version has 'pamphlets', but this could not be correct, because Malthus' second pamphlet
on the Corn Laws – *The Grounds of an Opinion on the Policy of Restricting the Importation of Foreign
Corn* – was not published until 1815; and because its protectionism would not have raised Jeffrey's
'admiration'.

[60] Three words indecipherable.   [61] Word indecipherable.   [62] Word indecipherable.

Write me a line or two in friendship in spite of my apparently ungrateful   12 May 1814
conduct – from which I have suffered enough already – and tell me something
of Bonaparte too – and Alexander[63] and the future destiny of the world[64] – you
are much nearer the ...[65] you know than I am.

What is your Edition of Smith doing?[66] And how do your labours go on at
Haylebury* – By the way, what do you know of a colleague Dr Spineto who
teaches languages in Cambridge? He has lately married a young lady of this
country, rather against the will of her friends and they are anxious to hear tell
what is his character, his estimation and his true connection at the university –
Do not give yourself any trouble, nor go a gossiping on purpose to answer this
– but if you happen to know anything about the man tell me if you think it right.
Remember me most affectionately to the excellent Hamilton,[67] and tell him if
he will come down to me this summer I will provide him with a wife – but I am
afraid he is going with the ...[68] to Paris – are you? I dare not leave here again so
soon tho' I should be much tempted if I could get certain companions. Playfair
has just gone to London and I instruct you to make a point of seeing him. Scott
too is in that great assemblage of wickedness. At this moment I envy you your
blossoms and nightingales – yes and more – I heard so much about you and
your family from my excellent friend Mr Wilkes while I was in America that I
should have fancied myself an old friend of yours in consequence of my marriage
even if I had not been so before. Do believe me Ever
Most Faithfully yours

F Jeffrey

PS I am in unfortunate and unprecedented need of a lot of reviews. Could you
do nothing for me? Or get Hamilton to do anything. You would both feel the
most lively compassion for me if you knew how stupid and how busy I am.

---

[63] Alexander I (1777-1825), Tsar of Russia, who defeated the French when they invaded Russia in 1812.
[64] Cockburn's reproduction of the letter ends here.   [65] Word indecipherable.
[66] This was a proposal by Malthus to publish an annotated edition of the *Wealth of Nations*. He had
conceived the idea as early as 1804, and was again pursuing it in 1812–14, but abandoned the project
when an edition of the *Wealth of Nations* was published along similar lines by David Buchanan in
1814 (*DNB*; James 1979; Malthus 1989b, Vol. I, pp. xxvi–xxvii).
[67] 'Hamilton', 'Playfair', and 'Scott' were presumably: Alexander Hamilton (1762–1824), professor of
Hindu literature and the history of Asia at the East India College (1806–18); William Playfair (1759–
1823), writer, who had also published (1805) an edition of the *Wealth of Nations* with notes and
supplementary chapters; and Sir Walter Scott (1771–1832), the novelist. The Malthus Library (Dalton
Hill) had forty works (mainly novels) by Scott.
[68] Two words indecipherable; second word possibly 'Malthuses'.

119

E. EAST INDIA COLLEGE

69. ROBERT GRANT[69]
TO MALTHUS[70]

5th. March [1817] – Linc[s]. Inn

My dear Sir,

5 March 1817   My father[71] wished me to write to you or to some other of the Professors; as he did not think he should himself find time for the purpose. You will have[72] seen the result of our apparently endless debate – a victory, – but hardly a triumph. I believe it was all we could get; & my father is so far well satisfied, that he thinks it was a great & triumphant victory as to argument, the enemy, under the most direct defiance, not only bringing forward no facts in proof of his charges, but abandoning all his principal points; till it came to this, that 5 disturbances ought not to take place without inquiry! Meantime, we have laid in ground to charge any future disturbance on the enemy.[73] One or two of the Directors deserted us basely. I happened not to be present, when M[r] Bosanquet[74] made some sharp remarks on your pamphlet. – However, you would, I am sure, only have been affected by them, with reference to their effect on the question; & I incline to think he at least did that[75] no harm, being very decided as to [76] letting things go on as at present, since they were going on well – M[r] Pattison

---

[69] Sir Robert Grant (1779–1838), second son of Charles Grant (1746–1823); BA 1801 (third wrangler and second chancellor's medallist); fellow of Magdalene College, Cambridge, 1802; MA 1804; admitted at Lincoln's Inn 1807; governor of Bombay 1834; knighted 1834 (*DNB*).

[70] No address. The letter was written the day after the decisive General Court of the Proprietors of the East India Company when a motion to close down the East India College at Haileybury was defeated. Malthus had written two pamphlets in defence of the College: *A Letter to the Rt. Hon. Lord Grenville, Occasioned by some Observations of his Lordship on the East India Company's Establishment for the Education of their Civil Servants*, 1813; and *Statements Respecting the East-India College, with an Appeal to Facts, in Refutation of the Charges lately Brought against it, in the Court of Proprietors*, 1817.

[71] Charles Grant, a director of the East India Company, and at various times deputy-chairman or chairman of its court of directors. He 'originated the scheme of education for the company's servants fulfilled by the establishment of the East India College at Haileybury' (*DNB*). Malthus' letter of 10 July 1805 to Charles Grant, accepting his appointment at the East India College, is held in the India Office.

[72] 'have' is ins.

[73] The pricipal spokesmen for the opponents of the East Inda College were Joseph Hume and Randle Jackson. See James 1979, pp. 234-44..

[74] Jacob Bosanquet, a director of the East India Company, supported the College and the professors, but was critical of Malthus' suggestion (*Statements*, p. 103n.) that the number of appointments made by the Company in any year should be less than the number of students completing their College studies, so that the students would be encouraged to compete for appointment, and appointment would be considered 'as a prize to be contended for, not a property already possessed'. See James 1979, pp. 242–3. Malthus' proposal for a competitive examination for appointment to the East India Company (at the conclusion of studies at the East India College) differed from the proposal (discussed by Robert Grant in the following letter, no. 70) for a competitive examination for entrance to the College.

[75] 'that' is ins.   [76] 'things being' is del.

spoke very effectively in our favour; the more so, from his making some 5 March 1817
exceptions in assenting to our doctrines.

But we must not expect complete rest; & my father thinks that a parliamentary inquiry is highly to be desired, & if possible, to be promoted. That consideration, however, may for the present be reserved. My immediate object in now[77] writing is to suggest (in my father's name) the expediency of preparing some other short work, setting forth the case of the College; with a view of having it ready, & publishing as soon as the occasion calls for it. He thinks it very likely that the Professors, or some of them, may have some juvenile Academic friend, with more leisure than themselves, who would execute such a work with spirit and success.[78] Will you excuse my suggesting this [79] (I mean the preparing such a work, not the employing a friend, for of course it would be still better from your own pen,) for the consideration of yourself and Dr Batten[80] & M^r LeBas?*[81]

For myself, the Quarterly Review fills my hands. The article was so cut up by my speech[82] that it will in fact require re-writing. Besides, it must be done with a peculiarly impartial & neutral air; which I must own it was not before. – I remain,

Dear sir, Y^r serv, R. Grant

---

[77] 'now' is ins.
[78] There is no record of any such publication by either Malthus or a 'juvenile Academic friend'. However, Robert Grant himself published in 1826 *A View of the System and Merits of the East-India College at Haileybury*, containing the substance of a speech made at a meeting of the court of directors in 1824 (*DNB*).
[79] '(which' is del.
[80] Revd Joseph Hallet Batten (1778–1837), BA (third wrangler), Cambridge, 1799; MA 1802; DD 1815; fellow of Trinity College, 1801; classical professor, East India College, 1806; principal, East India College, 1815–37 (*DNB*).
[81] Charles Webb Le Bas (1779–1861); BA (fourth wrangler), first chancellor's medallist, Cambridge, 1800; fellow of Trinity College, 1802; MA 1803; called to the Bar, 1806; dean and professor of mathematics and natural philosophy, East India College, 1813–37; principal, East India College, 1837, succeeding Dr Batten, resigned 1843 (*DNB*; Venn; James 1979).
[82] Probably a reference to his speech on 20 February 1817 at the Court of Proprietors on behalf of the College. The speech lasted over three hours. See James 1979, p. 241. These statements by Grant suggest that he was the author of the article 'East India College', *Quarterly Review*, Vol. 17, No. 73, April 1817, Art. 5, pp. 107–54. The article was mainly a review of Malthus' *Statements Respecting the East India College*, 1817. It strongly supported Malthus' defence of the College and paid glowing tribute to Malthus' character and literary skills: 'The pamphlet of Mr. Malthus seems to have acquired a considerable reputation, and, we think, very deservedly. It throughout exhibits a clear good sense and calm ability, which are highly impressive and satisfactory; and with these qualities are united others to which we cannot help attaching peculiar value, – great fairness and sincerity' (p. 111).

70. ROBERT GRANT
TO MALTHUS[83]

Private Westm[r] 8th. Nov. 1822.

My dear Sir,

8 Nov. 1822   I have thought much, since we met, of the plan suggested by M[r] Lebas*
for maintaining Haileybury under a[84] more open system of appointments than
has hitherto prevailed; & I am concerned to say that I cannot regard[85] it as
satisfactory. On the supposition therefore that the open system in question is
resorted to, I much fear that we must abandon Haileybury; & the question will
then fully arise, in what way the qualifications of the candidates for appointments
are to be ascertained.

I make no apology for consulting you on this point; assured that the great
object of providing good men for India is duly appreciated by you, [86]
independently of any personal interest in the mode of accomplishing that end.

The plan of a *completely* open system, that is, of inviting all the world to
be candidates, & of deciding the matter (testimonials of respectability being
produced) purely by a contested examination, meets with both ridicule &
objection.

The ridicule must be stingless if there be no force in the objection. Therefore
I go to the latter.

It is objected that the examination will gradually become nominal, & that
patronage will, after all, govern the decision.

I cannot think this; & yet I feel that one ought not to meet it by generalities;
but that some plan of tuning a field of competitors, & of examining them, should
be prepared.

There is certainly *some* danger of lures of patronage being held out to
Examiners to induce them in their turn[87] to patronise particular candidates. But
I should conceive that regulations, backed by publicity, would prevent the evil.
Only, what are they to be?

It has struck me that there ought, *perhaps*, to be two examinations of each
candidate, with the interval of a year between them; the one *initiatory*, the other
conclusive; by way of narrowing down the field of competition. In point of
principle, this would resemble the system at Colleges. The first examination
selects merely[88] the raw material; the second, the finished fabric. Only, on the
open plan, you must get the raw material manufactured where you can. –

---

[83] No address; the letter was apparently delivered by hand. It expresses Grant's concern over a proposal
       to adopt a system of open competitive examinations for admission of students to the East India College,
       replacing the existing system of patronage exercised by the directors of the East India Company.
[84] 'a' changed from 'as'.   [85] 'think' is del. and 'regard' is ins.   [86] 'without' is del.
[87] 'in their turn' is ins.   [88] 'only' is del and 'merely' is ins.

There is something so vast & vague in the idea of[89] throwing open the   8 Nov. 1822 contest to all [90] mankind, that it is not unnatural for those who consider the subject practically, to take [91] refuge in partial openness; such as, the allowing the *Directors* to name a determinate & yet an excessive number of competitors; or the Grenville project of throwing the burden of Selection on the great Seminaries;[92] or some modification of the latter idea.

I should be sorry to encroach much on your time & thoughts; but being most anxious on this whole Subject, and thinking it probable that you will throw light on it, I shall be thankful for any hints, however cursory, when you have leisure to communicate them.

Believe me
Yours very truly,

Rev. T. R. Malthus.   Robt Grant

F. Stagnation and General Glut

71. KARL HEINRICH RAU[93]
TO MALTHUS[94]

Erlangen 15 Juni 1821.

Werthender Herr Professor

Ihr "Essay on the principle of population", mit welchem uns Deutsche die   15 June 1821 Hegewischische Übersetzung bekannt gemacht hat, ist mit allgemeiner Theilnahme aufgenommen und verbreitet worden, und hat seinem Verfasser eine Hochachtung erworben, wie sie nur dem Verdienste um die menschliche Gesellschaft gewiedmet zu werden pflegt. Auch auf mich hat das Gewicht Ihrer

---

[89] 'the idea of' is ins.   [90] 'the world' is del.   [91] 'the' is del.

[92] William Wyndham Grenville (Lord Grenville) (1759–1834) was critical of the conduct of the East India Company in India, and of the method of private patronage used to select entrants to the East India College. He proposed that appointments to the East India Company should be made 'by free competition and public examination from our great schools and universities'. See Pullen 1987b, pp. 218–19.

[93] Karl Heinrich Rau (1792–1870), born in Erlangen, where he studied at the university and became a professor; later, professor at the University of Heidelberg (1822); elected to the Frankfurt Parliament (1848). This letter with its reference to 'deviations from Smith' and its advocacy of government intervention illustrates the influence of Cameralist ideas on Rau's early thinking. He was later to become a defender of Adam Smith's system of natural liberty. See *The New Palgrave*, Vol. IV, p. 96. This letter refers mainly to the debate between Malthus and Say on the possibility of a general glut. Rau asserts that he is 'for' Malthus and 'against' Say, but then paradoxically adds that he contests the possibility of a general glut. Rau, apparently aware that Malthus could not read German, supplied his own translation of the letter. Obsolete spellings in the German MS (e.g. 'seyn' for 'sein') are retained in this transcription without being individually signalled by the addition of a star (*).

[94] Address missing.

123

15 June 1821   Gedanken lebhaften Eindruck gemacht, und es freut mich Gelegenheit zu haben um Ihnen dieses zu sagen.

Diese Gelegenheit bieten mir Ihre "Principles of political economy" dar. Englische Bücher verbreiten sich nicht sehr geschwinde in meinem Vaterlande, daher mir Ihr Werk mit Say's Briefen zugleich zukam. Anderen schien es noch gar nicht bekannt zu seyn, wie aus dem Mangel von Anzeigen zu schliessen war. Da nun gerade jetzt in Deutschland über Handelsverhältnisse viel verhandelt wird, und darunter viel Unreifes, Einseitiges laut geworden ist, so schien es mir nützlich die Streitenden auf einen Standpunct zu führen, von welchem, sie die Besprechung eines Britten und eines Franzosen, und zwar zweyer ausgezeichneter Gelehrten, vernehmen könnten. Die gleichen Klagen über stockende Gewerbe in mehreren Ländern von ganz verschiedenen Verhältnissen, die Untersuchungen über die Ursachen des Übels muszten tiefer in das Wesen der Sache zu führen dienen, während sowohl die Anhänger als die Gegner des Süddeutschen Handelsvereins (die ersteren wollen Ihre und die französische Praxis, die leztern "Smith's" Theory in der Handelspolitic geltend machen) häufig etwas ungründlich aburtheilen. Daher gab ich eine Kleine Schrift heraus, welche erstens einen Auszug aus dem 7. Capitel Ihres Werkes, von Abschnitt zu Abschnitt, dann Say's Briefe, wörtlich übersezt, endlich Zusätze aus meiner Feder enthält. Sie heiszt

Malthus und *Say*, über die Ursachen der jezigen* Handelsstockung.

Aus dem Englischen und Französischen, mit einem Anhange von...

Hamburg, by* Perthes u. Besser, 1821. 301 S. 8°.

Ich weisz nicht, ob Sie mit den neueren Forschungen der Deutschen im Fache der polit.Oeconomy bekannt sind. Der Graf von *Loden, Hufeland, Lotz*, Graf von *Buquoy, Sartorius*, vorzüglich aber von *Bosse* in *Braunschweig*, an den ich mich im Gange meiner Arbeiten am meisten angeschlossen [habe], haben eine ziemlich selbstständige Schule zu bilden beygetragen. Der neuere Aufschwung der Wissenschaft wurde dadurch bewürckt, dasz man aufhörte, bey der Masse des Vermögens stehen zu bleiben, dasz man auf seine Bestimmung sah, und in ihm den Begriff von Hülfsmitteln für das häusliche und öffentliche Leben erkannte (Conf. Aristot. Politic. I, 8) Das Wirthschaftliche ward mit dem Sittlichen in genaue Beziehung gesetzt, und demnach der Zustand, in welchem der Mensch zufolge seines Vermögens, Verhältnisses[95] sich befindet, ins Auge gefaszt. Disz war nicht möglich, ohne häufige Abweichungen von Smith und den Franzosen; denn eine solche tiefere Ansicht gar fremd ist; *Simonde*'s nouveaux principes stimmen desto besser in unsern Gedankengang. Wir (das

---

[95] This is confusing. In the English version which follows, it is translated as: 'with regard to his relative Wealth'. But 'Verhältnisses' is a noun in the genitive case, not an adjective. Perhaps a closer translation would be: 'with regard to his Wealth, [and his] Circumstances'.

heiszt, die nicht grosse Zahl derer, welche an dieser neuen Wendung der Wissenschaft mitarbeiten) sind daher entschieden gegen den Satz, dasz Alles sich von selbst mache, und dasz die Regierung gar nichts zu thun brauche.

Ich will für dieszmal nichts weiter hinzusezen,* als dasz diese Richtung mit der Ihrigen vielfältig zusammentrifft, und dasz ich in dem erwähnten Anhange fast durchaus mich für Sie und wider Say ausgesprochen habe. Doch verschweige ich nicht (da die Wissenschaft hoch über persönlicher Rücksicht steht), dasz ich die Möglichkeit eines *General glut of commodities* bestreiten zu müssen geglaubt habe.

Es wäre mir sehr angenehm, wenn diese Eröffnung zu einem fortgesetzten literarischen Verkehre Anlasz gäbe. Gemeinschaftliche Liebe für Wissenschaft und Menschenwohl bindet die Menschen leicht und schnell an einander, und es scheint mir, als ob unmittelbare briefliche Mittheilungen von einem Lande ins andere manches Missverständnisse besser vermeiden, manchen Gedanken tausch leichter bewürcken könne, als der langsamere und unvollständige Verkehr durch Druckschrifften.* Sie werden mir erlauben, Ihnen schlüszlich zu erzählen, was ich bis jetzt geschrieben; ohnehin ist der Abstand zwischen Ihnen und mir gross genug, da Sie in halb Europa hoch geachtet sind. 1816: ein in Göttingen gekrönte Preisschrifft über das Zunftwesen (Ihre guilds oder Corporations) – 1819, 1820: eine Übersetzung von Storch's Cours d'Econ.polit. mit 17 Bogen Zusätzen von meiner Hand – 1821: mehrere einzelne Aufsätze unter dem Titel: Ansichten der Staatswirthschaft – Kleinere Arbeiten übergehe ich natürlich.

Mit aufrichtiger Hochachtung grüsze ich und bitte um Ihr freundschaftliches Andenken

Dr. Carl Heinrich Rau, Prof. der Cameral Wissenschaften

Im Fall Sie mir das Vergnügen machen wollen, mir zu schreiben, so bitte ich den Brief nach Hamburg an die Buchhandlung Perthes und Besser zu senden.

Translation (as provided for Malthus by Rau)

Erlangen, 15 June 1821

Sir!

Your essay on the principle of population, with which we Germans have been made acquainted by "Hegewisch's" translation[96] has been received with general approbation and in its wide circulation it has gained to its Author an [97] esteem, which uses* to fall only to the lot of those, who deserve well for the

---

[96]   Franz Hermann Hegewisch (1783–1865), MD, translated Malthus' *Essay on the Principle of Population.* The translation was published in Altona in 1807. See James 1979, pp. 362–4.

[97]   Word del.

15 June 1821 Good of mankind. Also upon me the strength of your reasoning has made a lively impression, and I am happy of the opportunity to tell you so.

This opportunity is offered me by your "Principles of political economy".[98] – English publications do not circulate so immediately in my country, which is the cause of your work reaching me only at the same time with "Say's letters".[99] To others it appeared not to be known at all yet, as was to be concluded from the want of Announces. The relations of commerce being much discussed at the present period, in which discussions many ill digested arguments and partial views are entertained, it appeared to me incumbent, to place the contending parties on a point of view, from where they might be within reach of the Arguments of a Briton and of a Frenchman, both distinguished Authors. The same complaints of stagnation in several countries of perfectly different relations, & the earnest enquiries into the causes of the evil were well adapted to lead to a deeper sounding of the matter, whilst the Partisans as well as the Opponents of the South German Commercial Union (the former adhering in Commercial politics to you and the French practice, the latter to "Smith's" theory) decide often somewhat superficially. For that reason I published a small pamphlet, containing, 1) an extract of [100] the 7th. chapter of your Work from article to article; 2) Say's letters literally translated, 3) Additions of my Own. It is entitled:

Malthus and *Say* on the causes of the present stagnation in trade

From the English and French, with an Appendix by [101]

Hamburg, printed for Perthes & Besser, 1821, 301 pages, 8⁹

I do not know, if you are acquainted with the later researches of the Germans in the province of Political Economy. – The Count *von Soden*,[102] *Hufeland*,[103] *Lotz*,[104] Count v. *Buquoy*,[105] *Sartorius*,[106] but principally *von Bosse*[107] in *Brunswick*, with

---

[98] T. R. Malthus, *Principles of Political Economy Considered with a View to their Practical Application*, London, 1820.

[99] J.-B. Say, *Lettres à M. Malthus, sur différens* sujets d'économie politique, notamment sur les causes de la stagnation générale du commerce*, Paris, 1820; translated by John Richter, *Letters to Mr. Malthus, on Several Subjects of Political Economy, and on the Cause of the Stagnation of Commerce*, London, 1821.

[100] 'your' is del. Ch. VII of Malthus' *Principles* is entitled 'On the Immediate Causes of the Progress of Wealth'.

[101] Here, and in the German version, MS has an ellipsis.

[102] Count Friedrich Julius Heinrich Reichsgraf von Soden (1754–1831). See Schumpeter 1954, pp. 501, 505; *Palgrave's Dictionary*, Vol. III, p. 440.

[103] Gottlieb Hufeland (1760–1817). See Schumpeter 1954, p. 501; *Palgrave's Dictionary*, Vol. II, pp. 336–7.

[104] Johann Friedrich Eusebius Lotz (1771–1838). See *Palgrave's Dictionary*, Vol. II, pp. 644–5.

[105] Count Georg Franz Buquoy-Longueval (1781–1851). See Schumpeter 1954, pp. 502, 711; *Palgrave's Dictionary*, Vol. I, p. 192.

[106] Georg Friedrich Sartorius (1766–1828). See *Palgrave's Dictionary*, Vol. III, pp. 352–3.

[107] Rudolph Heinrich Bernhard von Bosse (1778–1855).

whom in the course of my labours I have mostly sided, have helped to form a 15 June 1821 new School in this respect. The Science has obtained fresh impulse by people ceasing to stop at a given quantum of Wealth, by more considering its employment,[108] and by acknowledging it as the essence of every comfort in domestic and public Life (Conf. Aristot. Polit. I. 8).[109] The Economical was put into close relation to the Moral, and consequently a juster view taken of the situation in which Man stands with regard to his relative Wealth. – This was not possible without frequent deviations from Smith and from the French, who are entire strangers to a deeper conception; Simonde's nouveaux principes[110] are so much more analogous to our System. We (viz. a moderate number of those who are coadjutors in this new direction of the Science) are therefore decidedly against the proposition, that Ill should work its own cure and that Government need not interfere.

For the present I will not add more but that this direction coincides with yours in many points, and that in the above mentioned Appendix I have throughout declar'd myself *for* you and *against* Say. I will not conceal however (as Science should be far above personal consideration) that I have felt it necessary to contest the possibility of a general Glut of Commodities.

I should be very happy if this were to be the introduction to a permanent literary intercourse. Love of Science & the Good of Mankind will easily connect Men together, and it appears to me, as if immediate epistolary communications between different countries would sooner contribute to prevent misunderstandings, and to produce an Exchange of Ideas with more facility than the slower & imperfect intercourse by publications. You will permit me to tell you briefly, what I have lately published altho' fully aware of the distance between a Man so deservedly praised all over Europe and myself. 1816: An Essay on Guilds or corporations,[111] which obtained the prize at the University of Göttingen. 1819. 1820: A Translation of Storch's Cours d'Econ. polit.,[112]

---

[108] 'its employment' is ins.

[109] Aristotle, *Politics*, Bk. I, Ch. 8, l. 30: 'such things necessary to life, and useful for the community of the family or state, as can be stored ... are the elements of true riches; for the amount of property which is needed for a good life is not unlimited...' (tr. B. Jowett, in *Works of Aristotle*, Vol. IV, Oxford, 1921).

[110] J. C. L. Simonde de Sismondi, *Nouveaux principes d'économie politique*, 2 vols., Paris, 1819.

[111] *Ueber das Zunftwesen und die Folgen seiner Aufhebung* ..., Liepzig, 1816.

[112] Heinrich Friedrich von Storch (1766–1835), *Cours d'économie politique, ou exposition des principes qui déterminent la prospérité des nations*, 6 vols., St Petersburgh, 1815. Rau's German translation – described as 'a free, but very good, translation' – was entitled *Zusätze zu Heinrich Storch ... Cours d'économie politique, von D. Karl Heinrich Rau ... Aus der deutschen Übersetzung besonders abgedruckt*, Hamburg, Perthes und Besser, 1820. See *Palgrave's Dictionary*, Vol. III, p. 424; *The New Palgrave*, Vol. IV, p. 512; Schumpeter 1954.

15 June 1821 with 17 additional sheets of my own. 1821: Sundry essays, under the title: Views of Political Economy,[113] passing over of course several smaller pamphlets.
With sincere esteem and solliciting* your friendly remembrance,
I subscribe myself,
Dr. Charles Henry Rau,
Prof. of Cameral Wissenschaften
Should you do me the favour to write, I beg to direct the letter to Messrs. Perthes and Besser, Booksellers at Hamburg

G. MEASURE OF VALUE

72. MALTHUS
TO AN UNNAMED CORRESPONDENT[114]

[1825 or later]

My dear Sir

c. 1825   I am very much obliged to you for[115] your interesting letter, which I should have thanked you for before, but have been particularly engaged during the last ten days. The subject of value still retains all its interest with me, and will probably continue to do so, till the point is settled, – a[n] event which may yet be at a considerable distance.

I cannot help thinking with Col' Torrens[116] that you understand Ricardo's [117] measure of value differently from the majority of his readers. [118] As far as I recollect he[119] has nowhere proposed the measure that you propose. In his third and last edition[120] Chap. 1. sect 6. p. 44,[121] he says expressly, "May not gold be considered as a commodity produced with such proportions of the *two kinds of*

---

[113] *Ansichten der Volkswirtschaft mit besonderer Beziehung auf Deutschland*, Leipzig, 1821.

[114] Watermark date '1825'. The large number of corrections and the absence of a date and an address indicate that this is a draft. This letter, and the following letter no. 73, are concerned with the question of the measure of value. Malthus tries to substantiate his view that the best measure of value of a commodity is the quantity of standard labour that it can command in exchange, as opposed to Ricardo's view that the best measure of the relative value of commodities is the relative quantity of labour employed in their production.

[115] 'you for' is ins.

[116] Robert Torrens (1780–1864). A prolific writer on economics, his best known works are *An Essay on the External Corn Trade* (five editions, 1815, 1820, 1826, 1827, 1829), and *An Essay on the Production of Wealth*, 1821. He had been a professional soldier, rising to the rank of colonel in the marines.

[117] 'view' is del.   [118] 'In his last edition' is del.   [119] 'Ricardo' is del. and 'he' is ins.

[120] David Ricardo, *On the Principles of Political Economy and Taxation*, 3rd edn, 1821, a copy of which is in the Malthus Library. The three quotations are substantially accurate, but the underlinings/italics were not in Ricardo's text. The first two quotations were also quoted in Malthus' *Principles of Political Economy*, 2nd edn, 1836, p. 124.

[121] 'Chap. 1. sect 6. p. 44' is ins.

capital as approach nearest to the average quantity employed in the production c. 1825 of most commodities" and in the previous page he had distinctly stated that his gold "would be a perfect measure of value for all things produced under the same circumstances precisely with itself, *but for no others*". At the end of the section he further explains himself by saying : "It is necessary for me to remark that I have not said, because one commodity has so much labour bestowed upon it as will cost 1000£ and another so much as will cost 2000£ that therefore one would be of the value of 1000£ and the other of the value of 2000£; but I have said that their value will be to each other as two to one, and that in those proportions they will be exchanged. It is of no importance to the truth of this doctrine whether one of these commodities sells for 1100 and the other for 2200, or one for 1500 and the other for 3000£. Into that question I do not at present inquire. *I affirm only that their relative values will be governed by the relative quantities of labour bestowed upon their production*".

From these[122] passages nothing [123] can be more clear than that Ricardo's main view of a measure of value was an object so constituted that the quantity and rate of profits of which it was in part composed, should be proportionally[124] the same or very nearly the same as that of all other commodities, and that therefore all commodities would exchange with each other according to the only variable part of their value, namely[125] the quantity of labour worked up in them, of which his gold would be the measure.

It is true indeed that the exceptions which he had himself before stated might appear to his readers quite sufficient entirely to overturn the theory that commodities exchange with each other according to the quantity of labour worked up in them; and it is also true that he subsequently uses the quantity of labour worked up in a commodity to express not merely the relative value of commodities, but what he calls their real value. This appears particularly in his controversy[126] with Mr Say. But still I think it must be allowed that the passages which I have quoted express[127] that view of the subject which is most predominant[128] throughout his work, and [129] you must [130] allow that it is essentially different from mine.

With regard to the measure you propose, [131] namely[132] gold produced by a given quantity of immediate[133] labour, with the profits upon that labour for a year, you have not distinctly[134] stated whether the profits are to be constant, or

---

[122] 'this last' is altered to 'those'.   [123] 'surely' is del.
[124] 'proportionally' is ins.   [125] 'the only variable part of their value, namely' is ins.
[126] 'particularly in the controversy' is del. and 'This appears particularly in his controversy' is ins.
[127] 'which expressed' is altered to 'express'.   [128] 'generally prevalent' is del. and 'predominant' is ins.
[129] 'I think' is del.   [130] 'surely' is del.   [131] '[you have not explained,] you have s' is del.
[132] Misspelt 'namenly'.   [133] 'immediate' is ins.   [134] 'explained' is del. and 'distinctly' is ins.

c. 1825 to vary[135] with the general rate of profits in the country where the gold is produced. If the profits are to be constant, I do not know [136] that your measure would practically much differ from mine, though it would be a[137] forcd* [138] hypothesis to assume[139] that profits in the production of gold should remain constant, while they are altering in the production of all other commodities.[140] If on the other hand you suppose that[141] the rate of profits in the production of gold will[142] vary with the general rate of profits in the surrounding country, which I infer from your conclusions[143] then I should say that my measure essentially differed from yours,[144] and would lead to essentially different conclusions.

The grand distinction between my measure and Ricardo's is that my measure marks all the variations of value[145] which arise both from the[146] different quantities of profits [147] occasioned by the different quantities of fixed capital, [148] and [149] different *rates* of profits occasioned by the progress of cultivation or the abundance of capital,[150] as well as the variation [151] of value arising from the different quantities of labour; whereas Ricardo's only measures the latter, and the distinction of my measure from yours, [152] on the supposition that you consider the rate of[153] profits in the production of gold to vary [154] with the rate of general profits, is that mine having no such variable element in it,[155] will always[156] measure the variations of value in other commodities[157] occasioned by the varying rate of profits, [158] which yours will not.

Supposing for instance that a days common[159] labour had remained[160] of the same quality from[161] the time of Edward iii [162] to the present time, I should say that [163] a given quantity of such labour or the[164] gold immediately produced by it without profits[165] was the best measure of the varying values of all other commodities. You say that your measure would do as well. Let us see [166] what would be the difference in the results.

---

[135] 'variable' is altered to 'to vary'.   [136] 'whether' is del.
[137] 'is a much more' is del. and 'would be a' is ins.   [138] 'supposition' is del.
[139] 'suppose' is del. and 'assume' is ins.
[140] ', than to suppose what really takes place, that there are some commodities produced by [labour] immediate labour alone, and brought to market without delay' is del.
[141] 'you suppose that' is ins.   [142] '[are] is to' is del. and 'will' is ins.
[143] 'which I infer from your conclusions' is ins.   [144] 'it' is del. and 'yours' is ins.
[145] 'of value' is ins.   [146] 'the' is ins.   [147] '(' is del.   [148] '&c.&c.)' is del.   [149] 'the dis' is del.
[150] 'any other cause' is del. and 'the abundance of capital' is ins.
[151] 'and the distinction between my measure and yours according' is del.
[152] 'according to my latter' is del.   [153] 'the rate of' is ins.   [154] 'like the' is del.
[155] 'having nothing to do with profits' is del. and 'having no such variable element in it' is ins.
[156] 'always' is ins.   [157] 'in other commodities' is ins. and del.   [158] 'in other commodities' is del.
[159] 'common' is ins.   [160] 'was' is del. and 'had remained' is ins.   [161] 'in' is del. and 'from' is ins.
[162] 'as a days common labour' is del.   [163] 'the gold' is del.   [164] 'the' is ins.   [165] 'without profits' is ins.
[166] 'the result.' is del.

Suppose that an ounce of[167] gold and ten yards of cloth[168] in the [169] time of   c. 1825
Edward III were each[170] obtained by 50 days labour advanced for a year, and
that profits were 20 percent[171] then a purchaser[172] to obtain an ounce of gold, or
ten y^{rds} of cloth[173] must make the sacrifice[174] of 60 days labour, 50 as the advances,
and 10 the profits of the advances for the year. [175] Now supposing from the
increase of capital and cultivation, [176] without any alteration in the productiveness
of mere labour, profits had[177] fallen in the time of George IV to ten per cent[178]
and both gold and cloth had become more plentiful,[179] then according to my
standard[180] it would only be necessary to give 55 days labour for ten yards of
cloth instead of sixty and the diminished value of cloth would be correctly
marked;[181] whereas your gold, diminishing in value [182] at the same time with the
cloth owing to the fall of profits,[183] the cloth would cost the same quantity of
gold as [184] in the time of Edward III, and the greater plenty and cheapness of the
cloth owing to the abundance of[185] capital [186] would not be marked by your
measure.[187] The results therefore of the two measures would be essentially
different.

This is a case of a rise of proportional wages caused by a fall in the value
of the commodity, and the consequent fall of profits, just in the same way [188] as
when cottons fall, profits fall, and proportional wages rise, that is, the labourer
earns a greater quantity of the cottons which he produces.

The two cases stated in your letter are of a similar description, that is, they
relate to variations in proportional wages and consequent variations of profits[189]
which, if profits where they are one of the conditions of supply[190] be considered
as one of the elements of value, must always have a prodigious effect on the[191]
value of commodities.[192]

---

[167] '[a given quantity] an ounce' is del. and 'an ounce of' is ins.
[168] 'and ten yards of cloth' is ins.   [169] 'the' is repeated.   [170] 'had been' is del. and 'were each' is ins.
[171] 'per' is repeated.   [172] 'in order' is del. and 'a purchaser' is ins.
[173] 'of gold, or ten y^{rds} of cloth' is ins.
[174] 'give in exchange the value' is del. and 'make the sacrifice' is ins.
[175] '50 as the advances, and 10 the profits of the advances for the year' is ins. and 'And if 10 yards of
cloth were obtained in the same way, he must give in the same manner 60 days labour for the cloth.'
is del.
[176] 'profits had' is del.   [177] 'profits had' is ins.   [178] 'in the time of George IV to ten per cent' is ins.
[179] 'more plentiful' is ins.
[180] 'my labour or my gold would measure the [increased] diminished value of cloth' is del. and 'then
according to my standard' is ins.
[181] 'and the diminished value of [gold] cloth would be correctly marked' is ins.
[182] 'owing to the fall of profits' is del.   [183] 'owing to the fall of profits' is ins.   [184] 'before' is del.
[185] 'more' is del. and 'the abundance of' is ins.   [186] 'being employed in making it' is del.
[187] 'by your measure' is ins.   [188] 'just in the same way' is repeated and del.
[189] 'wages and consequent variations of profits' is ins.
[190] 'where they are one of the [elements] conditions of supply' is ins.   [191] 'the' is ins.
[192] 'of commodities' is ins. and 'and profits' is del.

c. 1825   In your first case the gross produce is increased while the *quantity* which goes to labour remains[193] the same, and consequently proportional wages fall and profits rise from 20 per cent to 44 per cent; and as the same quantity of labour as far as mere labour is concerned[194] still produces the same quantity of corn, while the other element of value has risen from 20 percent to 44 percent, it is quite natural that corn should become of much greater value, so that 20 days labour should only exchange for 16⅔ quarters instead of 20 quarters. If the gross produce be estimated in the[195] cloth the rise of[196] profits [197] would affect the price of cloth in the same way,[198] but it[199] would be more than counteracted by the increased productiveness of labour in making[200] cloth, and the purchaser would obtain 25 yards of cloth with the same sacrifice as he had before obtained 20 y^{rds}.

In your second case, the supposition of a sudden increase of labourers is tantamount to a comparative diminution of the funds for the maintenance of labour, in which case produce will be relatively scarce and profits will rise, and if profits be one of the elements of value, it is quite certain that a correct measure of value should shew* the increase in the value of produce occasioned by such increase of profits.

With regard to the[201] annuitant, paid as you propose in the[202] measure of value such a payment[203] does not pretend to secure to him [204] the command of a uniform *quantity* of commodities; if it did, it would [205] cease to be a correct measure of value;[206] because we will know that in the progress of cultivation & improvement[207] all commodities are liable to vary in reference to the sacrifice which must be made to attain them, both on account of the varying productiveness of labour, and the varying amount, and rate of profits. [208]

You ask whether your annuitant ought to have his power of purchasing impaired or augmented, not only by the varying productiveness of [209] labour, but by every alteration of proportional wages? The answer to the question is obvious. If every alteration in proportional wages alters the rate of profits, as it unquestionably does, and if [210] the rate of profits be an[211] element of value, as it unquestionably is, your annuitant *ought* certainly to have his power of purchasing vary accordingly. All that is secured to him is an income of uniform value. If

---

[193] 'is' is del. and 'remains' is ins.   [194] 'as far as mere labour is concerned' is ins.   [195] 'the' is ins.
[196] 'proportional wages and profits would fall and' is del. and 'the rise of' is ins.
[197] 'was in' is del.   [198] 'as it did that of corn' is del. and 'in the same way' is ins.   [199] 'it' is ins.
[200] 'the production of' is del. and 'making' is ins.
[201] 'your' is del. and 'the' is ins.   [202] 'paid as you propose in the' is ins. and 'a correct' is del.
[203] 'such a payment' is ins.   [204] 'a' is del. and 'the command of' is ins.
[205] 'be a most incorr' is del.   [206] 'of value' is ins.
[207] 'we will know [that] in the progress of cultivation & improvement' is ins. and 'we know that' is del.
[208] 'If from these causes commodities fall in value, your annuitant' is del.
[209] 'some' is del.   [210] 'every alteration rate[s]' is del.   [211] 'an' is repeated.

commodities fall in value[212] he has the advantage of obtaining more produce   c. 1825
with a given[213] sacrifice; if commodities rise in value he is necessarily subjected
to the disadvantage of obtaining less produce with [214] the same sacrifice. And I
contend that there is absolutely no other measure of this sacrifice than the
command of the quantity of labour which the purchaser of a commodity[215] is
required to transfer to the seller; or what comes to exactly the same thing, the
command of some commodity the relation of which to labour is known. If at
the present moment the relation of money to labour were not pretty nearly[216]
known, no person could form a guess of the price which he ought to offer for [217]
what he wanted to obtain.
[218]

According to your [219] mode of obtaining gold, its value would vary with
the value of the[220] corn and cloth. Your standard would not mark any alteration
of value arising from the increased rate of profits; and at the time when it was
necessary for a purchaser[221] to make a much greater sacrifice to obtain [222] the
same quantity [223] of corn and cloth as in your second example,[224] you would say
that the value of corn and cloth had remained the same. No doubt your annuitant
would be better off if he continued to have the same quantity of gold when gold
had greatly risen in value, but the person who had granted him the annuity
would be [225] worse off. And if profits were to fall instead of rise which is much
the more usual case, the fall in the value of [226] the given quantity of gold paid to
the annuitant would be a disadvantage to him, he would lose the benefit of the
cheapness of commodities occasioned by the fall of profits, and the granter of
the annuity might pay it with a less sacrifice. An annuity therefore of an uniform
value, though it cannot secure a uniform quantity of produce, seems to be on
the whole, the fairest both for the granter and the grantee.

You are inclined to prefer the use of the term gold for your[227] standard to
the term labour, in order not to disturb too much the language of commercial
men; my standard you know is easily convertible into gold,[228] but is there not
some danger of error and misunderstanding in using a very familiar term such
as[229] gold or money in a different sense from that in which it is generally and
practically used. I am convinced that both Mr Ricardo and Mr McCulloch[230]

---

[212] 'If the value of commodities fall with' is altered to 'If commodities fall in value'.
[213] 'the same' is del. and 'a given' is ins.   [214] 'less' is del.   [215] 'of a commodity' is ins.
[216] 'pretty nearly' is ins.   [217] 'commodities.' is del.   [218] 'You seem inclined to think' is del.
[219] 'standard' is del.   [220] 'value of the' is ins.
[221] 'for a purchaser' is ins.   [222] 'the same quantity of corn in your first example and' is del.   [223] *'both'* is del.
[224] 'in the' is del. and 'as in your second example' is ins.   [225] 'much' is del.   [226] 'his gold' is del.
[227] 'a' is del. and 'your' is ins.   [228] 'my standard you know is easily convertible into gold' is ins.
[229] 'such as' is ins.   [230] John Ramsay McCulloch (1789–1864).

c. 1825   have frequently been misunderstood by being supposed to be talking of common money, when they were talking of a money peculiarly constituted. I am disposed therefore to think that it is better to use the term *labour* in speaking of a measure of value, and [231] gold or money such as it practically exists when we are speaking of prices.

I should extend this letter to a most unreasonable length if I were to enter into the particulars of your paper marked No 1. I will only observe therefore that in your first[232] period an ounce of gold and a quarter of corn were in the ratio of equality, in your second period they are[233] in the ratio of 160 to 240. Consequently corn as compared with your standard gold will have risen [234] one half. According to my standard gold, only one fourth. The reason of this difference[235] is, that your gold gets cheaper at the same time that corn is getting dearer, whereas mine as I think[236] remains the same. [237]

73. MALTHUS
TO AN UNNAMED CORRESPONDENT[238]

[1828 or later]

c. 1828   Our discussion respecting value shews* the absolute necessity of a strict attention to definitions. The reason of our difference is that we are talking about two different kinds of value. These two different kinds you have stated in the latter part of your letter, and I am much pleased to find that when we advert to the same object there is no difference between us.[239] You say most justly, that it is one thing to make use of a measure of value with a view of marking the variations in the relative value of different commodities with reference to the conditions of their supply, it is another to employ a measure with a view of determining the command ˌwhich a person ought to have under any given circumstances over the commodities in which those variations have occurred. For the former purpose *labour is an accurate measure of value*. For the latter there is none either real or imaginary that can be deemed strictly correct.

Now this is exactly what I have said in substance both in my pamphlet on

---

[231] '[mere] the term' is del.   [232] 'first' is ins.   [233] 'are' is ins.   [234] 'from about' is del.
[235] 'of this difference' is ins.   [236] 'as I think' is ins.   [237] MS ends here.
[238] Watermark date '1828'. The large number of alterations and the absence of a date, a postal address, and the customary mode of address ('Dear ...') indicate that this is a draft. The similarity of subject matter and the use of expressions such as 'Our discussion' and 'your gold' suggest that the unnamed correspondent in this letter was the same as in the previous letter.
[239] '[you fully agree with me in regard to the object which I have adopted as the measure of the kind of value] what you say of them is exactly the same in substance' is del. and 'when we advert to the same object there is no difference between us' is ins.

the Measure of Value,[240] and in my Definitions.[241] And it is precisely because   c. 1828
there is no correct measure either real or imaginary for [242] a given command
over the mass of commodities, and because I think that[243] practically when the
[244] rise or fall in the value of a commodity is spoken of a [245] reference is hardly
ever made to the mass of commodities, that I consider it as [246] more correct, and
beyond all comparison more useful and practicable, [247] when the term value of
a commodity is used alone, to refer [248] to the former kind of value which you
describe, and not the latter. Consequently my definition of the value of a
commodity at any place and time, is, the estimation in which it is held at that
place & time,[249] determined in all cases[250] by the state of the supply compared
with the demand at that place & time and ordinarily by the elementary costs of
production, or conditions of the supply.[251] And of this kind of value you agree
with me that the labour of the same place & time[252] which the commodity will
command is the measure.

This [253] is the point on which I especially insist, and on this we are happily
agreed. I do not pretend to propose a measure of the power of commanding a
given amount of the mass of commodities and thinking with Ricardo[254] that
quantity is essentially different from *value*, I [255] cannot but be of opinion that
'the power of purchasing', is both a most[256] *indefinite* and incorrect definition
of value.

Yet even with regard to the power of purchasing by means of a[257] reserved
rent, it appears to me that the owner of such a rent ought to have the benefit in
the progress of society of the cheapening of commodities, not only from
improvements in machinery, but from the fall[258] of that almost universal element
of value – profits – arising from the [259] comparative abundance of capital. Let us
put a theory case and see the result. Supposing that in an early period of society[260]
from indolence and the almost total absence of the habit of saving,[261] the power
of making advances [262] and going without the returns for a year was possessed

---

[240]   *The Measure of Value Stated and Illustrated* ..., 1823.   [241] *Definitions in Political Economy*, 1827.
[242]   'the mass of commodities' is del.   [243] 'of commodities, and because I think th' is del. but then repeated.
[244]   'value' is del.; 'the' is repeated.   [245] 'real' is del.   [246] 'may' is del.   [247] 'to refer' is del.
[248]   'to the causes intrinsically affecting that commodity, which are measurable and not to the' is del.
[249]   '& time' is ins.   [250] 'at the moment' is del. and 'in all cases' is ins.
[251]   This definition is almost exactly the same as the one given in Malthus' *Definitions*, pp. 242–3: 'The
value, market value, or actual value, of a commodity at any place or time' is 'The estimation in which
it is held at that place and time, determined in all cases by the state of the supply compared with the
demand, and ordinarily by the elementary costs of production which regulate that state.'
[252]   'of the same place & time' is ins.   [253] 'alone' is del.   [254] 'with Ricardo' is ins.
[255]   'do not allow' is del.   [256] 'an' is del. and 'a most' is ins.
[257]   'to a' is del. and 'to the power of purchasing by means of a' is ins.
[258]   'cheapening' is del. and 'fall' is ins.   [259] 'abu' is del.   [260] 'in an early period of society' is ins.
[261]   'of Saving' is del. and 'of the habit of saving' is ins.   [262] 'for a year' is del.

c. 1828   by but very few persons, and that in consequence,[263] profits [264] were fifty per cent. The obvious result[265] would be that all commodities which[266] required such advances, and your gold among the rest would be extremely scarce and dear as compared with the [267] the producers and consumers. Now let us suppose that while a[268] reserved rent continues to be[269] measured in your gold, the habits of the society were to change, and a large proportion of persons were able to make advances, and go without returns for a year, and that in consequence profits had fallen to 10 per cent, and those commodities which before were so scarce and dear had now become plentiful and cheap compared with the producers and consumers, surely the owner of the reserved rent or of anything approaching to a constant value ought to have the benefit of this cheapness of commodities. But your measure would not give it him. You would give him the cheapness arising from improved machinery, and therefore your measure is not a measure of the power of purchasing generally,[270] you will not give him the [271] cheapness arising from the[272] abundance and cheapness of capital, and therefore your measure does not[273] remain constant while other things are varying. [274] In any sense in which the term value[275] has been taken, an object, a given quantity of which will neither continue to[276] command the same *quantity* of commodities, nor mark the same conditions of supply, cannot surely be considered as a good measure of value.

You object[277] to a reserved rent payable in my measure on account of its[278] having its power of purchasing empaired* or augmented by every variation of proportional wages; but this is only because a variation of proportional wages always accompanies the real cheapness or dearness[279] arising from comparative abundance or scantiness of capital and commodities.[280] A rise of proportional wages is not the primary *cause* of low profits, and of the fall in the value of commodities, but the *consequence*. The cause is the [281] previous fall[282] of commodities occasioned by the state of the supply & demand, that is, by the increased abundance of capital and consequent increase of the[283] supply of commodities compared with the producers & consumers. So far from agreeing

---

[263] 'all commodities in which advances were required were extremely dear' is del.

[264] 'being' is del.   [265] 'consequence' is del. and 'result' is ins.   [266] 'that' is del. and 'which' is ins.

[267] '[producers an] population, that is with' is del.   [268] 'the' is del. and 'a' is ins.

[269] 'is' is del. and 'continues to be' is ins.

[270] 'mass of commodities, but' is del. and 'power of purchasing generally' is ins.

[271] 'obvious' is del.   [272] 'the' is ins.

[273] 'it has no pretensions to constancy of value' is del. and 'your measure [has] does not' is ins.

[274] 'Ought such a measure to be considered as the best measure of value' is del.   [275] 'value' is ins.

[276] 'continue to' is ins.   [277] '[doubt] much' is del. and 'object' is ins.

[278] 'varying' is del. and 'on account of its' is ins.   [279] 'or dearness' is ins.

[280] 'and commodities' is ins. and 'Such a change' is del.

[281] 'increased abundance of commodities' is del.   [282] 'cheapness' is del. and 'fall' is ins.

[283] 'abundance of capital and consequent increase of the' is ins.

with M.ʳ Macculloch* that demand has nothing to do with profits, I hold it to be   c. 1828
a certain and most important truth that putting aside the question of prices[284]
profits *never* rise but [285] when the products of the same quantity of labour rise in
value from the state of the [286] demand compared with the supply and *never* fall[287]
but [288] when the products of the same [289] quantity of labour fall in value from the
same cause, operating either temporarily or permanently. Consequently there
can be no reason why the owner of a reserved rent should not have the benefit
of the cheapness arising from an abundant capital [290] as well as of the cheapness
arising from machinery.

But recollect that my main object is not an attempt to ascertain what a
reserved rent ou[gh]t to command, but to inquire whether there is any object
which may be considered as a fair approach to a standard measure of value, and
the nature of a standard measure is to measure the variations of all other
commodities while it remains constant itself. In this inquiry almost every thing
must of course depend upon the definition of the value of a commodity, and as
I cannot but think with Ricardo that *value* and *quantity* are essentially different,[291]
I continue to think after the maturest deliberation that my definition is both
more correct, and beyond all comparison more useful and applicable, than *the
power of purchasing*.

I have no objection to say that value is the power of purchasing but [292] I
have a great objection to go on and say that the value of a commodity is
proportioned to its power of purchasing. I ask, "power of purchasing" what? I
don't think[293] you can give me a consistent answer.

---

[284] 'putting aside the question of prices' is ins.   [285] 'from a rise in' is del.
[286] 'supply comm' is del.   [287] 'fall' is ins.   [288] 'fa' is del.   [289] 'kind' is del.
[290] 'from the state of the supply compared with the demand' is del.
[291] 'different' is ins.   [292] 'th' is del.   [293] 'think' is ins.

H. A LETTER FROM NEPAL

74. BRIAN HOUGHTON HODGSON[294]
TO MALTHUS[295]

Nepal Residency Feby 15. 1830.

My dear Sir,

15 Feb. 1830
    It is a long time since I had the pleasure of hearing from you or writing to you. The latter is indeed a gratification, you will say, which I have always held in my own hands: But consider your own reputation and how such an* one as I am should presume to write to you with nothing worthy of your notice to tell!

    I have not been unmindful of your wish to have some authentic particulars of the population, wages, & prices, of Nepal nor have I neglected the attempt to procure such particulars for you. But you need least of all men to be told that *accuracy* related to such points is indispensible* and what with the jealousy of the gorkha[296] gov^t & the extreme caution prescribed to me by my situation I have not yet been able to meddle effectually with these alarming topics. I do not despair however – will continue to exert myself – & shall have singular pleasure in hereafter presenting to you the results of my labours should they prove at all successful. For the last 12 months I have been in charge of this Residency[297] – a great honor* for so young a servant of the Company – and I believe I should ere this have been appointed Resident[298] in full but for my youth – a very remediable defect – and which may I hope prove such in regard to this Residency, unless some man much my senior in the service should press

[294] Brian Houghton Hodgson (1800–1894) had been a student at the East India College in 1816 and 1817. When he first went there he stayed as a guest in Malthus' house while waiting to pass his entrance examination. He attended Malthus' lectures and obtained a prize in political economy. See Hunter 1896; James 1979, pp. 243–4. In Hodgson's opinion, as reported by Hunter, Malthus was 'both the favourite and the hero' of the College. This letter was apparently written in response to a request from Malthus for information on population, wages and prices in Nepal, and as such attests to Malthus' continual search for authentic empirical evidence of economic conditions.

[295] Addressed: 'The Rev^d / T. R. Malthus / Hayleybury* College / Hertford'. No postmark.

[296] The Gurkhas are one of the dominant races of Nepal. *OED* gives as variant spellings 'Gho(o)rka', 'Ghurka', and 'Goork(h)a', but not 'gorkha'.

[297] In 1820 Hodgson was appointed assistant to the British Resident at the Court of Nepal. In 1829 the Resident (Edward Gardner) resigned, and Hodgson became Acting Resident. In a letter of 23 April 1829 to his sister he wrote: 'My superior in office here left this Residency March 1st, since which time I have been *chargé d'affaires*, and they tell me I shall soon be confirmed in the exalted post in which I now only officiate.' He held the position of Acting Resident for two years, but, because of his youth, had to wait until February 1833 before being appointed Resident (Hunter 1896, pp. 55–6, 70, 76–7; a sketch of the Nepal Residency faces p. 84).

[298] i.e. 'a representative of the East India Company ... residing at a commercial station ...' (*OED*).

his superior claims before my toga virilis[299] be furnished by that slow-fingered   15 Feb. 1830
tailor ...[300] Time!

Here, as in England, new fangled* politics are in vogue. But I doubt if this
be a meridian[301] as well suited to the trial of their quality as England. The local
gov¹ can hardly "pay their way" and the consequence is that a system of
retrenchment has been adopted which has cut off from a third to a half of the
former salaries of all branches of the service. This bitter pill has not been gilded
– and, what is worse, it has been thrust down our throats without a moment's
notice for preparation. Some folks hesitate not to cry aloud "*Breach of faith*"
insisting that we entered the service with known & permitted expectations and
that these have been grossly violated in circumstances which leave the option
of resignation unavailable – for what man that has served in India for 10 years
can adopt a new means of livelihood going home to seek it? This is not without
truth. Then again, we are all for a Free Press – the laws on the subject are
allowed to sleep & the "Radicals" of the East, intoxicated with liberty of speech
are playing some very drunken pranks. Some people tremble, – others laugh,
according as dispositions vary – But, I believe, the laughers upon this occasion
are very seldom the discerning few: and though I am *no* dupe to the prevalent
exaggeration respecting the political influence of the Press ("the rebellions of
the belly are the worse") yet I think a most fearful experiment is making without
any adequate prospect of advantage from its success under the present
circumstances of Hindoo mind nor do I consider the Press to be the *first*
instrument we should use in our endeavours to alter those circumstances ...[302]
the better. But enough of ...[303] Permit me to ...[304] my Brother Edward[305] to your
attention. I hope & trust that he will give a large portion of his time to your
department & the College pursuits – and shall be deeply indebted to you if you
will endeavour to make him perceive the superior importance, with a view of
his future active duties, of pol. economy, history & law. With kind regards to
M⁷ˢ Malthus & my other College acquaintances I remain my dear sir
Most truly Yⁿˢ B. H. Hodgson

[299] In Ancient Rome the 'toga virilis' was the plain white toga given to young men at about the age of
seventeen to mark their progression from adolescence to manhood. It was the customary dress of a
man (AT).
[300] Word(s) indistinct.
[301] i.e. 'The point or period of highest development or perfection, after which decline sets in; culmination,
full splendour' (*OED*).
[302] Word partially obscured by torn seal; probably 'for'.
[303] Word partially obscured by torn seal; probably 'politics'.
[304] Word partially obscured by torn seal; probably 'commend'.
[305] His second and youngest brother, Edward Legh Hodgson (1813–1835), was at the East India College,
Haileybury, for three terms from 1829 to 1831, and gained a number of prizes. He served in India as
Assistant Commissioner at Meerut from 1832 to 1835, and died from a fever caught while shooting in
the swamps (Hunter 1896, pp. 11, 71, 81–2).

I. Société Française de Statistique Universelle

75. CÉSAR MOREAU[306]
TO MALTHUS[307]

Société Française de Statistique Universelle
Protecteur Sa Majesté Louis Philippe 1ᵉʳ Roi des Français

Paris, (Place Vendôme No. 24) le 1ᵉʳ Décembre 1830

Monsieur et cher Collègue,

1 Dec. 1830

Sur le rapport du Comité des Finances, le Conseil a décidé que votre Diplôme vous serait transmis et que vous seriez prié d'en faire passer le montant qui est de 25 francs, ainsi que celui de la cotisation de 1830, qui est, à votre choix, de 30 francs par an (ou 300 frs une fois payés) et 15 frs par an (ou 150 frs une fois payés) comme membre honoraire non co-propriétaire.

J'ai l'honneur de vous annoncer que les Bulletins de la Société sont sous presse et vous seront prochainement expédiés.

J'ai l'honneur d'être avec une haute considération,

Monsieur & Cher Collègue,

Votre très humble & très obéissant serviteur,

Par ordre du Conseil

Le Directeur du Bureau d'Admᵒⁿ

César Moreau

Enregistré sous le Nº 590
J. Leivsey

A Monsieur Robert Malthus, membre de plusieurs Sociétés Savantes &c[308]

---

[306] César Moreau (1791–1860), French vice-consul in London, founder of the Société Française de Statistique Universelle (*Palgrave's Dictionary*, Vol. II, p. 818). He published numerous statistical works on the finances and foreign trade of England, France and Ireland.

[307] Addressed: 'Thomas Robert Malthus Esqʳ FRS / Maitre* ès arts de l'université de Cambridge &c &c &c / East India College / Hertford'. Postmark: 'Z DE 10 1830'. It is not clear from this letter whether Malthus had applied for membership of the Société, or whether Moreau had taken the initiative in conferring membership on him.

[308] The editors acknowledge the assistance of Dr Patrick Laplagne (University of New England) in deciphering this letter.